SULGR

THE WASHINGTONS

FRONTISPIECE

SULGRAVE MANOR HOUSE. THE SOUTH FRONT.

SULGRAVE MANOR
AND
THE WASHINGTONS

A History and Guide to the Tudor Home of George Washington's Ancestors

BY

H. CLIFFORD SMITH, F.S.A.

Author of 'Buckingham Palace: its Furniture, History and Decoration'

WITH A FOREWORD BY

VISCOUNT LEE OF FAREHAM

P.C., G.C.B., G.C.S.I., G.B.E.

Chairman of the Sulgrave Manor Board

NEW YORK

THE MACMILLAN COMPANY

1933

Contents

CONTENTS

List of Illustrations

PLATES

LIST OF ILLUSTRATIONS

LIST OF ILLUSTRATIONS

FIGURES IN THE TEXT

LIST OF ILLUSTRATIONS

Introduction

HERE at last we have the book for which all who are interested in the more intimate and romantic aspects of Anglo-American history have been waiting, and, for the first time, we can read an authoritative, scholarly, and exhaustive account of the English home of George Washington's ancestors. To Mr. Clifford Smith the expenditure of time and thought which this monument of patient research represents has been a labour of love, but we are none the less deeply in his debt for the skilful and engrossing manner in which he has discharged a task of international importance. His presentment of the story of Sulgrave Manor and its environment is happily designed to satisfy the tastes and needs of historians, antiquaries, and pious pilgrims alike. Even for the professional architect Mr. Clifford Smith's careful analysis of the structural vicissitudes through which the house has passed is a mine of technical information and disposes once and for all of many legends and misconceptions. These latter have been fostered in some cases by a patriotic but misguided desire to confer upon the Washington family a social and territorial importance to which they themselves certainly had never aspired. They were worthy representatives of the worthiest English stock, but in no sense county magnates, and the Manor House was never a 'nobleman's seat' – even in miniature. To equip it, therefore, if only in imagination, with stately approaches, such as an avenue or towering gate-house, or with extensive 'pleasaunces' would be entirely inappropriate, and those responsible for the recent restorations have striven, in a spirit of truth and reverence, to revive only such features of this typically English home as are in conformity with surviving traces or documentary records. As always in such cases, original wills and deeds constitute one of the most fruitful sources of information, and fortunately, as Mr. Clifford Smith has demonstrated, a wealth of material is still available to give authority and local colour to his admirable narrative. From its original purchase by Lawrence Washington in 1539 for the sum of £324, 14s. 10d., down to 1659 when the last Washington left it, Sulgrave Manor led an uneventful but dignified existence, whilst the thoughts and fortunes of its successive owners were concerned more with sheep-farming and the wool trade than with any dreams of a transatlantic destiny.

It is said of George Washington that he professed to have little knowledge of, or concern with, his English ancestors, but he undoubtedly owed to them his absorbing interest in wool and sheep, 'that part of my stock [at Mount Vernon] in which I most delight.'

Apart from these prosaic and commercial preoccupations, it is pleasant to find that Lawrence Washington was a man of taste and a lover of things beautiful. He makes special mention in his will (dated 1581) of a 'goblet, parcel gilt, with a cover for the same,' and he leaves to his son no less than 'four pounds to buy him a Salt,' although his bequests to his various grandchildren average only five shillings apiece! What would we not give to recover those precious items of plate, the market value of which to-day might well exceed that of the Manor House itself. There is also a touch of romance in Lawrence Washington's relations with his tenants; he bequeaths to one of them a cottage 'without paying any rent therefor, other than one red rose at the feast of Saint John the Baptist yearly,' and he then goes to his grave in all the odour of kindliness and sanctity, wrapped doubtless in the woollen shroud which later was made compulsory by law in order to encourage the industry which had been the mainstay of his fortune.

Less worthy were some of his Sulgrave neighbours, for we learn with regret that the village had, in later times, an unenviable reputation as the resort of a band of highwaymen and poachers. One of the most prominent of these was no less a personage than the parish clerk who was accustomed to secrete his ill-gotten gains in the church strong-box, and who 'never performed his part in the church services without loaded pistols in his pocket.' Have we perhaps here the hereditary germ of the 'gangster' industry which has played so prominent a part in recent American history – at any rate according to Hollywood?

After the departure of the Washingtons in 1659, Sulgrave Manor fell upon evil days, and eventually 'degenerated into a common farm-house.' Indeed, so obscure had it become that it was not even mentioned in Murray's *Guide to Northamptonshire* in 1878, and it was not until 1885 that the first proper description of the house was published by Sir Henry Dryden, the erudite local historian, and a near neighbour at Canons Ashby.

In 1890 a contemporary visitor describes it as 'a place that has lost its ancient dignity, and is now frowsy and neglected' with 'nettles, docks, and thistles as the only things that flourish.'

This was the state of things until January 1914, when the derelict home of the Washingtons was purchased, for the sum of £8400, by British subscribers, the first names on the list of the subsequent restoration fund being those of the King and the Prince of Wales.

The pious initiative having thus been taken by friends of America in this country, it was natural and wholly fitting that Americans themselves should contribute to the restoration and upkeep of this shrine of Anglo-American kinship, which is only second in importance and sentimental appeal to Mount Vernon itself. Thanks mainly to the National Society of Colonial Dames, and to individual members thereof whose incomparable services in this connection have been fully recorded by Mr. Clifford Smith in Chapter XVII of the present book, the house has not only been faithfully restored, so far as may be, to its original condition, but also appropriately furnished in harmony with its various periods. The gardens and grounds have also been re-planned and made beautiful, and now at last Sulgrave Manor, reconstituted and preserved with taste, scholarship, and loving care, has become a worthy place of pilgrimage and an abiding monument of the common origin of the English-speaking peoples. Indeed, all that remained to be done was to record, in seemly and adequate form, the long and chequered story of the English home of the Washingtons, and how successfully Mr. Clifford Smith has performed this onerous duty will be at once apparent to every reader of this book, which must always remain the classic authority on Sulgrave and its history.

LEE OF FAREHAM.

Preface

My first sight of Sulgrave was on a summer day of 1920, when Lady Lee of Fareham suggested that I s houldaccompany her to the Manor House to discuss its furnishing. The restoration work was then in full swing under the supervision of Sir Reginald Blomfield, R.A., who had restored Chequers ten years before. The ancient decorative features of the rooms were being gradually cleared of modern accretions, and the harmonious beauty of the interior brought once again to light. The furnishing of the Manor House proceeded, and a year later, in June 1921, when it was dedicated and thrown open to the public, it had already acquired something of the appearance it had presented during the hundred and twenty years that the Washingtons lived there. By the time of the George Washington Bi-Centenary Celebrations, held at Sulgrave in July 1932, the repair and equipment of the house and the laying out and planting of the garden was at length complete.

In exploring the building, I have had as my guide, the steward and caretaker, Mr. Frederick Carter, who was placed in charge of it in 1919. Born in the neighbouring village of Middleton Cheney, where his family have been for nearly three hundred years, he has lived the greater part of his life within a few miles of Sulgrave.

During the restoration of the Manor House he was responsible for carrying out Sir Reginald Blomfield's designs for the laying out of the garden, and, as the work proceeded, he retrieved, put aside, and carefully guarded every ancient fragment as it came to light.

In conversation with me he recalled many Northamptonshire traditions, and explained the original purpose of each article of domestic use with which the Manor House is stored, especially the marvellous equipment of the ancient kitchen. Finally he placed me for ever in his debt by producing for me from the bottom of a drawer a thin, worn manuscript, bound in faded, marbled paper, entitled 'The History of Sulgrave,' signed 'J. Henn,' and dated 'April 1789.'

In offering my thanks to those who have helped me I must first place on record the debt of gratitude I owe to the memory of my friend, Rollo Laird Clowes. It was due to his knowledge and patient researches at the British Museum and the Record Office that so much new material has come to light in connection with the Washington family and the early history of Sulgrave, and it was he who drew the coats of arms which adorn my text.

I have to thank Lord Spencer, Vice-Chairman of the Sulgrave Manor Board, for allowing me the use of many books, papers, and pedigrees from Althorp dealing with the Washingtons; the Rev. H. Isham Longden, F.S.A., who has placed his special knowledge of the Washingtons at my disposal; Miss Joan Wake for information concerning early Sulgrave documents; Mr. T. Pape, F.S.A., the well-known student of the Washington ancestry; and Mr. H. D. Ziman for his expert help in the earlier chapters dealing with the history of Sulgrave and the Washingtons, as well as for other advice.

For my description of the garden of the Manor House I am under a special obligation to Miss Eleanour Sinclair Rohde. For architectural guidance I would thank Mr. Alfred J. Gotch, F.S.A., Past President of the Royal Institute of British Architects, who examined every detail of the Manor House with me; and Mr. R. Fielding Dodd, F.R.I.B.A., who most generously placed at my disposal his draughtsman, Mr. Arthur Gerrard, who is responsible for the architectural and freehand drawings and plans which illustrate my text. I must also thank Sir Reginald Blomfield, R.A., architect to Sulgrave Manor, and a Member of the Board of Governors, for the use of his plans of the house and garden; Dr. Allen Mawer, Hon. Secretary of the English Place-Name Society, for the loan of the field-map of Sulgrave; Mr. Hanslip Fletcher for his sketches of the church and village; and Mrs. J. P. Brown, of Sulgrave, for much useful information about the history of the village. I am grateful for the use of some unpublished notes on the surrounding country by the late Mr. W. E. Grey, of Moreton Pinkney, given to me by the Vicar of Sulgrave.

My chapter on the church owes a great deal to the generous help given me by the Vicar, the Rev. W. S. Pakenham-Walsh; also to Mr. F. C. Eeles, Secretary to the Central Council for the Care of Churches, and to Mr. F. E. Howard, who took for me the photographs of the Washington brasses.

For the history of the purchase of Sulgrave I am indebted to Sir Harry Brittain, K.B.E., C.M.G., an original member of the Board of Governors; and for the story of its endowment to Mrs. Joseph R. Lamar, Past-President of the National Society of the Colonial Dames of America, and Mrs. Edward Mitchell Townsend, a Colonial Dame and a representative of that Society upon the Sulgrave Manor Board.

My thanks are due to the Board of Governors for permission to use their records, and to their Secretary, Miss D. K. Palmer, for her help; and above all to Lord Lee for his great kindness in writing the Introduction to this book.

H. CLIFFORD SMITH.

VICTORIA AND ALBERT MUSEUM,
LONDON.

TO THE

VISCOUNTESS LEE OF FAREHAM

THIS BOOK IS DEDICATED BY

THE AUTHOR

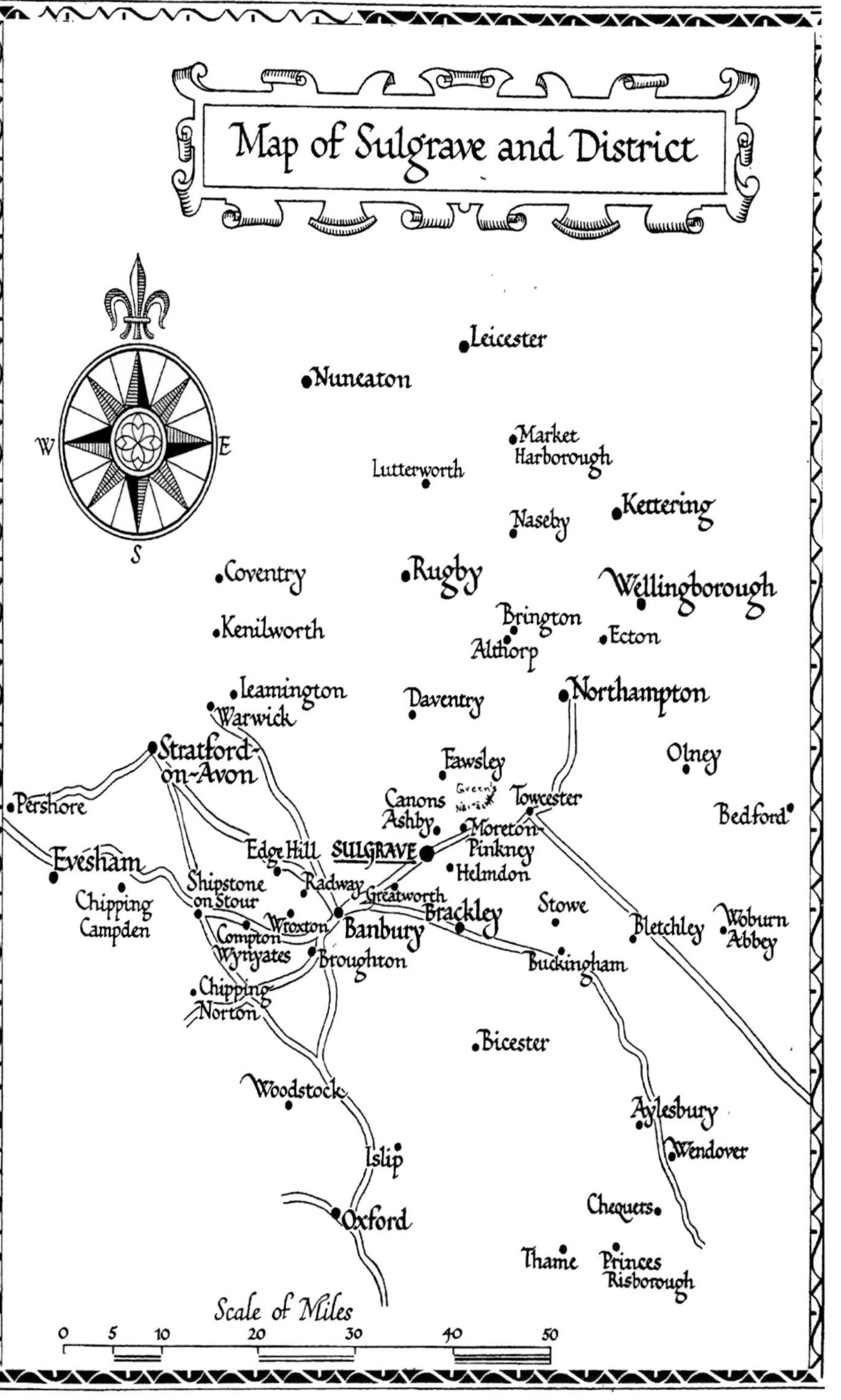

Map of Sulgrave and District
W
E
S
Leicester
Nuneaton
Market Harborough
Lutterworth
Naseby
Kettering
Coventry
Rugby
Wellingborough
Brington
Kenilworth
Althorp
Ecton
Leamington
Warwick
Daventry
Northampton
Stratford-on-Avon
Fawsley
Olney
Pershore
Canons Ashby
Towcester
Bedford
Moreton-Pinkney
Edge Hill
SULGRAVE
Evesham
Helmdon
Radway
Shipstone on Stour
Chipping Campden
Greatworth
Brackley
Stowe
Wroxton
Banbury
Bletchley
Woburn Abbey
Compton Wynyates
Broughton
Buckingham
Chipping Norton
Bicester
Woodstock
Aylesbury
Wendover
Islip
Chequers
Oxford
Thame
Princes Risborough
Scale of Miles
0
5
10
20
30
40
50

PEDIGREE (*in outline*) OF THE WASHINGTONS OF SULGRAVE AND VIRGINIA

(1) Elizabeth, widow of William Gough. = Lawrence Washington, builder of Sulgrave Manor, born *c.* 1500, died 19 Feb. 1583-4, buried at Sulgrave. = (2) Amee, da. of Robt. Pargiter, of Greatworth, Northants, died 1564.

(1) Elizabeth, da. and heir of Walter Light of Radway, Warwicks. = Robert Washington, of Sulgrave, born 1540, sold Sulgrave, 1610, to his nephew, Lawrence Makepeace, died 1619, buried at Sulgrave. = (2) Anne Fisher, of Hanslope, Bucks.

Lawrence Washington, died 1619, buried at Maidstone. = Martha, da. of Clement Newce, of Great Hadham, Herts.

Amye married Alban Wakelyn, of Eydon, Northants.

Lawrence Washington, of Sulgrave, born *c.* 1568, died 1616, buried at Brington, Northants. = Margaret, eldest da. of William Butler, of Tighes, Sussex, married 1588.

Abel Makepeace of Chipping Warden, Northants, died 1602. = Mary Washington,

Lawrence Makepeace, bought Sulgrave, 1610. = Elizabeth Croker.

Rev. Lawrence Washington, M.A. B.D., Fellow of Brasenose Coll., Oxford, Rector of Purleigh, Essex, died Jan. 1652-3. = Amphillis, da. of John Twigden, of Spratton, Northants.

Abel Makepeace, sold Sulgrave 1659, died 1666, buried at Middleton Cheney, Northants.

Colonel John Washington, born 1632 or 1633, settled in Virginia, died Sept. 1677. = Anne, da. of Lieut.-Colonel Nathaniel Pope, married 1658.

Captain Lawrence Washington, of Virginia, died March 1697-8. = Mildred Warner; on her husband's death she went to England and married 2ndly George Gale, of Whitehaven, Cumberland.

Jane Butler = Captain Augustine Washington, of Virginia, born 1694, died 1743. = Mary Ball.

General George Washington, born 11 Feb. 1732, first President of the United States of America, died without issue, 14 Dec. 1799. = Martha, widow of Daniel Parke Custis, and da. of John Dandridge.

SULGRAVE MANOR
AND
THE WASHINGTONS

Chapter I

THE SCENE

SULGRAVE lies almost in the very centre of England, in the south-west corner of Northamptonshire, which borders on the counties of Warwick, Oxford, and Buckingham. It is seventy miles north of London, eighteen from Northampton, eight from Banbury, and equidistant – twenty-eight miles – from Oxford and Stratford-on-Avon.

The village is in a most charming situation, on a low spur in a broad, deep-cut valley, resting as it were on the crest of a wave, and from some of the highest-lying points it commands extensive views. From Barrow Hill, supposed to be a tumulus, about a mile to the north of Sulgrave, nine counties at times are visible.

Its main approaches are by the London road on the south, and by the road from Banbury on the west. This latter road passes straight through the village to reach Sulgrave Manor.

Buried in the depths of the Midlands, the surroundings of Sulgrave possess all the peculiar characteristics of Midland scenery. Ridge upon ridge of undulating pasture land, valley after valley of flat meadows and shallow sluggish streams encircle it; while narrow roads bordered by broad margins of greensward and by giant hedges stretch out from it in every direction.

The scarcity of running water is one of the unexpected features which strikes one in this district. Row upon row of willows down the centre of a valley naturally suggest a fair-sized stream, and there are innumerable watercourses; but in summer they are almost invariably dry, while in winter the water which flows sluggishly along them is at best a very muddy apology for a running brook.

No one would venture to call this a thickly wooded country,[1] yet this southern district of Northamptonshire is by no means bare, for the bold outline of the rolling land is relieved by numberless fox-coverts, by frequent copses of birch and larch, and at intervals by the parks and avenues of stone-built country seats. The villages and the remoter farm-steads lie embowered in trees; and on a summer day one may wander for miles along high roads and bridle-lanes under the shade of abundant hedgerow timber.

Such is the landscape of the country-side where George Washington's ancestors in Tudor and Jacobean days had their home. One is impressed by the thoroughly English character of the scene. Here no mountains are in sight, 'no torrents, no cascades, no forests – nothing to excite the emotions of mankind,' but fields with luxuriant herbage, flower-filled hedgerows, and farms with grazing land.

The country has a fascination of its own, yet to most Englishmen it is unfamiliar ground. Artists seldom come to paint its unobtrusive beauties, and few travellers pass along its highways. The regular tourist in search of scenery goes further afield – to richer woodlands and more fertile valleys, to the grander surroundings of the Welsh mountains, the Scottish Highlands, or the Cumbrian Lakes. Yet Sulgrave itself has in recent years drawn as many as nine thousand visitors in a single season to see the Washington Manor House.

Though the social character of the country-side has changed,

[1] As early as 1789 Jeremiah Henn, the local chronicler whose manuscript history of the village is described in Chapter VI, writing in the *Gentleman's Magazine* on the derivation of the place-name 'Sulgrave,' says: 'Whatever woods or groves may formerly have been, no vestiges remain at this time, the article wood being very scarce.'

the outward features of the land are not greatly altered from the Elizabethan days when the Manor House was new, and John Norden the topographer was writing of Northamptonshire in his *Speculi Britanniæ Pars Altera* [1] as

'a most pleasant Shire, adorned both with salutarie and profitable Seates, manie and notable Sheepe Pastures, rich feedings for Cattle, firtile-Corne Groundes and lardge Feilds greatly inrichinge the industrious Husbandman. No Shire within this Land hath so little waste Grounds, for theare is not in a manner anie part thereof, but is turned to some profitable Use. It is very populous, and the Townes, Parishes, yea every *Hamlett* for the most parte, but most especiallie the Houses of the Nobillitie most healthfully Scituate in a most pure and pleasant Ayre. The Countrie most comfortable for Travaylers not only in regard of the open perspects which are delightfull to wayfaringe Men; But also in regarde of plentie of Townes, Parishes and Villages, which are so universallie dispersed, that in every two or three Myles at the most, is found a Place of ease to the wearisome Travylour. . . .

'The firtilitie, salutarie ayre, pleasant perspects and convenviencie of this Shire in all things to a generous and noble mynde have so allured Nobilitie to plante themselves within the same, that no Shire within this Realme can answere the like Number of Noblemen, as are Seated in those Partes. . . .

. . . 'No Shire within this Lande is so plentfullie stored with

[1] 'SPECULI BRITANNIÆ *Pars Altera*: or, A DELINEATION OF NORTHAMPTONSHIRE; Being a brief HISTORICALL AND CHOROGRAPHICALL DISCRIPTION OF THAT COUNTY. Wherein are also Alphabetically set down, THE NAMES OF CYTIES, TOWNES, PARISHES, HAMLETS, HOWSES OF NOTE, and OTHER REMARKABLES. BY THE TRAVAYLE OF JOHN NORDEN, IN THE YEAR M.DC.X. London: Printed in the Year M. DCC. XX.'

Though dated 1610 and not published until 1720, this book bears internal evidence that it was composed in the lifetime of Queen Elizabeth.

Gentry in regarde whearof this Shire may seeme worthy to be termed the Herralds Garden, whearin they may gather such varieties of Coates as in some degree or other match all their Coates in *Englande*.

'Manie other Things may be said . . . not only in regarde of Profitt but also of Pleasure. Ffor Hawkinge both on Land and River it will hardly be matched, such pleasant Fields and lardge perspects at will, to view the soaringe Ffawkon, and golden streames so interlaceinge the cheareful Hills and Dales replenished with Game of all sortes to delighte the noble Mynde. Deare, Red and Fallowe, both in Parks, Fforests, and Chases are so plentifull as noe one Shire yeeldeth lyke. . . .

'Thus is *Northamptonshire* furnished with Parkes, Forests, and Chaces yealdinge often recreation to the Mynde, exercise to the Bodie, and relief to the Table.'

The Northamptonshire farmer of those days, and, indeed, for centuries afterwards, was a happy man, so far as farmers are ever happy. Norden could not but wonder

'to call to Mynde the greate heards of Cattle longinge to every small Parishe, Village, and Hamlett, which when in my small Travayle I did behond by such generall multitudes I perswaded my selfe of an impossibilitie, that so small Parishes and Places of so slender Accompt could yeeld so great a Number of kyne and other Cattle, such mayne Fflocks of Sheepe and which made me most to marvayle were the greate heards of Swyne, a Beast altogether unprofittable, 'till he come to the Slaughter. Then his rustie Ribbs in a Frostye Morninge will please *Pearce* the Ploughman, and will so supple his Weather-beaten Lipps, that his Whipp and his Whistle will hamer out such harmony as will make a Dogge daunce that delights it. But howsoever they be fed, the baser sorte of Men prove wealthie, and wade through the World with good countenance in their calling, least beholden generally to the monied Men of any other Shire whatsoever that I knowe.'

It cannot be said that the farming life of Northamptonshire is now so brisk. Northamptonshire villages lie far apart, and here as elsewhere the fatal process of migration from country to town has gone on steadily. Villages which once were places of importance have sunk into obscurity, and the local industries of lace-making and boot-making have pined away under the competition of larger centres. Sulgrave itself, a parish of some 2000 acres, has seen a steady decrease in its population since the beginning of the nineteenth century – when the second of the two great monumental histories of Northamptonshire was compiled – having sunk from 578 in 1821 to 380 a century later. It is perhaps owing to the prevalence of pasture over arable land that one seldom meets a wayfarer along the 'No Drift Roads' and cross-country paths, and save in the actual neighbourhood of the villages a sense of unusual loneliness prevails.

Before the days of railways the village was almost as completely isolated as it was possible to be – so isolated, in fact, that Sulgrave and three neighbouring hamlets, Lois Weedon, Culworth, and Wappenham, were known as the 'Lost Villages.' Its distance from any large town cut it off from much communication with the outer world, and travelling was difficult in these parts. The soft stone of the country made execrable roads; they were indifferently looked after and often had ruts, we are credibly informed, of half a yard in depth; for the most part they were merely field roads, enclosed on the one side by a boundary hedge, but with no fence at all on the other, and wherever one went the way was impeded by a succession of field gates. Some of these former field roads still bear the ancient name of 'Welsh lanes,' being the routes along which the Welsh ponies were driven to seek a market in the Midland counties.

Situated on the belt of limestone which runs diagonally from the Dorset coast to Whitby in Yorkshire, the village of Sulgrave is built entirely of stone. We do not, however, find it in quite the same abundance here as in the Cotswolds; for while the walls of farmyards and cottage gardens are of stone, beyond the confines of the village hedgerows border the roads and fields. The village buildings are mainly of the local Helmdon stone, which is generally rubble, not hand-dressed, and laid in courses, the roofs being either thatched or of stone tiles. The farms and a few of the larger houses, such as the charming long low building known as the Thatched House, opposite the main entrance to the Manor House, are faced with hand-dressed Helmdon stone.

The quoins or corner-stones of the houses, and the jambs and lintels of doors and windows are of Hornton stone, as are the gable-ends and ridge tiles and the mullions of the windows, though these in many cases have been replaced at later times by stout oak window-frames. This stone, which is from the Hornton quarries, near Banbury, is of two colours, a warm brown and a sage-green with occasional brown splashes, while the dark-red iron sandstone from the neighbouring quarry of Eydon is sometimes used both for facing and for walls.

In earlier days the wool from his pastures and corn from his ploughed fields brought great prosperity to the farmer. Sulgrave contains no less than sixteen farms, most of which have their fronts upon the road, and their lands extending out behind them – a disposition rarely met with in the English country-side. Every group of farm buildings includes one or more fine, lofty barns for the unloading of wagons, and for the storage of farm produce. Each barn is in itself a noble piece of architecture in stone and timber-work, and the use of local materials and the existence of a strong local tradition in building result in such uniformity of style that often it is not easy in the case of a barn, a cottage, or even of a farmhouse, to say whether it was built in Tudor, Stuart, or Georgian times.

Chapter II

THE EARLIER HISTORY OF SULGRAVE

OF the early history of Sulgrave little is known, owing to the loss of the parish registers prior to 1659 in a fire which destroyed the vicarage at the beginning of the eighteenth century. The village was at no time large, or prominent in the history of the Midlands. Topographers took little notice of it, and it is barely mentioned by John Norden in his *Delineation of Northamptonshire*. The place-name Sulgrave (also termed Solegrave, Solgrave and, Soulgrove in early deeds) is said to be derived from the Saxon words for a plough and a wood, though Baker, who gives this derivation in his History of Northamptonshire, remarks that 'the union of arable and wood land would have equally applied to most parishes of Saxon nomenclature.'

It is stated in *Northamptonshire Place-Names* (1933) that the first syllable may be the Old English *sulh*, denoting a channel or passage, and that the second is perhaps *graef*, a pit or trench. The local historian, Jeremiah Henn, in an article in the *Gentleman's Magazine* of 1789, suggests that it may derive the first part of its name from the little rivulet Sou or Sow which rises at Holywell Spring in Sulgrave and journeys on to Towcester as the River Tove. In his manuscript 'History of Sulgrave' (to be referred to later) he remarks that the village name was then 'vulgarly pronounced Sowgruff.'

Seven hundred years earlier, at the time of the Domesday Survey (1086), Sulgrave was a single large manor extending over four hides (480 acres). It was the property of Ghilo, brother of Ansculf, who had as tenants Hugh, Landric, and Otbert. There was at this time arable land sufficient for ten ploughs. Three of these ten ploughlands formed Ghilo's personal demesne, with one serf attached to them. Five ploughlands were in the possession of twenty villeins and six bordars or cottagers. The remaining two had probably recently become waste, for the Domesday Survey notes that the annual valuation had decreased from £9 to £7. There were eight acres of meadowland, and it is observed that the whole manor lay within the Soke of Wardon. Four men had previously held it; they were not allowed to leave it, being apparently attached as villeins to the Soke.[1]

Ghilo, the lord of the manor, held a good deal of property in Northamptonshire. He was known as Ghilo de Pinkeney, and was ancestor of the family of Pinkeney, who held the barony of Weedon (of which Sulgrave formed part) by service of Castle Guard at Windsor. Ghilo himself was the founder of Weedon Pinkeney as a cell to the monastery of St. Lucien of Beauvais, in France. The probable site of his residence at Sulgrave may be identified in the mount called Castle Hill, which lies a little westward of the churchyard with a faint fosse on the north side. For the barony of Weedon Ghilo's successors paid to the Constable of Windsor Castle, towards the guard, the sum of fifteen shillings (as the equivalent of fifteen knights' fees) annually until, in 1301, Henry de Pinkeney alienated the barony to the King, Edward I.

[1] *i.e.* 'The franchise of holding a court' (Kenelm Digby's *History of the Law of Real Property*); the word being also applied to the extent of land covered by the franchise.

Long before this the estate at Sulgrave had been divided into several manors by the process known as sub-infeudation. Robert de Pinkeney, ancestor of the Pinkeneys of Moreton Pinkney, and probably a younger brother of Ghilo, was enfeoffed of a portion of the lordship. We find an undated deed in which Simon St. Lys, Earl of Northampton, testifies that in his presence, in the city of Northampton, Robert Pinkeney had granted to the church and monks of St. Andrew, in Northampton, 'all the fee which Godfrey and Gero held of him in Sulgrave by service of one knight.'

This grant was confirmed in the reign of Henry II by the paramount lord of the time, Gilbert de Pinkeney of Weedon, with the consent of his wife Eustachia and his son and heir Henry. The Priory was established in possession of the church of Sulgrave with pertinences 'of the gift of Godfrey and Bartholomew, and a moiety of all the land which Godfrey held in Sulgrave, as given to them by said Godfrey de Bartholomew, freed from all service to the said Bartholomew, but subject to the service due to himself of half a fee from Robert de Pinkeney.' Bartholomew de Sulgrave, the son of Godfrey, duly confirmed the Priory in their possession of half his lands in Sulgrave, and entered into an agreement with the Prior and monks, respecting the Castle Ward due to Windsor, for half a fee.

The Priory of St. Andrew in Northampton which thus became a corporate land-owner in Sulgrave was situated in the north-east part of the town, near the wall, and bordering on the River Nen. It was founded before the year 1076, and re-founded with Cluniac monks from the Abbey of St. Marie de Caritate on the Loire in 1084 by Simon de St. Lys, the Earl of Northampton already mentioned. He gave it, among much else, two hides of land in the adjoining manor of Stotesbury. By such gifts a manor of St. Andrew's was carved out of the parent Pinkeney Manor, and further grants increased its size. Bartholomew de Sulgrave himself added all his demesne in arable, pasture, and meadow land for ten years after the death of St. Hugh of Avalon, Bishop of Lincoln (September 1200), rendering yearly half the growing corn, apart from the tithe, and two loads of hay.

Henry, son of Bartholomew, apparently restored the church of Sulgrave to the Priory. Lands and houses in the same parish came to the monks by gift of the same Henry. Waleran de Sulgrave gave them thirty acres and five virgates in Sulgrave, and his grandson, William de Lyons, subsequently remitted the service of the land. William de Culworth gave them in free alms half the tithes of hay of his demesne of Sulgrave, and all the tithes of hay of his tenants there. He confirmed Waleran's gifts, and released the Prior and monks from attendance at his court, and from Castle Ward at Windsor. Before the year 1290 the St. Andrew's Manor must have been a complete entity, with its own lord (the Prior), its manor courts, and its privileges.

Meanwhile the remainder of the parent manor of Sulgrave had been divided into two portions, commonly referred to as the Elington and Culworth Manors. At the beginning of Edward I's reign (1273) Henry de Elynton[1] was certified to hold one knight's fee in Sulgrave of William de Pinkeney, and this remained in the hands of the Elington family until about 1359, when William de Elington conveyed the estate to John de Stotesbury. The direct line of Stotesburys died out about 1563, when the estate passed to Thomas Leeson, and in the following year, at the Court Baron of Lawrence Washington, 'the jurors presented that Thomas Leeson held a messuage and virgate and half of land as heir of Thomas Stotesbury who had died since the last Court.' Thomas Leeson was the grandson of Thomas Stotesbury, and in a later chapter we shall see how the Elington

[1] Brydges and others quote him as 'Glinton.'

Manor passed in due course from the Leeson family into the hands of a grandson of Lawrence Washington.

The remaining manor was in the hands of the Culworth family at least as early as the reign of King John, when Sir Robert de Culworth is observed to hold 'a carucate [plough] of land and tenants.' The William de Culworth who made so generous a gift to the Priory of St. Andrew was the sòn of Sir Robert. Sir Robert's father, another William, had made a bargain with Henry, the then Prior of St. Andrew's, and it appears that the family was already established in his generation, *i.e.* before the reign of King John.

Hugh de Culworth, the great-grandson of Sir Robert, sold the estate to Walter de Gayton, who in turn disposed of it to Sir John de Montalt, who acquired another carucate of land, and after some disputes, retained it until his death in 1293. Through his son, Adam de Montalt, whose daughter Elizabeth married Stephen de Trafford, it passed into the Trafford family, in whose hands it remained (with one brief interval when it was taken into the possession of the King) until 1371. It was then purchased by Sir Henry Ardern, in whose family it remained until, in 1439, it was conveyed to Robert Danvers, later Justice of Common Pleas. The Danvers family retained the Culworth Manor for the greater part of two centuries. It never came into the hands of the Washingtons or their descendants, being purchased about 1604 by the Crewe family.

Side by side with the Elington and the Culworth Manors of Sulgrave, which continued to be held by laymen as of the Honour of Pinkeney, the Manor of St. Andrew remained in the hands of the monks. Like other foreign monasteries in England, St. Andrew's Priory lost its revenues by confiscation to the Crown during the wars with France, but in the time of Henry IV the monks obtained the liberty of retaining their temporalities on payment of twenty shillings yearly to the King. In the sixth year of Edward IV (1466), the Priory was 'made denizen' and became discharged of all pensions due to the Crown. The last three Priors were William Rekner, who was appointed about 1523; John Petie, mentioned in 1538; and Francis Abree, *alias* Leicester, who had not long been in office when the religious houses in England were dissolved by Henry VIII.

These Priors and their predecessors were lords of the manor of Sulgrave, and possibly stewards, visiting the manor in person at least twice a year. There would have been a room in the manor buildings where manorial business would have been conducted. Henn in his notes on Sulgrave in the *Gentleman's Magazine*, says that these stood in a sequestered situation near the former church, five or six hundred yards north-west of the present church, where there was 'antiently a grange belonging to St. Andrew's, a monastery in Northampton, of which there are at this time [1789] no remains.'

There are in existence two copies of the Deed of Surrender of the Priory, one in English, dated 1st March 1537-8, the other, in Latin, dated the following day. The former contains a confession by the monks of their mismanagement of the House: '... the revenues of which we the said Prior and Convent, voluntarily only by our proper conscience compelled, do recognise neither by us nor our predecessors to have been employed according to the original intent of the founders, that is to say, in the pure observance of Christ's Religion, according to the devout rule and doctrine of holy St. Benedict, in virtuous exercise and study according to our profession and avowal, nor yet in the charitable sustaining, comforting, and relieving of poor people by the keeping of good and necessary hospitality. But as well we as others, our predecessors, called religious persons, within our said monastery, taking on us the habit or outward vesture of the said rule only to the intent to lead our lives in an idle quietness and not in virtuous exercise, in a stately estimation and not in obedient humility, have under the shadow or colour of the said rule and habit vainly, detestably, and also ungodly, employed, yea, rather devoured, the yearly revenues issuing and coming of the said possessions in continual ingurgitation and farcing[1] . . . to the most notable slander of Christ's holy Evangiles.'[2]

The Visitor General had reported that 'the House was greatly in debt, the lands sold and mortaged, the farms let out and the rent received beforehand for ten, fifteen, and twenty years; chanters founded to be paid out of the lands, and great bonds of forfeiture for non-payment.'

Among the possessions which the Priory relinquished were the manor, impropriate rectory, and advowson of the vicarage of Sulgrave.

In the Valuation of Ecclesiastical Properties (*Valor Ecclesiasticus*) of the twenty-first year of the reign of Henry VIII (1529-30), it is stated that there was a rent of twenty-one shillings yearly, called 'Windsor Reint,' issuing out of Sulgrave, payable to the College of Windsor. In the same valuation, under 'Rents and Farm in divers villages and hamlets,' Sulgrave is valued at £6, 18s. 9½d., but the rents-of-assize (about £6, 8s. od. gross) are not included, and it is likely that the part of the manor in Stuchbury was valued separately, as part of another manor.

From an undated Rental in Latin in the Public Record Office of all the possessions of the Priory of St. Andrew, made in 1538 for Henry VIII after the Dissolution, it appears that Lawrence Washington already held from the Priory a lease of a house in Sulgrave, and that he assisted the surveyors in their labours. As it shows the name and rents of the free and customary tenants who, in all probability, were holding when Lawrence took possession of the lordship, an abridg-

[1] Guzzling and stuffing.

[2] The Gospels.

ment of the part of the Survey referring to Sulgrave is appended here: –

'Free tenants in Sulgrave.

Thomas Humfrey, certain lands with appurtenances, rent, at Michaelmas, 4s. and 2 capons.

John Coll, certain lands, rent 9½d.

William Lovell, certain lands, rent 8d.

Thomas Stuttesbury, certain lands, rent 4s.

William Stephyn, certain lands, rent 22d.

The same William, certain lands, rent 1 lb. cumin.[1]

Sum, 11s. 3½d. [The rents in kind ignored.]

'Tenants at will in Sulgrave.

John Warrenne holds at will according to the custom of the manor a messuage and certain lands, rent, at Ladyday and Michaelmas, 23s. 8d.

John Kyng, a cottage, rent 3s. 4d.

Richard Baker, a messuage and certain lands, rent 14s. 6d.

Edward Raynndon, a messuage with appurtenances, rent 14s. 6d.

Sum, 56s.

'Rents of divers lands and tenements anciently received by the hands of Christopher Tomson payable at the Feast * * * 60s.

Sum, 60s.

Lawrence Wasshyngton holds by indenture a messuage with appurtenances in Sulgrave, and renders therefore yearly [*his rent*] *at the Feasts of the Annunciation and St. Michael the Archangel*, 20*s*.[2]

[1] An aromatic garden herb.

[2] This proved that he already had a *house*, with yard and the accompanying buildings. As the name of the house (*i.e.* messuage) is not given, it is not possible to say whether it stood on the site of the present Manor House.

Christopher Tomson holds by indenture a tenement and two yard lands with appurtenances, rent 18s.

Sum, 38s.

Robert Bull holds * * * certain lands with appurtenances in Sulgrave, rent 31s. 6d.

Sum, 31s. 6d.

Sum total, £18, 17s. 9½d.

'Stuttesbury.

Christopher Tomson holds by indenture one close[1] with appurtenances, these called the "Welkys," rent, at Lady-day and Michaelmas, 26s. 8d.

The same holds by indenture another close called the "Mylfeld" with appurtenances, rent 106s. 8d.

The same holds by indenture, two other closes called "Westfeld" and "Townesfeld," rent £23.[2]

John Mellys holds by indenture another close called the "Pooles," with appurtenances, rent 26s. 8d.

The same holds in ferm by indenture two other closes which are worth yearly £12, nevertheless the same John renders therefor during a term of years granted to him £6.[3]

Sum £37 [*sic*].

'*Outgoings :*

'Sulgrave and Woodford.

Rent resolute[4] to the Earl of Derby issuing out of lands in Woodford, yearly 3s. 4d.

Annual and perpetual pension anciently paid to the Dean and Chapter of the College of Windsor out of the issues, 11s. 3d.

[1] A field.

[2] This must have been a very large acreage.

[3] Then follows the word *quousque*, probably as a query: 'Until when?'

[4] Rent paid away by the lord of the manor to some other lord.

A like pension anciently paid to the Archdeacon of Northampton for procuration, issuing from the church in Sulgrave, 6s. $6\frac{3}{4}$d.'

In the margin of the manuscript under the heading 'Stuttesbury,' is a note which does not appear to have been recorded by any previous writer on the history of Sulgrave. It is to the effect that the 'particular' was made by Lawrence Washington, gent.; while below, in a different hand, is a memorandum: 'that the aforesaid closes were granted to Robert Durwyte (or Turwyte) and his heirs for ever, and are now granted and have been sold (*conceduntur et vendebantur*) to John Melles and his heirs for ever by the said Robert.'

Chapter III

THE ARRIVAL OF THE WASHINGTONS

THOSE who visit Sulgrave come there, for the most part, for its Washington associations. It is for the sake of the Washingtons that the Manor House, whose beauties both inside and out it is one purpose of the present book to illustrate, has been carefully restored since the War, and its formal garden re-created. The walls and ceilings, the open hearths, the timbered roof and ancient plaster work are those which it first possessed, and, in the main, the features which now meet the eye are those which it was given about the year 1540 by Lawrence Washington, the founder of the family at Sulgrave, and the direct ancestor at seven removes of George Washington of Virginia, the first President of the United States.

The stages by which the Washington family arrived at Sulgrave will be outlined in the present chapter. George Washington himself professed to have little knowledge, and indeed little interest concerning his ancestry, but all that is known to-day of the descent of his Sulgrave forebears follows from a somewhat inaccurate clue which he himself gave.

Sir Isaac Heard, Garter King of Arms, who wrote in 1791 to question the President, was told that Colonel John Washington, the President's great-grandfather, had emigrated to Virginia about 1657 with his brother Lawrence.[1] Whence they had come was unknown, but there was a family tradition that the line had its origins in the north of England. Sir Isaac Heard was not discouraged from following up these scanty clues, and when he found in a Visitation of Northamptonshire, made in 1618, the names of a John and a Lawrence Washington, both sons of a Lawrence Washington of Sulgrave, who had died two years earlier, he assumed, though with some doubts, that he had tracked down the emigrants of forty years later.

This identification was accepted for a time, without Sir Isaac's reservations, by writers on the Washington pedigree. But in 1866 it was definitely disproved by the researches of Colonel J. L. Chester, who ascertained that the John Washington of the Visitation of Northamptonshire died in England about 1668 as Sir John Washington of Thrapston,[2] while his brother had become the Rev. Lawrence Washington,[3] Rector of Purleigh in Essex, and was buried at Maldon in 1652-3. Since neither of these could have been the founder of the family in Virginia, it seemed possible that the emigrants might be dissociated from Sulgrave altogether. The thread, however, had only temporarily disappeared, and the coincidence of names seemed to demand further research.

An American genealogist, Mr. H. F. Waters, succeeded in re-establishing the connection by the discoveries he made between 1884 and 1892. The Rev. Lawrence Washington, though not himself an emigrant was, so Mr. Waters made it clear, the father of two sons who bore the same names as his brother at Thrapston and himself, and who actually crossed the Atlantic after their father's death. The great-great-grandfather of the President was thus the Lawrence Washington who was Rector of Purleigh; and the Rev. Lawrence Washington who was Rector of Purleigh was the great-

[1] For a more accurate statement, see pp. 68-69.
[2] See p. 66. [3] See pp. 67-68.

grandson of the Lawrence Washington who built Sulgrave Manor. Thus the line was re-established, and through the founder of the Sulgrave branch Mr. Waters traced their ancestry backwards to the Washingtons of Warton and Whitfield (or Tewitfield) in Lancashire, whence this first Sulgrave Washington came.

The President's belief that his forebears had come from the north of England was thus satisfactorily confirmed. It was, however, possible to trace the line still farther backwards. Washington Irving, in his *Life of Washington*, had plunged boldly towards the Washingtons who had settled in the twelfth century at a village of their own name in Durham, but he had worked out no definite connection. There was a rival theory that the Washingtons of Warton (and hence of Sulgrave) were a branch of those Washingtons who drew their name, also in the twelfth century, from Whashton in Yorkshire. Researches since that time have made it certain that it was Washington Irving's guess which was the right one: the Washingtons of Sulgrave and of Virginia came from Durham and not from Yorkshire. This village of Washington (anciently Wessington) lies not far from the River Wear, four miles distant from Chester-le-Street. The place-name (according to Harrison's *Surnames*) signifies the estate or farm of the family of Hwǣs. Hwǣs, an Anglo-Saxon personal name, meant sharp or keen.

The story may now be re-opened at a point over three hundred and fifty years before the building of Sulgrave, when the earliest traceable members of the family appeared in the village in Durham from which their surname was derived. We are indebted to Mr. Edward Lee McClain[1] (who holds the copyright in the authentic

[1] *The Washington Ancestry, and Records of the McClain, Johnson, and Forty Other Colonial American Families.* Prepared for Edward Lee McClain by Charles Arthur Hoppin. Three volumes. Privately printed, 1932. A copy of this important work was presented to Sulgrave Manor House by Edward Lee and Lulu Johnson McClain, 'as their Contribution to American History and Genealogy,' 8th March, 1932.

Washington genealogy prepared by Mr. C. A. Hoppin[1]) for allowing Mr. T. Pape to write the following partial summary of the earlier direct paternal ancestry of the Sulgrave Washingtons.

The family name of Washington is first mentioned in *Boldon Buke*, a great rental compiled by Bishop Hugh Pudsey in 1180, which is kept in Durham Cathedral Library. William de Hertburne quit-claimed the vill of Hertburne and held Wessington instead for a rent of £4. In 1227 we are told that William de Wessington holds the vill of Wessington, so that either William de Hertburne assumed the name *de Wessington*, or his son did. Thereafter, chiefly by deeds still extant in England and given in Mr. McClain's book, one can trace the senior male line through quite a number of generations of Washingtons whose Christian names were either William or Walter. Their heraldic device seems to have been a lion. The earliest Washington seal, attached to a deed dating from about the middle of the thirteenth century, is circular with the design of a lion passant, and the legend states that it is the seal of Walter, son of William de Wessington. Near the beginning of the fourteenth century Walter de Wessington's seal showed a rampant lion, over all a bend.

But before the middle of the fourteenth century we find a junior branch of the Washington family using the well-known mullets and bars (the 'stars and stripes') of the Washington coat.

Now there are no memorials of the family in the mining village of Washington in County Durham, either in the church, which is quite modern, or at the old manor house, which has been divided into tenements and is rapidly falling into decay. But the two bars

[1] Mr. C. A. Hoppin, by his original research, was the author of most of the Washington genealogy, as published by Mr. McClain – Mr. Pape collaborating in proving the very early English genealogical information which is his copyright in England. For the complete authentic pedigree substantiated by documentary proofs Mr. McClain's book should be studied.

and three mullets in chief of the Washington coat of arms occur on a stone shield on the west front of Hylton Castle in the valley of the Wear. If we omit seals on deeds, that is perhaps the oldest Washington coat of arms in existence. The oldest seal, however, rather damaged, but showing the two bars with three mullets in chief on a shield surrounded by geometrical tracery, is attached to a deed dated 1346, among the Duke of Norfolk's muniments. It is a grant of Helton Flechan in Westmorland to William Norton by Sir William de Wessington, and it is given at Wessington. This deed and the seal are of the greatest importance, for they link up the family of Washington in the county of Durham with the same family in Westmorland. This branch of the Washington family held half the manor of Helton Flechan in Westmorland through the marriage of an heiress, Margaret de Morville, with William de Wessington of County Durham. It was most likely his brother, John de Wessington, who, about the year 1260, married a Westmorland heiress and thereby received lands in dowry round Kendal.

Robert de Wessington, who married Johanna (or Joan) Strickland of Sizergh Castle, was in all probability John de Wessington's son, and we know from deeds and documents quoted in Mr. McClain's book, and now in the muniment rooms at Lowther Castle and Sizergh Castle, that he received not only lands round Kendal but also half the manor of Carnforth in North Lancashire from his brother-in-law, Walter de Strickland, whereby the Washingtons were brought into territorial association with the district between Carnforth and Lancaster. In the direct line of descent from Robert de Wessington by his wife Joan (*née* Strickland) came another Robert, whose only daughter and heiress, Agnes de Wessington, married Edmund Lawrence of Ashton Hall, near Lancaster. The line of George Washington's paternal ancestry was carried on by an uncle of Agnes, viz. John de Wessington, who, in the late fourteenth century, married Joan Croft. Soon afterwards the name definitely takes the modern form, so that, when one looks at the copy (published as aforesaid) of a long inquisition taken in 1484, a year after his death, one finds Robert's surname in the form *Wasshington*.

He held many lands in North Lancashire for various services and payments. In all probability the Washington coat of arms carved in stone on the outer western wall of Warton church tower was a record of this Robert Washington's generosity in the building of the church. That is the only memorial of one of George Washington's direct ancestors at Warton, though there is, in the churchyard under the east window, a gravestone to an eighteenth-century Elizabeth Washington and her grandson, the Rev. Thomas Washington, who died in 1823, the last of the junior local branch.

The branch which concerns our narrative descends from another Robert Washington, second son of the Robert Washington who died in 1483. This Robert, the grandfather of Lawrence Washington, the builder of Sulgrave, was married three times: to Elizabeth Westfield, to Jane Whittington, and to Agnes or Anne Bateman. His eldest son by his first marriage was John Washington, who married Margaret Kytson, the daughter of a neighbour at Warton, and the sister of Sir Thomas Kytson, the merchant adventurer, of Hengrave Hall, Suffolk. Of the six children of John Washington and Margaret Kytson, the eldest, Lawrence Washington, was the builder of Sulgrave Manor House. He is presumed to have been born at Warton about 1500.

The ancestry of Lawrence Washington has been traced here somewhat perfunctorily, for despite all the researches of recent years it frequently remains obscure whether the John or the Robert Washington mentioned in one document is the same as the John or the Robert of another, and not a son or a nephew of the same name. A Visitation of Northamptonshire for 1564 is, however, fairly detailed as to the immediate descent of Lawrence of Sulgrave. We know the names of his brothers, Nicholas, Leonard, Peter, and Thomas, and of his sister Jane, who married Humphrey Gardener of Cockerham. Nicholas, it appears, moved to the neighbourhood of Morecambe Bay in Lancashire. Leonard remained at Warton. Peter died young.

Lawrence, the eldest, and Thomas, the youngest, both went into the wool trade, in which it is clear they were helped by their uncle, Sir Thomas Kytson, a man of considerable importance, who became a freeman of the Mercers' Company in 1507, Sheriff of the City of London in 1533, and Warden of his Company in 1535. Between 1507 and 1525, when he began to build Hengrave Hall upon the Manor which he had purchased in Suffolk, Kytson had apparently acquired great wealth by dealing in Kendal cloths and taking part in the Flanders trade. He finished building Hengrave Hall in 1538, and died in 1540, leaving a widow who subsequently married, first, Sir Richard Long, and later, John Bourchier, Earl of Bath. Among the coats of arms inserted in the windows of the banqueting hall at Hengrave Hall is one commemorating the marriage of Sir Thomas's sister with John Washington.

Thomas Washington, the nephew of Sir Thomas Kytson (and we may believe his godson), was apprenticed to him, and became a freeman of the Mercers' Company in 1541. A number of letters from him to his widowed aunt, which he wrote in 1551 from London and from Antwerp (where he became first Governor of the Merchant Adventurers' English Bourse), are preserved. His brother, Lawrence Washington, did not become a member of the Mercers' Company; he is said to have been educated for the Law and to have become a Bencher of Gray's Inn, but there does not appear to be any authority for this oft-repeated statement.[1] The success of his uncle in the wool trade was not, however, lost upon him, and he evidently entered the trade quite young in London and became, in due course, a successful woolstapler. Some time before 1530 he married Elizabeth Gough, the widow of a wealthy mercer, and settled with her in the town of Northampton. His cousin Catharine Kytson had married Sir John Spencer, a prosperous Northamptonshire landowner, and lived at Althorp a few miles away. Sir John Spencer, who owned as many as twenty thousand sheep at one time, may well have sold wool to his wife's cousin in Northampton. Lawrence himself had, in any case, his wife's connections, and his uncle, Sir Thomas Kytson, to forward his interests in London. He was in a position to make a fortune, and evidently did so.

In 1531 he acquired land in Northamptonshire at Higham Ferrers, Chelveston, and Caldecott, and in the next year he became Mayor of Northampton. At the same time he leased from the Priory of St. Andrew at Northampton an estate called Millefield at Sulgrave[2] upon which, with a partner, he began to raise sheep. Before 1535 he had also taken the lease of a house at Sulgrave. When, four years later, the property of the monks was confiscated by Henry VIII, he seized the chance to purchase for the sum of £324, 14s. 10d. the Manor of Sulgrave, and the Millefield estate which he had hitherto leased.

[1] See Rev. H. Isham Longden, *The History of the Washington Family* (1927).

[2] Part of the land given in Stuchbury, see p. 42.

Chapter IV

LAWRENCE WASHINGTON THE BUILDER OF THE MANOR HOUSE

THE earliest mention of Lawrence Washington in the County of Northamptonshire appears to be on a deed of 24th March 1530-1, in which the Dean and Chapter of the College of St. Mary of the Newark, Leicester, demised to Lawrence Washington and Elizabeth his wife the appropriate Rectory of Higham Ferrers, Chelveston and Caldecott, for a term of forty years. His wife had already inherited land in these parishes from her first husband, William Gough, by his will dated 24th August 1528. Lawrence Washington evidently married her about 1529, or 1530, and he must already have been resident and fairly well known in the town of Northampton, since in 1532 he was elected mayor. No doubt he was assisted by the fact that his wife's first husband had been a bailiff of the borough.

Lawrence Washington's coat of arms is to be seen in the upper corridor of Northampton Town Hall, where there is an almost complete series of shields bearing the names of the mayors from 1377 onwards. On the 15th April 1532 he witnessed the will of one, Margaret Whelers of All Hallows, Northampton, who bequeathed 'to Master Wasyngton a gold ring.' On the 29th May 1535 he witnessed the will of Christopher Foster of the same parish. Richard Morton, on the 14th July 1539, named him among the four 'indifferent men' (*i.e.* impartial men) who should appraise his goods, and left him 'a gowne furyd wyth foxe.' He is named, in June 1541, by Thomas Chipsey, a Northampton grocer, as an original trustee of the Free Grammar School which Chipsey founded there. He was Mayor of Northampton for the second time in 1545, when (perhaps owing to the dispersion of the religious houses which formerly dispensed charity) the corporation formulated certain enactments to keep down the price of bread. Evidently Washington retained throughout this period a place of business and possibly a residence in the town of Northampton, where he could stay from time to time. During his two periods of mayoralty, at any rate, he must have lived there, and he is frequently named on documents as Lawrence Washington 'of Northampton.'

At Sulgrave he already held, probably as early as 1533, a 'messuage with appurtenances,'[1] that is, a dwelling-house with yards and garden, and also leased of the Priory of St. Andrew's the estate of Millefield. When the monastery was dissolved in 1539 he acquired the possessions which had belonged to it at Sulgrave by purchase from the King, paying (as has been stated in an earlier chapter) £321, 14s. 10d. for the grant, which is thus described in the Letters Patent of the 10th March 1538-9 preserved in the Public Record Office: –

> 'The Manor of Sulgrave with appurtenances . . . late belonging and pertaining to the Monastery of St. Andrew . . . and all . . . messuages, mills, lands, tenements, meadows, feedings, pastures, rents, reversions, services, woods, underwoods, wastes,

[1] See Rev. H. Isham Longden, *The History of the Washington Family*, p. 10.

commons, moors, waters, fisheries, knights'-fees, escheats, reliefs, fines, heriots, courts-leet profits, views of frank-pledge, and all that pertains to view of frank-pledge; and all and singular our [1] hereditaments, profits, commodities, and advantages whatsoever, together with all rights, liberties, jurisdictions and franchises whatsoever, within the towns or parishes of Sulgrave and Woodford in the said county, lately belonging and pertaining to the said monastery; and also the close of land and pasture called Millfeldes with the appurtenances in the tenure of the said Lawrence Washington and Christopher Tomson in Stuchbury in the county aforesaid, lately belonging to the said monastery; and a close, lands and pastures with appurtenances in the tenure of John Averey, and lately in the tenure of Richard Bowers in Cotton in the same county, lately belonging to the said monastery.'

The King excepted and reserved the Rectory of Sulgrave and the advowson of the vicarage of the church there, and all houses, tithes, offerings, profits, and emoluments belonging to them. He added, however: –

'All messuages, lands, tenements, mills, meadows, feedings, pastures, woods, underwoods, wastes, commons, moors, waters, fisheries, rents, reversions, services, and other hereditaments profits commodities and advantages lying in the town or parish of Sulgrave lately belonging to the nunnery [2] of Catesby in the same county, as fully and entirely as Joyce Bykley, late Prioress, had held and enjoyed or ought to have enjoyed them.'

Also:

[1] *i.e.* the King's.

[2] Benedictine Nunnery.

'All lands, tenements, messuages, mills, meadows, feedings, pastures, woods, underwoods, wastes, commons, moors, waters, rents, reversions, services and other hereditaments etc. lying in the town or parish of Sulgrave lately belonging to the monastery or priory [of Austin Canons] at Canons Ashby in the same county, as fully and entirely as Richard Colles, late Prior, had held and enjoyed or ought to have enjoyed them.'

These lands, etc., of Catesby and Canons Ashby were set down as being of the clear annual value of 45s. 4d. and no more.

Lawrence Washington his heirs and assigns were to have, hold and enjoy the Manor of Sulgrave, the lands in Woodford, the Millefelds in Stuchbury, and the close in Cotton from the King and his Successors for ever by the 20th part of a Knight's fee, and a yearly payment of 31s. 3d. at Michaelmas; and to hold the lands in Sulgrave lately of the monasteries of Catesby and Canons Ashby in chief by a thirtieth part of a Knight's fee, and a yearly payment of 4s. 7d. by the name of title, or a yearly tenth part, at Michaelmas.

In all the premises he was to have such views of frank-pledge, courts-leet, chattels of waif and chattels of felons, of fugitives, strays, rights, jurisdictions, privileges, franchises, liberties, commodities, profits and emoluments as fully as the former owners had enjoyed them. He was also to have all issues and rents of the premises from Michaelmas, 1538, as the King's gift.

Then follows a warranty clause, which mentions that there is a certain rent of 11s. 3d. issuing from a part of the premises, and payable to the Dean and College of Windsor, and a certain annual rent of 3s. 4d. issuing from a part of the premises, and payable to the Earl of Derby and his heirs.

As the sale to Lawrence Washington did not include the rectory and vicarage, he was not burdened with the procuration fee (mentioned in the survey) which was a payment by the incumbent in lieu of entertainment for the Bishop, Archdeacon, or Visitor when they came to the parish. Some other landowner must have had to pay the remainder (9s. 9d.) of the payment to the College of Windsor.

We thus learn that Lawrence Washington, though he did not receive from the King the whole of the lands of the Manor of Sulgrave (St. Andrew), became possessed of the lordship, which gave him the responsibility of appointing a steward, and holding Courts-Baron and Courts-Leet there, but such jurisdiction would not extend to his lands outside the Manor.

From the above Survey and Letters Patent it appears that the Millfield in Stuchbury had been 'concealed land,' and, as we have seen, Lawrence Washington drew the attention of the Crown Surveyors to it.[1]

Lawrence Washington was not content with this estate; he acquired by purchase additional lands and possessions in the neighbourhood, which we shall find referred to in the Inquisition *post mortem* which was held in 1584 on behalf of the Crown (of whom he held the land in the first place) to determine his full possessions and the identity of his heir. In Sulgrave he was evidently the principal person of his time, not only in his own manor but apparently in the neighbouring manors as well. We have already seen[2] that he presided at the Court-Baron which decided in 1564 the claim of Thomas Leeson, as heir of Thomas Stotesbury, to the Elington Manor. In the

[1] This information is of importance as showing that Washington was already sufficiently interested in Sulgrave to assure the Crown Surveyors that no part of the Manor was lost. Probably he was already interested in one of these fields in Stuchbury (which lies south of Sulgrave), and having a desire to buy the whole Manor, or as much of it as possible, pointed out to the Crown Surveyors that it was 'concealed land,' *i.e.* a part of the Manor of Sulgrave, belonging to the Priory of St. Andrew, which had been omitted in the Valuation of Ecclesiastical Possessions made in the twenty-first year of the reign of Henry VIII.

[2] See p. 37.

'Book of Harnes' for the Wardon Hundred, compiled in September 1559, we observe that the contributions to the militia of Northamptonshire were these: 'Mr. Washynton is charged to fynd an archer on foote & the rest of yt. towne an archer.'

Lawrence's first wife, Elizabeth (formerly Gough), had died before 1543, and he married Amee Pargiter, the daughter of a neighbour, Robert Pargiter of Greatworth, whose name occurs not infrequently with that of Washington himself on deeds. Whereas his first marriage seems to have been childless, he had no fewer than eleven children by his second marriage: Robert, Lawrence, Frances, Anne, Elizabeth, Magdalen, Barbara, Mary, Margaret, Christopher, and another son. Their portraits, etched in ascending and descending order in the conventional manner of the time, may be seen on two of the brasses attached to the tomb of Lawrence Washington and his second wife in Sulgrave Church.[1] From the tombstone we learn that she died on the 6th October 1564. He himself lived on until the 19th February 1583-4, and no doubt built the Manor House to house his family within the first few years of acquiring the estate. The fur-bordered gown shown in the effigy upon his tomb is no doubt the gown which Richard Morton left him.

He was over eighty when he died. His will, made on the 18th October 1581, and proved on the 11th February 1584, has been preserved in the Register of the Prerogative Court of the Archbishop of Canterbury. It runs as follows: –

'LAWRÉNCE WASHINGTON of Souldgrave in the Co. of Northampton, gentleman, 18 October 1581, proved 11 February 1584.

'As concerning my body, which, as it was made of earth, so must it return to dust and earth again, I desire therefore and require mine exequitor to cause the same to be inhumate and buried in the

[1] See p. 190.

parish church of Souldgrave aforesaid, in the South Aisle there before my seat where I usually use to sit, according to his discretion. To Mr. Walter Light a whole sovereign of gold and to his now wife a ducate of gold. Towards the amending of Stanbridge Lane twenty shillings. And I will that Roger Litleford shall have the oversight in amending the said lane and bestowing the said twenty shillings. And for his pains in that behalf to be sustained I will him two shillings.

'And I will to every one of my sons' and daughters' children five shillings apiece, and to every one of my brother Leonard Washington's children six shillings eight pence a piece willed to them by Parson Washington. Also I give to my brother Thomas Washington's children by his last wife forty shillings. Also I devise to my son Lawrence Washington one goblet parcel gilt, with the cover for the same, and four pounds of currant English money to buy him a salt.

'And I further will to him one featherbed in the gate-house, one feather bed over the day-house, one coverlet with a blue lining, one coverlet in the gate-house chamber, two boulsters, two pairs of blankets, four home made coverlets & four mattresses. Also I give to Lawrence Washington, son to Robert Washington my son and heir apparent, the ring which I usually wear. Also I forgive and acquit my brother Thomas Washington of all such debts and duties as he by any manner of means oweth unto me. And I forgive and discharge John Lagoe, sometime my servant, of all such sums of money as he oweth unto me and of all rents and arrearages of rents due unto me for such lands, tenements or hereditaments as he holdeth of mine, by lease or otherwise, for term of my natural life. And I will to every one of my servants which shall be in service with me at the time of my decease twelve pence.

'Also I will that the said Robert Washington shall yearly give to my servant Symon Wood a livery coat and forty shillings of currant English money for his wages yearly during his life. And whereas I stand charged by the last will and testament of William Bond, gentleman, for the amending and repairing of Preston Lane and for the repairing of the way between Dalington and the Westbridge at Northampton called Spangstone, I earnestly require my executor and overseers to call upon the said John Balgoye for the amending of the said places, for that I have, long time heretofore, delivered into the hands of the said John Balgaye the sum of ten pounds of currant English money for the repairing of Preston Lane and twenty shillings for the amending of Spangstone, for that only use and purpose.

'Also I will and devise that widow Compton shall have, hold, possess and enjoy for term of her life so much of one cottage as she now possesseth in Sulgrave, so as she well and honestly behave herself during her life, without making or doing any reparations thereupon and without paying any rent therefor, other than one red rose at the feast of Saint John Baptist yearly, if the same be demanded. And my further meaning and intent is that the said Robert and his heirs shall from time to time forever appoint some honest aged or impotent person to inhabit the same cottage for term of life, and that such aged or impotent person shall not pay to my heirs any manner of rent therefor for term of his life other than a red rose payable as aforesaid, nor shall be charged to repair the same cottage during his or their lives. And my mind, intent, and meaning is that if any doubt, ambiguity or controversy shall appear to arise or grow in respect of these presents then I will the same shall be decided and determined by my overseers or any one of them.

'And of this my last will and testament I constitute, ordain and appoint the said Robert Washington my sole executor, and of the same I make and ordain my well beloved and trusty friends the said William Baldwyn and William Pargiter my overseers, desiring them to call on my executor if any default or slackness shall evidently in him appear, for or towards the performance of this my last will and testament, and for their pains I will to either of them forty shillings.

'Witnesses, WILLIAM BALDWIN, WILLIAM PARGITER, ROBERT CALCOTT, GEORGE WOODWARD.'

LAWRENCE WASHINGTON'S ESTATE AT HIS DEATH

The Inquisition *post mortem* taken at Rothewell, co. Northants, on 24th August 1584, states that at the time of his death Lawrence Washington was seised in fee of the Manor of Sulgrave, and of all the lands and possessions granted to him by King Henry VIII in 1538-9. He also held a great barn and stable in Stuchbury, a parcel of meadow and a close called the 'Lordes Closse,' another close called Oxhey, and a piece of land called Sulgrave field with appurtenances in the vill of Stuchbury, late in the tenure of Lawrence Washington and Christopher Tomson or their assigns, formerly belonging to the Prior of St. Andrew; also a close called Broddistes lying in the parish of Hardington, co. Northants, formerly belonging to the said Priory; also the advowson of the rectory of Stuchbury likewise formerly belonging to the said Priory and lately purchased by the deceased from Sir John Williams, knight, and Anthony Stringer, gent.; also a messuage or tenement in Woodende in the parish of Blakesley, Northants; an acre and an end of a close in Sulgrave,[1] late of Thomas Stutesburie or his assigns lately purchased by the deceased from Sir Ralph Sadler, knight, and Laurence Wennington,[2]

[1] This last also had been church-land given for the upkeep of a lamp in Sulgrave Church.
[2] or Wemmington.

gent. In addition, woods called Greate Crannis and Lytell Crannis in Blakesley containing twenty-six acres purchased from Henry, Duke of Suffolk and * * * Dewport, gent.; lands, messuages, etc. in Pattishill, Ascote and Eastcote in the parish of Pattishill, Northants, lately purchased from William Molle of Falcott, Northants, gent.; and also a dovecote, orchard, and one close in the parish of St. Giles in the town of Northampton, lately purchased from John Molle, deceased.

The 'Inquisition' goes on to state that by an indenture dated 10th December 1564 made between the deceased Lawrence Washington of the one part and Walter Light of Radway, co. Warwick, gent., of the other part, in consideration of a marriage afterwards solemnised between Robert Washington, gent., then son and heir apparent of the said Lawrence, and Elizabeth Light, then daughter and sole heiress of the said Walter Light, Lawrence agreed for himself and his heirs with the said Walter, his heirs and administrators, that before the Easter following he would make a firm estate in two messuages in the parish of Pattishill, to hold the same to the use of the said Lawrence so long as the said Robert should live, after his death to the use of Elizabeth Light for life for her jointure; after her death to the use of the heirs male of Robert Washington, and in default of such issue to the use of the heirs male of Lawrence Washington, younger son of the said Lawrence; for default of such issue to the use of the right heirs of Lawrence (the father) for ever.

The jury added that the Manor of Sulgrave and other premises in Sulgrave, Woodford, and Cotton were held of the Crown by the 20th part of a knight's fee and were worth yearly £15, 12s. 6d.

Chapter V

THE DESCENDANTS OF THE BUILDER

THE descendants of Lawrence Washington, the builder of Sulgrave Manor House, continued to live there for just seventy-five years after his death. Though the estate changed hands in 1610, it was bought by a grandson of his, Lawrence Makepeace. Another grandson, the Lawrence Washington who was the father of the emigrants to Virginia, was, it is believed, born in the Manor House in the last year of Elizabeth's reign and brought up there in boyhood.

Though Norden mentions Sulgrave in the list of Northamptonshire villages, the name of Washington does not occur among those he picks out from his *Herralds Garden*, nor is Sulgrave Manor selected as a seat comparable to, say, Sir John Spencer's at Althorp. Indeed Sulgrave was not comparable, and though its builder might well be described as a 'monied man' when he purchased the estate, those of his descendants who remained at the time in Northamptonshire, were not, as it happened, the most prominent of their family. Of the four sons, the most distinguished was the second son, Lawrence, for whom his father purchased the living of Stuchbury, and who subsequently became a member of Gray's Inn and Registrar of the High

Court of Chancery,[1] and died in 1619 at Maidstone. His son, Sir Lawrence Washington of Garsdon in Wiltshire, was likewise a Registrar in Chancery. Concerning the two youngest sons of Lawrence the builder we know little or nothing; the eldest, Robert, succeeded his father at Sulgrave, and must be dealt with at greater length. Of the daughters we need mention only Frances, who married John Tomson of Sulgrave (perhaps the son of the Christopher Tomson who shared Millefield with her father)[2] and Mary, who married Abel Makepeace of Chipping Wardon in Northamptonshire, and was the mother of Lawrence Makepeace, who purchased Sulgrave from his uncle in 1610.

Returning to Robert Washington, the eldest son of the founder of Sulgrave, and the direct ancestor of the American president, we find that he was born in 1540, the year after his father had secured the Manor of Sulgrave, but probably before the house had been completed. He had married Elizabeth Light, the daughter and heiress of Walter Light [3] of Radway in Warwickshire, and had six sons and three daughters. His father appears to have bought Pattishall as a dower-house for Robert and his wife in 1564. Robert inherited Sulgrave twenty years later, and after the death of his first wife he married Anne Fisher of Hanslope in Buckinghamshire, by whom he had three further sons and three more daughters.

With a family considerably larger than that of his father, and possibly without his father's ability, Robert was unable to preserve

[1] From Letters Patent dated 26 March, 35 Eliz. (1593), it appears that among the Chancery Registrars of that date were Lawrence Washington esquire, Lawrence Washington esquire junior, and Leonard Makepeace esquire (? a relative of Lawrence Makepeace). 'Lawrence Washington esquire junior' is evidently the future Sir Lawrence Washington of Garsdon, who did not succeed his father in office on his death as is usually stated, but overlapped with him. The fact that his father is called 'esquire' seems to indicate that he was never ordained to the living of Stuchbury, but was a layman who held the gift of it. This would explain a puzzling lawsuit described in Hoppin (*op. cit.* p. 83) where complaint is made that no parson had been installed for sixty years.

[2] See p. 54.

[3] Mentioned in Lawrence Washington's Will, p. 58.

the estate. In 1610, nine years before his death, he sold the Manor, with the consent of his eldest son, Lawrence Washington, to his nephew, Lawrence Makepeace. The portion of the estate which lay in Stotesbury was disposed of in the same year to Simon Heynes.[1] Lawrence Makepeace had already purchased, in 1606, the Elington Manor from its then holder, Thomas Leeson, which may perhaps account for the fact that Robert remained at Sulgrave for the last nine years of his life, as is shown both by letters and by his will dated 1619, in which he describes himself as 'Robert Washington of Souldgrave in the County of Northampton, Esq.,' and asks to be 'buried in the South Aisle of the church before my seat where I usually sit under the same stone that my father lieth buried under.'

Of his sons, the eldest, Lawrence Washington, who died in 1616 and was buried at Brington, must receive the most attention. The second, Robert, married in 1595-6 Elizabeth Chisull, and established himself at Great Brington, where he seems to have been fairly closely associated with the lord of that manor, his relative, Sir John Spencer of Althorp. His marriage with Elizabeth Chisull had taken place in Wormleighton, another village owned by the Spencers, and his wife had been bequeathed the sum of £20 by Sir John Spencer in 1599 'in regard of her pains about me in my sickness.'[2]

The Althorp grain-book for 10th October 1610 contains the entry: 'After this week Robert Washington did take a windmill of me,' and in Lady Penelope Spencer's housekeeping book for 12-18th January 1622-3, Mr. Robert Washington is seen to have presented to the household of Althorp '5 chickines, 2 cupp. hennes, and 1 Flitch of Bacon.' He died on the 10th March in the same year, and his wife nine days later. They were buried together, as

[1] This man is usually said to have been another nephew, but the reason is not obvious.

[2] 'Robert Washington' was also one of those appointed to make an inventory of all the goods and chattels of Sir John Spencer after his death, but the signature to be seen on the manuscript inventory in the Althorp library appears to be that of his father, who was still living at Sulgrave.

the inscription on their tomb in Great Brington Church reads: 'after they had lived lovingly together many years in this parish.'[1] Elizabeth Washington named the then Lord Spencer as her executor.

The house in which Robert and his wife lived was probably the large double house with an oriel window which is still to be seen at Great Brington. The house in the adjacent village of Little Brington, with an inscription, 'The Lord Giveth and the Lord Taketh Away,' which has been named as the 'Washington House' and supposed to have been the home in turn of Robert's elder brother Lawrence, and of himself, does not seem for certain to have sheltered either, though the discovery of a circular horizontal stone sundial at Little Brington[2] with the Washington arms, the initials 'R W,' and the date, 1617, suggests that Robert and Elizabeth may have lived there for a time. When, where, and for how long Lawrence Washington, the elder brother, lived at Brington appears somewhat indefinite. Of his seventeen children one, Gregory, was baptized at Great Brington on the 16th January 1606-7, and buried there the next day, and Lawrence himself was also buried there. Beyond that we can only surmise. The names of none of his other children occur in the Brington register.

This Lawrence Washington was, as we have said, the most important of the brothers to the historian. He was the eldest grandson in the senior line of Lawrence Washington, the founder of Sulgrave,[3]

[1] An entry in the seating roll of Brington Church made in 1606 states that the uppermost pews on the south side were reserved for Robt. Washington, 'Gent, and his wife,' and the benches next to this pew for the menservants of the same 'Robt. Washington' – indicating that they were people of some social standing.

[2] The sundial, which was found face downwards, and had been used as a 'saddle-stone' for a corn rick, is now at Althorp. A replica was presented in 1917 by Earl Spencer to the State of Massachusetts, and is now preserved in the State House at Boston.

[3] He was the nephew of the Lawrence Washington who became Registrar of Chancery, and the cousin of this man's son, Sir Lawrence Washington of Garsdon. During the founder's lifetime there were at least four namesakes in the family alive together.

and the direct ancestor of George Washington. He was born at Sulgrave Manor House about 1568, and married at Aston-le-Walls in Northamptonshire, Margaret Butler, the eldest daughter of William Butler of Tighes (Ticehurst) in Sussex. His wife was of good family, tracing her descent from the Plantagenets. Before his death in 1616 he had had by her eight sons and nine daughters.

He is alleged, rather doubtfully, to have been in the service of the first Lord Spencer from about 1604 onwards, and more certainly to have lived, after the sale of Sulgrave, at Wickamon, or Wick Hamon, now Wicken, as a tenant of Lord Spencer. He was there at the time of his death in 1616, and Lord Spencer's grain-account book shows that a year earlier 'Mistress Washington' paid him five quarters of malt as rent on behalf of one Sandon. He may then have managed Lord Spencer's estates at Wicken.[1] Several of his sons are of interest. The eldest, Sir William Washington, later of Packington in Worcestershire, married Anne, daughter of Sir George Villiers of Brooksby, and half-sister of Charles I's favourite, George Villiers, Duke of Buckingham. He was knighted by James I in 1621-2, and was prominent on the Royalist side in the Civil Wars. His son, Colonel Henry Washington, held Worcester against the Parliamentary army. The second, Sir John Washington of Thrapston in Northamptonshire, knighted in 1623, was also on the Royalist side. His second wife was Dorothy Pargiter of Greatworth, Northants, a relative. Both of these were frequent guests at Althorp, as were other

[1] The story of Lawrence, his brother Robert Washington, and other members of the family and their kinsmen the Spencers, was woven by the Rev. John Nassau Simpkinson, Rector of Brington, into a novel, published in 1860, entitled *The Washingtons: a Tale of a Country Parish in the Seventeenth Century*. The special value of this book consists in the appendices, which include long extracts from inventories of the contents of Althorp, and of the Althorp household books of the time of James I and Charles I, compiled from manuscripts in the Althorp library. The copy given by the author to his wife on its publication, was presented to Sulgrave Manor by their son, H. W. Simpkinson, in 1922.

members of the family. The sixth son, Thomas Washington, went as page to Madrid in 1623, to the future King Charles I, and died there.

It was the fourth son, again a Lawrence Washington, who was the father of the emigrants to Virginia, and the great-great-grandfather of George Washington. He is presumed to have been born at Sulgrave about 1602. At the age of seventeen he went up to Brasenose College, Oxford, took his degree early in 1623, and became a Fellow of his College on the 27th May in the same year; he was appointed to the office of Reader in 1627, and was proctor in 1631. He married Amphillis, the daughter of John Twigden, of Little Creaton in the parish of Spratton, Northants, probably a year or two before he resigned his Fellowship. He did this on the 30th November 1633, having been already inducted to the rectory of Purleigh in Essex, on the 14th March 1632-3. In the following year he received the degree of Bachelor of Divinity.

When the troubles between King and Parliament were at their height he was naturally suspect by the rebels because he had two brothers in the Royal army.[1] In order that they might sequester the benefice he was subjected to cruel libels by the Parliamentary party. It was alleged that he was 'a common frequenter of Ale-houses, not only himself sitting dayly tippling there, but also incouraging others in that beastly vice, and hath been oft drunk, and hath said "That the Parliament have more Papists belonging to them in their Armies than the King had about him, or in his Army, and that the Parliament's Army did more hurt than the Cavaliers, and that They did none at all"; and hath published them to be Traitours, that lend to or assist the Parliament.' On the other side of the question there are statements that he was a 'very Worthy,

[1] As proctor in 1631, moreover, he had displaced a proctor expelled from office as 'Calvinistic, and displeasing to the King.' (See Isham Longden, *op. cit.*, p. 28.)

Pious man, and a very Moderate, Sober Person; . . . a Loyal Person, and had one of the best Benefices in these Parts, and this was the Only cause of his Expulsion.' Deprived of his rectory in 1643, he went to Little Braxted, in Essex, where Thomas Roberts, a Royalist, who held the right to appoint a parson there, gave him the living, a very poor one in a very small parish. He died in January 1652-3 and was buried at Maldon.

Of his three sons and three daughters the eldest son, John, generally known as Colonel John Washington, was born in 1632 or 1633; of his early history little is known. In November 1640 Charles I presented him to a 'scholar's place' at Sutton's Hospital (Charterhouse School), but owing to a long waiting-list of other boys previously nominated by the King, he seems to have been educated elsewhere. Possibly he had some experience as a sailor, and may have made a voyage or voyages to America before he decided to leave England permanently.

In 1656 he entered into a business partnership with Edward Prescott of Barbados and Virginia, and arrived in the Potomac River in Virginia at the end of that year. Owing to disagreements they separated. John soon began to acquire land, and imported from England men whom he settled there as his tenants. He married Anne, daughter of Lieutenant-Colonel Nathaniel Pope, by whom he had a son, Lawrence, born on his parents' plantation near Mattox Creek in Washington parish, Westmorland County, Virginia, in September 1659. This son, Lawrence Washington, married Mildred Warner and died in March 1697-8. His widow, who married again, died in England and was buried on the 30th January 1700-1 at Whitehaven, in Cumberland. Captain Augustine Washington, the son of Lawrence and Mildred, was born in 1694, and married first Jane Butler, by whom he had four children, and secondly Mary Ball, by whom he had six, the eldest of whom was General

George Washington, the first President of the United States of America.

Two other members of the family of the Rev. Lawrence Washington of Purleigh crossed the Atlantic. Lawrence Washington, the second son, who was baptized at Tring in Hertfordshire on the 18th June 1635, made a journey to Virginia and acquired land there in 1659. On returning to England he married Mary, daughter of Edmund Jones of Luton. His interests in the New World necessitated frequent journeys to America, and he eventually settled there. Martha Washington, youngest sister of the two emigrants, went to Virginia about 1677 with the aid of a legacy left by her eldest brother, Colonel John Washington. She married Samuel Hayward, Clerk of the County of Stafford, Virginia, and died childless.

To go further into the history of the Washington family after they left Sulgrave lies outside the scope of the present book. The interested reader can but be referred to the researches of Colonel Chester, Mr. H. F. Waters, and, in the present generation, the Rev. H. Isham Longden, Mr. C. A. Hoppin, and Mr. Thomas Pape. Their discoveries make, even for the amateur of genealogy, a fascinating story.

Chapter VI

SULGRAVE AFTER THE WASHINGTONS

AFTER the death of Robert Washington, the son of the builder of the Manor House, in 1619, Lawrence Makepeace, his nephew, must have entered into the property which he had actually purchased nine years before. Indeed, it is more than probable that he was living in the Manor House already, and that Robert Washington was his tenant upon the estate. Makepeace had bought the Elington Manor in Sulgrave from the Leeson family in March 1606-7, and the two manors were, for the first time in five hundred years, united.[1] The possibility that he was living in the Elington Manor House up to 1619 has already been mentioned, but the

[1] The original deed, dated 7th March 1606-7, for the sale for the sum of £1310, by Thomas Leeson to Lawrence Makepeace, of the Elington or Leeson Manor, was presented to Sulgrave Manor by J. G. Butler, of Youngstown, Ohio, in 1924.

The peculiar value of this document lies in the fact that it bears the signatures, as witnesses, of three members of the Washington family–Robert Washington, and his two elder sons, Lawrence and Robert, who sign their names as follows: –

'Robarte Wasshingtō the Elder.
Law: Wasshingtō:
Roberte wasshington the yunger.'

One of the three other witnesses is William Pargiter, whose father, Robert, was cousin to Robert Washington (see Plate VIII, *b*).

Washington Manor House seems to have been the more desirable and the more substantial or it would not have lasted until our own time.

That Lawrence Makepeace did live at Sulgrave, and not merely own the property, is clear from a remonstrance addressed to him by Rouge Rose, Marshal to Clarenceux, King of Arms, for having, while entering his pedigree in the Visitation of 1618, usurped certain quarterings. It runs as follows: –

'To MR. LAWRENCE MAKEPEACE of Sulgrave, these - Whereas, by virtue of his Majesty's Commission under the great seal of England, you were warned and accordingly did appear before me, Rouge Rose Pursuivant of Armes, at Daventry, where I sat in his Majesty's behalf and service to register all the gentlemen of name and arms within the hundred of Warden according to the tenor of his Majesty's Commission; and forasmuch as you then brought in and showed unto me as proper to your family a scocheon or coat of arms, vid't, *Quarterly of four, the first Azure, 3 eaglets in bend between two cotisses Argent, the second Or, two bends Gules, the third bendwayes of eight Or and Azure, and the fourth Gules, a fess counter-componie Argent and Sables between six cross crosses formy fitche of the second*, borne by the several names of Belknap, Sudley, Montford, and Botelar, and lawfully quartered by many worthy families in this kingdom; these are therefore to require you, and in his Majesty's name straightly to charge and command you that from henceforth you do not only forbear the using and bearing of the said arms which you have hitherto usurped against all right and custom of the Law of Arms, but also any other arms whatsoever, until you know the Earl Marshall's pleasure therein. Hereof fail you not, as you will answer the contrary at your peril. Given under my hand at Toscester the xxiiijth day of December An. D'ni 1619.[1]

Abel Makepeace, the son of this too-forward owner of the Manor, succeeded his father and, in 1659, at about the time that the two Washington emigrants were settling in Virginia, he sold Sulgrave to Edward Plant of Kelmarsh. Edward Plant is described as 'of Overston, late of Sulgrave' when selling the Manor in 1673 to the Rev. Moses Hodges of Over Norton in the county of Oxford. Descendants of this gentleman held the estate for more than a century and a half. Moses Hodges himself enjoyed the estate for only three years before he died on the 21st May 1676, and left the Manor to his son, John Hodges, probably the most important person in the history of Sulgrave since Lawrence Washington of Northampton.

John Hodges united to the double manor which Lawrence Makepeace had created, a third manor of Sulgrave, the Culworth or Trafford Manor, which Lord Crewe's trustees sold to him in 1700. He held the now completely united manor until 1723-4, and it was evidently under him that the main rebuilding took place. His brother, the Rev. Dr. Moses Hodges, who followed him, died in less than a year. An abstract of his will is preserved by Mr. J. P. Brown of Sulgrave: –

'Abstract from the Will of Moses Hodges of Sulgrave co. Northants, doctor of Divinity. Nov. 2, 1724.

'To my daughter, Mary Hodges, my manor of Sulgrave, also that capital messuage or manor house standing and being in Sulgrave, wherein my brother John Hodges did lately inhabit and dwell; also the orchard, garden, homeclose, foreclose, etc.

[1] *The Visitations of Northamptonshire made in 1564 and 1616-19.* Edited by W. C. Metcalfe (1887). The copy of this remonstrance, printed in Baker's 'History of Northamptonshire,' contains many inaccuracies.

adjoining . . . I also give to my said daughter Mary my household goods, furniture, plate, linen in the said manor house at Sulgrave.

'To my daughter Lydia Hodges, that cottage in Sulgrave in the tenure of John Humfrey; also that barn and close near adjoining to the said cottage, commonly called Pargiter's Close.'

Mary, who married Goddard Smith, died in 1726 without children, and settled the reversion of her estate upon her three sisters, Theodosia, Anne, and Lydia, who died in turn, leaving no children, though Lydia, who was married to the Rev. Dr. Launcelot Jackson of Launton and Bletchington in Oxfordshire, buried a daughter, also named Lydia, in the Washington tomb while she was living in Sulgrave. She herself and her sisters left their shares of the estate in turn to their kinsman, the Rev. Moses Hodges Bartholomew, a grandson of their father's half-sister, Frances. He was a Fellow of Queen's College, Oxford, and does not seem ever to have lived on the estate, being described at one time or another as 'of Oxford, of Edgcote and Netherpayford in Northamptonshire, and of Wardington in Oxfordshire.'

That the absence of a squire as occupant of the Manor House was detrimental to the place is clear, for Sulgrave we learn, in earlier days, had an unenviable reputation as the resort of a band of highwaymen and poachers. Known as the Culworth gang, from the adjacent village where many of them lived, for twenty years they terrorised the neighbourhood. In the ancient iron-bound chest which stands in Sulgrave church, one of the most daring members of the gang, no less a person than the parish clerk, one William Abbott, shoemaker by trade, was accustomed to secrete his share of the spoil; and tradition relates that he 'never performed his part in the church services without loaded pistols in his pocket.' The end came in 1787 and four of the gang were executed at Northampton. Abbott, however, escaped with a sentence of 'Transportation' – a light punishment in times when many a man was hanged for stealing a sheep or even a lamb.

The story is confirmed by the following entries in the church books: –

> 'Aprill the 22nd, 1787. John Wilcox Labourer first officiated as a parish Clerk of Sulgrave on the dismission of William Abbot, by appointment of the Reverend Richard Wykham, Vicar of Sulgrave.
>
> 'July 1787. William Abbott parish Clerk was condemned at Northampton Assize to lose his Life for High Way Robbery, but was afterwards reprieved for Transportation for Life.
>
> 'For the Good and future safety of this parish Minuted down.
>
> 'By Rd. Wykham Vicar of Sulgrave, June the fifteenth 1788.'[1]

We have mentioned more than once in the preceding pages an account of Sulgrave set down by Jeremiah Henn in 1789. We know little of this local chronicler save that he was a native of Stoke Line in Oxfordshire, and was married at Sulgrave church to Martha Castle of Sulgrave in 1788. There is no reference in the parish register to the name of Henn before that date, so presumably he settled in Sulgrave on his marriage. The Henns still live in Sulgrave, and various fields bearing the name 'Henn's Close,' are scattered round about the village, one of them nearly facing the entrance to the Manor House. Henn contributed three articles on Sulgrave to the *Gentleman's Magazine* of May, August, and September 1789. The manuscript which he composed, and drew upon for these articles has survived, unpublished, and was presented to Sulgrave

[1] Information supplied by the Rev. W. S. Pakenham-Walsh, Vicar of Sulgrave.

Manor in 1933 by Mr. Frederick Carter, steward and caretaker of the Manor House. This, with various documents, now also in the possession of the Sulgrave Manor Board, forms our principal authority for a picture of Sulgrave in the eighteenth century. Mr. Henn's introduction to his little manuscript is so naïvely written that it is worthy of quotation: –

'*Licetne pauca?*

'To trace the Origin of Names, & investigate the state of remote Country Parishes from ye earliest period, through succeeding ages, to ye present, would be a task which perhaps very few, if any, could accomplish.

'In this Book I have endeavoured to give such accounts as I have received, partly from my own knowledge, and partly from Manuscripts with which I have been favored; One of which was an extract from Mr. Bridges's History of this County, from which I have found it necessary to deviate in some particulars, and new-model others; In this, I hope to stand excused, when it is considered that perspicuity & veracity have been my objects throughout. There are doubtless many errors and mistakes, Grammatical & Orthographical, many of which are obvious to the meanest capacity: But, as I drew up the following, *without first making a correct Copy to go by*; I hope, also in this, to avoid censure.* This feeble effort of mine being only a rough sketch, which, some abler hand may (perhaps hereafter) bring to a better conclusion. An obscure person, unassisted by books, or connexion with the Learned, cannot be expected to yield those Hesperian fruits which are produced only from the *early initiated* Scholar.

* 'A learned Divine once observed to me: "What doth the *Style* signify, if the *Meaning* be understood?"'

'I have hereto prefixed a Ground Plott of this Parish, which was done (not from an actual Survey and Admesuration, but,) from my own idea of the situation of the place; therefore, let the distances therein, not be depended upon as exact proportionals, but only considered as the *form* & *fashion* of the town, whereby a stranger might have conception thereof, & travel therethrough, as well as if familiarized. Into whose hands this may fall, is uncertain; therefore, let diffidence plead for error.

'J. HENN.'

At the end, as a postscript, he writes: –

'Some particulars not met with in this Book will appear in the Gentleman's Magazine, and are now under inspection of the Editors for that purpose. *April*, 1789.'

Bridges, writing before 1724, describes the land of Sulgrave as consisting of open fields, except for some small enclosures which belong to particular farmers. But in 1760 an Act of Parliament was passed for 'dividing and enclosing the open and common fields, common meadows, common pastures, common grounds, and commonable lands within the Parish Township and Liberties of Sulgrave,' and Henn tells us that the fields were duly enclosed in 1761.[1]

Bridges, in whose time the Hodges family were still in residence, makes no allusion to the state of 'Washington's Manor,' but Henn notes that 'The Old Mansion House' – or 'Great House,' as he also calls it – 'is now much dilapidated.' Further on he remarks: 'Part of it was taken down a few years ago.' No record of this pulling down has so far been discovered, nor, except by conjecture, is it possible to form any estimate of what was actually destroyed.

[1] A contemporary certified copy of the 'Award of the Parish of Sulgrave,' under the Enclosure Act was presented to the Manor House by Mr. Frederick Carter in 1933.

Baker, in his 'History of the County of Northamptonshire' (1822-30), speaks of the Manor House as 'formerly the residence of the Washingtons,' adding the information that it had 'degenerated into a common farm house.' In 1840 the estate was sold by the Bartholomew trustees to Colonel the Hon. Henry Hely-Hutchinson, from whom it passed by a rather circuitous route to his son-in-law, Lieutenant-Colonel Arthur Reynell-Pack, who died in 1860 and was succeeded by Mr. Arthur Reynell-Pack, of Netherton in Devonshire, who sold it to the British Peace Centenary Committee.

How the Manor House itself and the surrounding estate was purchased in 1914 and eventually vested in the Sulgrave Manor Board will be described in a later chapter of this book. We have already seen that it had 'degenerated into a common farm house' when Baker wrote a century ago. Washington Irving, in his *Life of George Washington*, published in 1855, says: 'I visited Sulgrave a few years since. It was in a quiet rural neighbourhood, where the farmhouses were quaint and antiquated. A part only of the manor-house remains, and was inhabited by a farmer.'

From this time onwards until towards the close of the nineteenth century the house seems to have sunk into almost complete oblivion. The lack of interest taken in it may be judged by the fact that in the first edition of Murray's *Handbook for Travellers in Northamptonshire and Rutland*, published in 1878, there is no mention whatever of the Manor House. It is to Sir Henry Dryden, of Canons Ashby, the well-known Northamptonshire antiquary, that we owe the first, and to this day the only, complete and accurate description of the building. This was published in *Northamptonshire Notes and Queries* of April 1885, under the title of 'The Washington Manor House at Sulgrave,' and provided the editor of the second edition of Murray's *Handbook* (1901), and all subsequent writers, with concise and reliable information.

It is difficult to discover the names of the farmers who first occupied the Manor House. The Stuchfields, a family long established in Sulgrave, are said to have lived there during the first half of the nineteenth century. From about 1870 until 1884 Henry Webb Cook was the tenant. One of the earliest of references to the house as being the ancestral home of the Washingtons, by writers who visited Sulgrave, is in an article contributed by E. W. Tuffley to the American magazine, *St. Nicholas* (November 1883), entitled 'The Origin of the Stars and Stripes.' In it he says: –

> 'The ancient home of the Washingtons belongs now to a farmer by the name of Cook, and is little more than a quaint and interesting ruin. A few signs of its former stability and grandeur may be traced; but the window with the Washington crest, which Washington Irving mentions in his *Life of Washington*, is no longer to be seen. . . . The porch, or entrance, to the old manor-house still speaks, though somewhat shakily, of the early glory of the place; . . . above it is the now familiar shield bearing on its face the Stars and Stripes.'

On Cook's death in 1884, the then owner of the property, Mr. Arthur Reynell-Pack, being unable to let the farm, 'had to take it up himself,' and from 1884 to 1890 his three sisters lived there and helped him to farm it. He recollects spending £500 on the house, and he also glazed in the Royal Arms in the gable of the porch to save them from the weather.[1]

After having been for six years once more the home of gentlefolk, in 1890 the Manor House stood empty for a while. During that period it was visited by Moncure D. Conway, well known in his day, who, in an article entitled, 'The English Ancestry of Washinton,' in *Harper's Magazine*, remarks: –

[1] From a letter from Mr. Reynell-Pack to the writer, dated 25th September 1932.

> 'I saw the placard for its sale, and considering its old royalist associations, found something picturesque in its advertisement as HOMESTEAD OF THE ANCESTORS OF THE GREAT AMERICAN PRESIDENT. . . . We found it unfurnished and unoccupied except by the housekeeper.'

Later on in the same year we have another description by a visitor, William Clarke who, writing in the December issue of the *English Illustrated Magazine*, in an article entitled 'The Ancestral Home of the Washingtons,' says: –

> 'The house itself consists of two wings at right angles to one another. In the adjacent yards and courts, nettles, docks and thistles are the only things that flourish. It is a place that has lost its ancient dignity, and is now frowsy and neglected. The traditions of the ancient monks who once held the lands of Sulgrave, and the stalwart, knightly, loyal race of gentlemen who succeeded them, have alike vanished, leaving the present reality of a neglected, degenerated, unused farm-house which no one lives in or cares for. . . . This old manorial estate is now in the hands of a non-resident proprietor, comprises some 213 acres, and can be let . . . for £200 per annum.'

The article goes on to describe the building and its surroundings in considerable detail and, together with the admirable woodcuts which illustrate it, forms a valuable contribution to the history of Sulgrave.

In 1891 the house again found a tenant and was occupied for about ten years by a farmer, William Pryce Seckington. He was succeeded by Frank James Cave, who lived there until 1914 when the Manor House was purchased by the British Committee for the Celebration of the Hundred Years' Peace between England and America.

That the building, during these latter years, had fallen into considerable decay is made clear by the writers already quoted. Indeed, when it passed into the hands of the Centenary Committee one of the spandrels of the stone archway of the entrance porch showed a crack which extended across the Washington coat of arms, almost obliterating it. The arch itself had already begun to sink, and the whole porch might have collapsed at any moment. From about 1900 onwards the estate was known to be for sale and advertisements of it were published from time to time. In 1902 a report appeared in the *Banbury Guardian* to the effect that the house had been purchased and was to be taken down and re-erected in America, but this proved to be without foundation.

The War delayed the work of restoration, only a few very necessary repairs being undertaken early in 1915, and a caretaker put in charge. In October 1919 Mr. Frederick Carter was appointed Steward and Caretaker, a post which he still holds. The restoration of the house and the laying out of the garden was put in hand during the following year, and in June 1921 the reinstated Manor House was thrown open to the public.

Chapter VII

THE EXTERIOR OF THE MANOR HOUSE

THE Manor House, set in a formal garden, bounded by meadows and shaded by chestnuts and ancient elms, occupies the centre of an estate of two-and-twenty acres on the eastern outskirts of Sulgrave village. It is a two-storied building of limestone, partly faced with roughcast, and roofed with stone tiles.[1] It consists of two blocks; the Tudor portion with a high-pitched roof, red-brick chimneys at one end set at an angle in the Elizabethan manner, and a gabled porch facing south; and a later, Queen Anne, wing with a roof of lower pitch, which runs at right angles to the north (Plate III, *a*). (See Fig. 29, p. 163.)

It is approached through a gateway flanked by tall stone piers, which stands at the point where 'Great Street' joins 'Little Street.' Passing along the drive that runs between the Manor meadows known as 'Little Green' and 'Madam's Close,' the visitor reaches the house by a footpath, and enters through a doorway in the corner of the stone-flagged courtyard (Plate I, *a* and *b*).

This doorway on the north side, which is in the Queen Anne

[1] The walls, which are three feet thick, are of coursed rubble, quarried in the adjoining parish of Helmdon. The quoins and dressings are of Hornton stone, a finer quality of the native iron-bearing limestone, from the neighbourhood of Banbury. The stone tiles of the roof are probably from the Northamptonshire quarries at Colley Weston.

wing, is now the first part of the Manor House to meet the visitor's eye.

Originally, however, the house was entered from the south through the ancient porch in the centre of the main front which bears the Washington shield, and it is with this Tudor porch as a starting-point that the exterior of the house will be described (Plate II, *a*).

Until a century and a half ago the porch, as was customary in a Tudor house, occupied the exact centre of the main front, with the kitchen and buttery on one side and the family apartments on the other. The entire portion west of the porch, containing the original kitchen and domestic offices, disappeared at some date between 1700 and 1780, and wings which extended outwards at either end were pulled down at the same time. The Manor House remained in a curious, truncated form, with the porch at one end, until 1929, when the missing section of the front west of the porch was rebuilt upon the ancient site by Sir Reginald Blomfield, R.A. This reconstructed part of the Tudor building is faced with stone to harmonise with the ancient work which it adjoins, but without roughcast. It is designed internally as a residence for the steward, releasing rooms hitherto occupied by him in the Queen Anne wing, which, restored to their original condition and suitably equipped, were opened to the public in 1931 (*Frontispiece*).

The south front – the original Tudor portion of the Manor House, begun about 1540 – was completed by Lawrence Washington about 1560, soon after the accession of Queen Elizabeth. He then added the porch, and with due loyalty[1] placed the great Queen's coat of arms and initials in plaster-work upon its gable.[2] Far below,

[1] The use of the Royal Arms and initials does not (as often stated) imply that Queen Elizabeth once stayed here.

[2] These arms and initials might equally be those of Edward VI, but the 'ovolo' which forms one of the mouldings round the doorway, cannot be considered earlier than 1560.

(a)

(b)

PLATE I

(a) APPROACH TO THE MANOR HOUSE. ON LEFT, THE ANCIENT ELMS; ON RIGHT, 'THE WASHINGTON ELM' IN CENTRE OF LAWN. (See pp. 81 and 160)

(b) NORTH ENTRANCE. THE STONE COURTYARD. (See p. 161)

in a comparatively inconspicuous position in the spandrels of the moulded stone arch of the entrance, he carved his own coat of arms with the 'stars and stripes' (mullets and bars) – *i.e.* two bars with three mullets (or five-pointed stars) above – which had been borne by his ancestors from the middle of the fourteenth century, was borne by his descendant, George Washington, and is widely believed to have inspired the American national flag (Plate II, *b*).

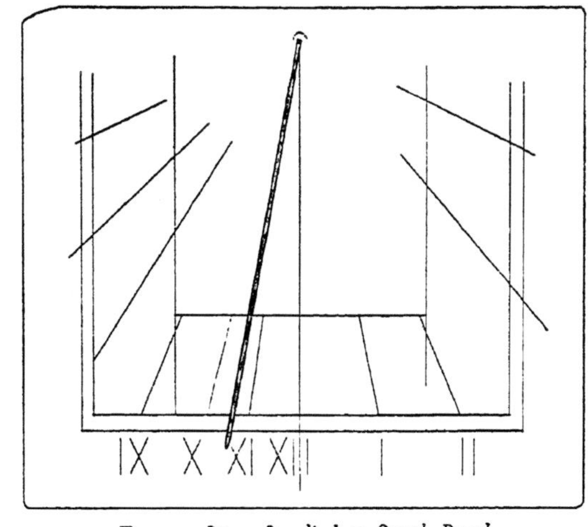

FIG. 1: *Stone Sundial on South Porch*

The external angles or quoins of the porch are constructed of massive blocks of Hornton stone. Their projection from the rougher stone of the walls is about $1\frac{1}{2}$ inches, the surface wall-covering of roughcast being of that thickness throughout. The face of one of the quoin stones high up on the right, on a level with the little window of the room above the porch, is engraved as a sundial (Fig. 1), of which the gnomon or dial-pointer, a beautiful little piece of sixteenth-century wrought iron-work, is supported by a dragon with an elongated neck (Fig. 2).

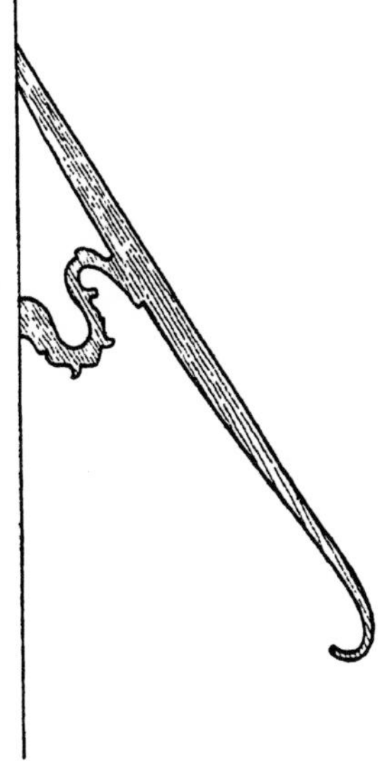

FIG. 2: *Wrought-iron Gnomon (pointer) of Sundial*

The four-centred entrance archway of the porch is surmounted by a square head and a label or 'hood-mould' – a projecting moulding designed to throw off rain. The arch itself is formed of two large blocks of stone, each one 34 inches long by 21 inches high. The Washington arms in raised shields, with the mullets and bars sunk, not standing out in relief, are carved on both spandrels. In the right spandrel they are in perfect condition; but the left spandrel, which is of softer stone, is split. The split runs down the centre of the shield and the surface of the stone has so flaked away that only one of the stars and the lowest of the three bars are now discernible.[1]

Jeremiah Henn, in his *History of Sulgrave*, thus describes the shields in 1789: 'The arms of Washington, cut in stone, are on each side of the doorway, one of which has the crescent for difference.' He naïvely adds: 'I think, 'tis wonderful that Mr. Bridges omitted these.' All trace, however of this crescent – the heraldic device used to denote descent from a second son[2] – which this shield originally contained in addition to the bars and mullets, has long since disappeared; and Sir Henry Dryden, writing in 1885, states definitely that there is 'no crescent.'[3]

The jambs supporting the archway are also, like the quoins, formed of large blocks of Hornton stone. They, with the archway, are elaborately moulded above, the mouldings ending in high vase-shaped 'stops.'[4]

[1] Before the restoration of the house was taken in hand the portion of this stone towards the centre of the arch had sunk nearly half an inch at the point where the crack occurs. It has now been permanently fixed by a copper bar set in behind it and embedded in cement.

[2] Lawrence Washington's grandfather, Robert Washington of Warton, was second son of Robert Washington of Warton, Lancs. (see p. 49).

[3] *Northamptonshire Notes and Queries*, Vol. I, p. 189.

[4] The whole doorway presents a very interesting comparison with the doorway of the south porch of Sulgrave church, which bears the date 1564, and may, as suggested, have been erected by Lawrence Washington in memory of his wife (see p. 186).

(*a*)

(*b*)

PLATE II

(*a*) THE PORCH OF THE SOUTH FRONT, SHOWING THE ARMS OF QUEEN ELIZABETH UPON THE GABLE. (See p. 82)

(*b*) THE WASHINGTON COAT OF ARMS CARVED UPON SPANDREL OF STONE ARCHWAY OF PORCH

On the inner face of one of the jamb-stones is cut the following name and initials: –

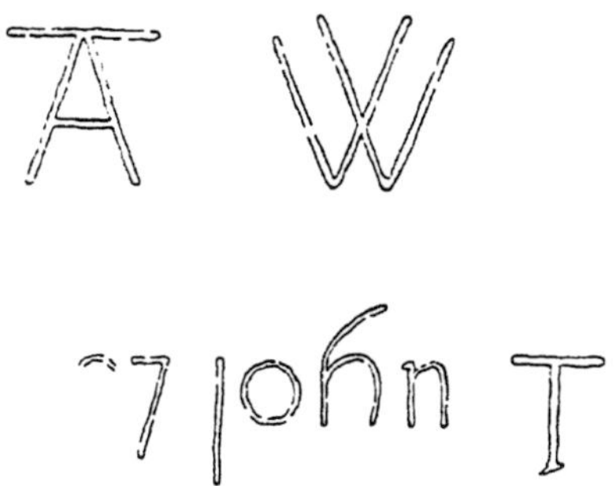

Fig. 3: *Initials on South Porch*

Of this no satisfactory explanation is so far forthcoming; though on the stone opposite to it are two initials: –

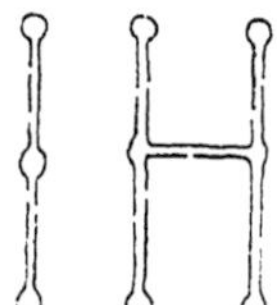

Fig. 4: *Initials on South Porch*

which may possibly be those of John Hodges, successor of the Washingtons, and builder of the Queen Anne wing.

Above the centre of the arch, half-way between it and the little porch-room window, is a plaster panel in a raised moulded frame about 18 inches square, showing the outline of a shield, but the coat of arms or other device which it once held is indecipherable. Henn, writing of it, remarks: 'Another shield, or rather the shadow of one, appears underneath the beforementioned [the Royal Arms], over the doorway, but time hath long since devoured the characters thereon.'

Above the window of the porch are the Royal Arms of Queen

Elizabeth (azure three fleurs-de-lys or; and gules three lions passant or; quarterly) and her heraldic supporters – dexter, a lion guardant imperially crowned, or, and sinister a dragon gules – and her initials, E.R. (Elizabeth Regina), together with a fleur-de-lys and a Tudor rose.

All this has unfortunately suffered severely from the weather, and much of its surface has been lost. The central shield bearing the Royal Arms and the crown above it were originally in the same relief as the supporters – the lion and the dragon – on either side.

Henn tells us that the first quarter of the royal shield showed '3 fleurs-de-lys,' and the third '3 lions passant guardant,' but that the second and fourth quarters were 'quite defaced.' All that now remains of it is the first coat of plaster showing the cross lines of the four quarterings. The crown, however, still retains the second coat of plaster. The method of working was to apply coat upon coat, about half an inch at a time, until the desired relief was obtained, and the scratches now visible on the shield are the craftsman's key-marks made to form a grip for the next coating of plaster.[1]

In the apex of the gable, which is finished with a moulding in oak under the tile verge, is a quaint triangular ornament, modelled in plaster-work, resembling a little pyramid with birds perched on its sloping sides; and with a full-faced head below on either side. That on the left represents a lop-eared sheep (of the kind to be seen on the monuments of the wool-staplers in the churchyard at Chipping Campden) wearing a falling collar; that on the right a lamb adorned with an Elizabethan ruff. They are evidently humorous allusions to the source from which the Washington fortune was derived (Fig. 5). The four little birds above resemble plovers, but

[1] This information has been kindly supplied by Mr. Lewis Smallcorn of Bath, a practical plasterer of wide experience.

may conceivably be intended for jackdaws or starlings which the plasterer of Tudor times would see perched on the backs of the sheep grazing below him in the meadow. A close examination reveals the fact that both the birds and the sheep and lamb have their eyes filled in with little points of charcoal.

Fig. 5: *Plaster-work on Gable of South Porch*

There are deep holes in the eyes of the lion and the dragon supporters of the Royal Arms which at one time were certainly filled in the same curious way, but the filling is now gone, together with the outer layer of modelled plaster-work.

The entrance porch, since the restoration of the missing wing, again occupies the centre of the main front. How much further to the left of it the Tudor house may have extended westward it is now impossible to say; but in 1920 a huge, unhewn boulder, weighing four or five hundredweight, which had the appearance of a foundation stone, was dug out from under the corner of a former building some 50 feet west of the present house, and rolled into the adjoining yard where it now lies. Similar rough boulders which appear to have served the same purpose were found in a line with the south front of the Manor House, and now lie hidden under the present garden wall.[1]

That the Tudor house also extended further to the east there is definite evidence; for the present exterior wall at the east end of the main building proves on examination to be an inside wall. Not only is the surface partly covered with interior plaster-work, but a fireplace of Tudor pattern, with stone jambs and massive oak lintel, now filled in, can be seen built into it at first-floor level; while under

[1] Similar boulders, called 'foundation stones,' resembling sarsen stones, but of flint, were found a short time ago at Grove Manor, an Elizabethan house near Wantage in Berkshire.

the gable can be seen the projecting ends of the oak roof-purlins which were sawn through when, for some unknown reason, the house was reduced in size (Plate XIII, *a*).

It is believed that this missing east wing actually extended some 70 feet further to the east, foundations of buildings having been uncovered at this distance away, beyond the present rose-garden, the surface of which had been raised to its existing level at an early date as a site for this vanished part of the old Tudor house.

Further evidence of these former buildings is afforded by the low wall on the south side of the rose-garden, of squared ashlar stones, in deep and shallow courses, constructed many years ago of facing stones of Tudor date. Worked also into the wall are numerous lichen-covered coping stones – ridge tiles from vanished roofs.

Passing onwards round the house from the east we see the Queen Anne wing stretching some 50 feet northwards at right angles to the Tudor block. It has two well-designed chimney stacks, in the traditional Northamptonshire style, of solid stone, each with a projecting base and moulded cornice uniting two separate shafts [1] (Plate III, *a*).

The east front of the Queen Anne wing has few features of architectural interest, for the living-rooms look out chiefly to the west, where lattice windows open on to the stone courtyard, and the stone roof is pierced by picturesque gabled dormers to light the attics. Opening on to the courtyard are three handsome doorways surrounded by moulded stone architraves. One leads into the kitchen. The second, the present main entrance, in the corner of the courtyard, is a copy of the first. The third doorway is of similar design, but slightly larger than the kitchen doorway, and was made

[1] There are similar chimney stacks on the 'Thatched House,' opposite Sulgrave Manor.

PLATE III

(a) GENERAL VIEW OF THE MANOR HOUSE FROM THE SOUTH-EAST. (See p. 88)

) and (c) THE LION OF ENGLAND, AND THE TUDOR DRAGON OF WALES. PLASTER FIGURES ON THE WALLS INSIDE THE PORCH. (See p. 93)

at the same time (about the year 1700) in the wall of the Tudor building on the south side of the courtyard, to give access to the great hall. This doorway, now closed on the inner side, still has its original oak frame and a massive oak door made of wide vertical boards tongued together and 'ledged' behind.

The third side of the courtyard is formed by the gabled end of the great early-eighteenth-century barn, formerly the brewhouse, which has, as the apex stone of its gable at either end, a beautiful hexagonal Tudor finial. These early finials, as well as the Tudor 'kneelers' – the stone corbels at the bases of the gable coping – were made for a roof of steeper pitch than that of the brewhouse barn. They are actually of the same pitch (52°) as the existing Tudor portion of the Manor House, and clearly came from some part of it which has disappeared.

On the western gable of the barn is a weather-vane of wrought iron, its upright rod decorated with a spiral twist, the points of the arrow adorned with two volutes, and the top terminating in a fleur-de-lys. It was rescued from an ancient barn at Middleton Cheney, a village five miles away, and was set up here in 1927.[1]

At the same end of the barn is an outside stone staircase leading to the granary above; and here, during the restoration of the Manor House, a number of most interesting pieces of carved stone-work from former buildings – fragments of windows, doorways, and the like – were found built into the stairway and into the walls near by.

The earliest of these include a square stone with a quatrefoil opening sunk within a circle (Fig. 6), and the top of a small window with a trefoil head, both dating from the early sixteenth century. They are unglazed, and were probably fixed high up in the gable-

[1] This charming example of eighteenth-century iron-work was presented to the Manor House by the Garden Club of America.

ends of two ancient barns for purposes of lighting and ventilation.[1] The barns to which they once belonged may have been part of farm buildings of pre-Washington date, which were held by a tenant-farmer on behalf of the earlier monastic owners of the property.

Fig. 6: *16th Century Stone Ventilator from Gable-end of Barn*

Another set of stone fragments, six in number, dating from the middle of the sixteenth century, belonged to parts of Lawrence Washington's buildings which have since disappeared. They comprise two portions of a square window-head with a mullion and sunk spandrels, both once glazed; the sill of a window with the marks of mullions, and holes for iron bars; half the head of a doorway with an inner moulding; and two fragments of door-jambs.

The fragment latest in date consists of half the head of a chimney-piece with a spandrel, decorated with lozenge-shaped ornaments (Fig. 7). It is of particular interest since, dating as it does from about the year 1600, it is the most substantial evidence we possess of the architectural work carried out by Lawrence Washington's son

Fig. 7: *Head of Stone Chimney-piece About* 1600

[1] There is a sixteenth-century quatrefoil of somewhat similar design in the gable-end of a barn attached to a house called 'The Three Ways,' in the centre of Sulgrave; and a small window with a trefoil top of the same date can be seen in a barn belonging to the Dial House, upon the road to Banbury. Unglazed slits similar to the window with the trefoil head give light to

and successor, Robert Washington, which, judging by the handsome nature of this example, was of a somewhat over-ambitious character, and lends colour to the theory put forward by the late Sir Henry Dryden that he may possibly have over-built himself, and so have been forced to sell the property.[1]

The existence of three deep, ancient wells, one under the Queen Anne wing, another under the present reconstructed west wing (the site of the Tudor kitchen), and a third some eighty feet to the west, is further proof of the former extent of the building.

The stone courtyard is enclosed on the north by a low wall with a small gate set in the middle. Roughly carved upon one of the stones on the inside of the wall are the letters 'C.S.' – the initials of Christopher Stuchfield,[2] an occupant of the Manor House in the early years of the nineteenth century.

No record, unfortunately, is preserved of the position of the ancient gatehouse to which Lawrence Washington refers in his will. That it must have been a building of some size may be inferred, since it contained a bedstead of sufficient importance to be specified as a bequest to his second son, Lawrence. There is, however, a tradition that the building stood just north of the stone courtyard; and the discovery of a paving of small pebbles, said to have formed the gatehouse yard, which was laid bare a few years ago during the reconstruction of the footpath leading from the drive up to the north entrance, supports this supposition.

the winding stone stairway of the early sixteenth-century priest's house at Easton-on-the-Hill, near Stamford at the northern end of the county.

[1] *Northamptonshire Notes and Queries* (1885), p. 189.

[2] For centuries the Stuchfields, like the Malsburys, the Whittons, the Wilcoxes, and the Taylors, have been residents of Sulgrave village. Some of them were long-lived; the gravestone of one, Thomas Stuchfield, dated 1825, records that he lived to ninety-one and his wife to exactly the same age. Another Thomas Stuchfield died in 1850 aged eighty, and his wife soon after at the age of eighty-three. I can, however, find no record of a Christopher Stuchfield in the Sulgrave churchyard.

As the result of a close examination of the present structure, inside and out, and of all existing fragments, together with such documentary evidence as has survived, the architectural history of the Manor House may be summarised as follows.

The complete absence of any traces of medieval work leads to the definite conclusion that the house was built anew by Lawrence Washington, all visible traces of any previous buildings, monastic or otherwise, that may have existed upon this site, having been obliterated. Towards the year 1560, when his young family was growing up, he enlarged the house, made certain alterations to the great chamber, and added the south porch. His son, Robert, who succeeded him, made further additions to it for the accommodation of his fifteen sons and daughters.

A hundred years later John Hodges built the Queen Anne wing, the brewhouse barn, and other outbuildings – using for them certain material from parts of the house which he had pulled down.

Finally, about the year 1780, when the Manor House had become a farm, further portions were destroyed, reducing it to its present dimensions.

Chapter VIII

THE INTERIOR OF THE MANOR HOUSE: THE PORCH, THE 'SCREENS,' AND THE GREAT HALL

PASSING beneath the stone archway of the gabled porch in the centre of the south front, the visitor enters the outer porch of the Manor House – a stone-flagged vestibule seven feet square. On its side walls, facing one another, are two large heraldic animals in plaster, boldly modelled in high relief, the Lion of England and the Tudor Dragon of Wales (Plate III, *b* and *c*). These spirited figures closely resemble those on the gable outside which support the arms of Queen Elizabeth, and are presumably by the same hand. They are exceptional examples of Tudor plaster-work, and no other instance of the use of great heraldic beasts of the kind placed in a similar position is on record. Indeed it is difficult to point to an exact parallel to them in any position elsewhere. Writing in 1789 Henn supplies us with the following descriptions of them:

> 'In a back porch leading to the garden are two antient figures in plaster, very rude and uncouth, on each side against the wall; the one a Lion, the other a Dragon: these probably once were

SULGRAVE MANOR
AND
THE WASHINGTONS

supporters to a coat of arms, or perhaps placed in the porch as emblematical of the rank of the family then resident at the mansion.'

As has been said, the lion and dragon on the gable outside once had the hollows of their eyes filled in with minute points of charcoal.

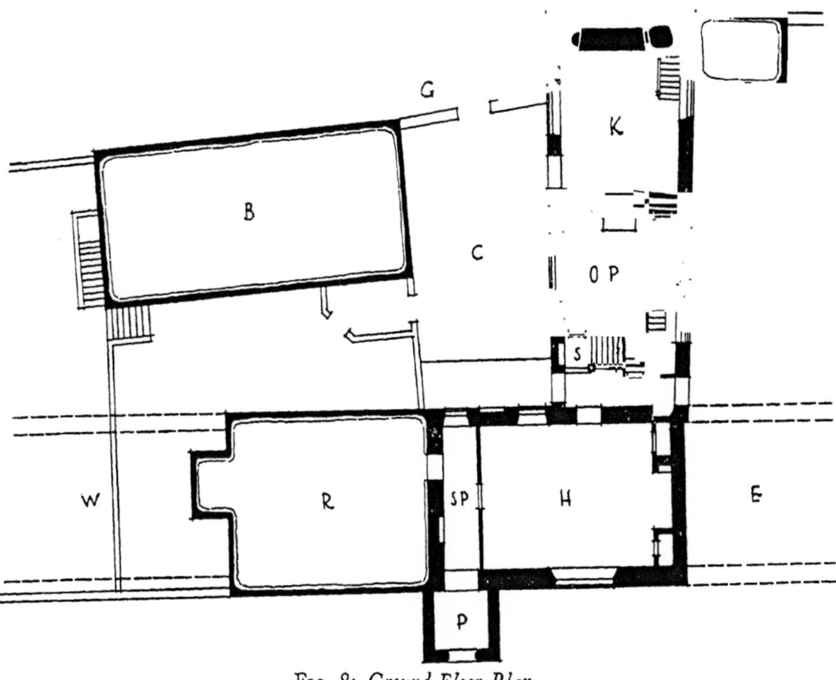

Fig. 8: *Ground Floor Plan*

P Porch
SP Screens Passage
H Great Hall
S Staircase
OP Oak Parlour
K Great Kitchen
C Stone Courtyard
B Brewhouse Barn
R Steward's Residence
E Reputed Site of former East Wing
W Reputed Site of former West Wing
G Reputed Site of former Gatehouse

The eyes of these magnificent beasts in the porch are filled in with oval-shaped pieces of blackish glass. Now, the use at this period of such glass, above all for a purpose of this kind, is most remarkable, for it is not known to have been made in England in Elizabethan times; though pale green potash-glass for domestic use and white glass for window panes was made by glass-workers in the forests of

Sussex. It has been suggested that the glass eyes of these figures may be the work of the optical glass-makers who at this time flourished in the Netherlands.[1]

THE 'SCREENS'

Facing the entrance archway is a massive oak door by which the visitor enters the passage known from medieval times as the 'Entry,' or, more commonly, the 'Screens,' which originally ran between the domestic offices and the great hall. This passage, which is five feet wide, had, as was usual, a door at either end, the further door leading into the court beyond. The back door was replaced about the year 1700 by a window, and another larger doorway – now closed – made into the yard a few feet to the east. In the wall on the left-hand side were originally two doorways, one leading into the Tudor buttery and fitted with a buttery hatch, as is still commonly in use in college halls, the other leading into the pantry or other serving apartment, beyond which lay the Tudor kitchen. The existing doors, which occupy the exact positions of the former buttery and pantry doors, now give access to the steward's residence.

The 'Screens' passage was sometimes fitted with a niche for holding plates and dishes and for washing them; and it is possible that the little recess in the wall of the 'Screens,' close to the doorway as one enters, was originally used for this purpose, though from its position it may have served to hold a lamp or lantern. The theory that it had a religious use and had anything to with a chapel is untenable. In it now rests a cannon ball from the battlefield of Edgehill. Here, on 23rd October 1642, some sixteen miles from

[1] Glass made for optical purposes was a speciality of the Netherlands. Antwerp was an active centre of its manufacture, and it was also made in Venice. Harvey, the discoverer of the circulation of the blood, who was physician to James I, and Charles I, obtained the glass for his scientific instruments from the Low Countries; and, later in the century, Spinoza, the philosopher, earned his living in Holland by grinding lenses for optical glasses.

Sulgrave, while Lawrence Washington's great-grandson was still living at the Manor House, Cavaliers met Roundheads in the first engagement of the Civil Wars, in which great-great-grandson, Colonel Henry Washington, the defender of Worcester, is recorded to have fought for King Charles with conspicuous bravery.[1]

On the right-hand side is a fine timber screen reaching to the ceiling, with an arch in the centre opening into the Great Hall. The original screen had disappeared, but the actual position of its upright timbers was indicated by a series of mortice-holes in the ceiling beam; and at the restoration in 1920 a screen of oak, set in chamfered uprights, taken from a Tudor model, was erected (Plate IV, *a*).[2]

Facing the visitor on entering the Screens passage from the porch is a finely modelled bronze bust of George Washington made by Frank Ordway Partridge after the Houdon life-mask. It stands on a tall marble pedestal draped with two splendid silken banners – the British and American flags. Houdon made this mask during his visit to Mount Vernon in October 1785, for the purpose of modelling a bust of Washington for the State of Virginia. We have a record that he stayed at Mount Vernon for a fortnight, leaving there on 19th October: '. . . in my barge,' wrote Washington in his diary, 'to Alexandria, to take a passage in the Stage for Philadelphia.' President Harding was the honorary chairman of the Committee of Presentation of this important gift to Sulgrave Manor from the American people. The unveiling took place at the re-opening of the Manor House on 21st June 1921 by the late Marquess of Cambridge, President of the Management

[1] The cannon ball was purchased in 1933 at a sale by Lord North of the contents of Wroxton Abbey – the home of his ancestors for over three hundred years – and was presented to the Manor House by Mr. Edmund Bushill.

[2] The screen from which it is copied is in the neighbouring Manor House of Weston-on-the-Green in Oxfordshire.

Committee of Sulgrave Manor, and a signatory to the deed of purchase of the Manor in 1914. The two great banners – the one the gift of the English-Speaking Union, the other, the 'Old Glory,' the gift of the Sons of the American Revolution – were accepted, dedicated, and placed in the position they now occupy on the same occasion.

On the left of the Screens passage and facing the entrance into the Great Hall is a bronze plaque engraved with the coat of arms of the National Society of the Colonial Dames of America. It bears the following inscription: –

IN COMMEMORATION OF THE RAISING OF THE

FIRST PERMANENT ENDOWMENT OF SULGRAVE MANOR

in the year 1924 by

THE NATIONAL SOCIETY OF THE COLONIAL DAMES OF AMERICA

Mrs. Joseph R. Lamar, President.

This Tablet was erected by the Board of Governors.

July 1925

Attached to the oak screen beside the archway into the Great Hall is a bronze tablet erected by the Stars and Stripes Club of Manchester in honoured memory of the one hundred and twelve American soldiers who died and were buried at Manchester during the Great War.[1]

Near the front door is a smaller plaque recording the participation of the Society of the Colonial Dames of America [2] in the restoration of the Manor House in 1917.

[1] This tablet is reproduced in *American Shrines on English Soil*, by J. F. Muirhead.

[2] This is a sister society to the National Society of the Colonial Dames of America.

THE GREAT HALL

Though the great hall in Tudor times was no longer, as in the Middle Ages, the only room of any importance in the house, where everybody lived and the retainers often slept, it still remained the principal apartment, being well adapted as a centre of family life. It served also as a reception-room for guests, and as a general meeting-place on festive occasions for the entire household.

The Great Hall at Sulgrave, a finely proportioned room, measuring twenty-four feet by eighteen, now presents much the same appearance as when completed by Lawrence Washington towards the middle of the sixteenth century (Plate IV, *b*). About a hundred years ago it had been divided roughly in half by a brick partition to provide both a dairy and a sitting-room for the tenant farmer, and when purchased by the Peace Centenary Committee the open fireplace had been filled in and fitted with a modern grate, the walls covered with many layers of wall-paper, and the moulded timbers of the ceiling hidden by plaster. In 1920 the brick partition, wall-paper, and plaster ceiling were taken down, and the oak screen re-erected; and on the removal of the grate, a magnificent Tudor fireplace with a huge four-centred oak chimney beam was revealed.

The Hall is lighted by two windows with moulded oak mullions and transoms. The great four-light lattice window on the south side, with its leaded panes, overlooks the garden, and a similar but smaller two-light window on the north side, the stone courtyard. Inserted in the windows is a series of vividly coloured panels of heraldic glass emblazoned with the Washington arms and marriage alliances, the history and description of which will appear later in the present chapter.

On entering the Hall from the 'Screens' the visitor should glance

(a)

PLATE IV

(*a*) THE SCREENS PASSAGE, WITH A VIEW INTO THE GREAT HALL. (See p. 96)

(*b*) THE GREAT HALL, SHOWING PORTRAIT OF GEORGE WASHINGTON OVER THE FIREPLACE, AND HERALDIC GLASS PANELS IN THE WINDOW. (See p. 98)

(*c*) THE STAIRCASE, WITH A VIEW INTO THE GREAT CHAMBER. (See p. 117)

for a moment at the stone-paved floor, which in Tudor times would have been strewn daily with fresh rushes or sweet-scented herbs. The floor slabs are of blue Hornton stone, the deeper tone of those at the western end of the Hall exactly marking the limit of the former dairy; the darker colour being due to the action of buttermilk and salt. The salt, it seems, still 'works out' at times of atmospheric change, acting as a weather-glass to indicate the approach of a sudden storm.

The magnificent timber ceiling claims special attention, not only on account of its imposing character, but for the information it provides regarding the date of the building. Constructed on a rectangular plan, the great main beams, of bold projection, which run across the ceiling, are fixed into the wall beams which lie like a cornice round the top of the wall. The beam running in sections down the centre of the ceiling is tenoned into the larger of the cross beams, forming square panels. These squares, six in number, are again subdivided by wooden fillets, of similar section but of lesser size, into twenty-four smaller squares, their lengths being supported on the thickness of the larger beams. Above them are laid the wide oaken boards forming the flooring of the Great Chamber directly overhead, which is covered on the under-side with plaster-work and shows whitewashed squares between the cross beams of the ceiling of the Hall. The great beams and lesser beams are of the same moulded sections, boldly chamfered (*i.e.* bevelled) to half their depth; and the timber-work as a whole produces an effect that is simple yet at the same time most imposing (Plate v, *b*).

A similar ceiling exists at Fawsley Manor, six miles from Sulgrave, where, in the kitchen and buttery, beams of precisely this design are found. This part of Fawsley was built by Sir Valentine Knightley, who succeeded his brother, Sir Edmund, in 1542, and died in 1566; and it is likely that the two ceilings are the work of the same craftsman.

The fireplace of the great hall was the focus of English domestic life from earliest times and was always an important decorative feature of the room. Until the middle of the sixteenth century the opening for the hearth was supported by a brick or stone arching, or more frequently, as we see here, by an oak beam or 'bressumer' resting on stone jambs. An interesting point in connection with these early fireplaces is that they were part of the construction of the house, being built up as the work proceeded, differing in this respect from the mantelpiece of later times, which has always been merely an ornamental addition to the room. In most houses of similar standing a raised daïs would have been placed across the end of the hall opposite to the screen; but here there is no space for it, since the ancient fireplace occupies almost the whole of this wall.

The oak chimney beam of the Great Hall at Sulgrave is of immense size – no less than 9 feet 6 inches wide, 18 inches high, and 13 inches deep from front to back. It is decorated with long, shallow, sunk spandrels, and the jambs on which it rests are formed of large blocks of blue Hornton stone. The beam is four-centred and the chamfer on its edge is carried down the jamb on each side, the chamfer on the jambs being 'stopped' twice – a rare variation of the single stop usual in early sixteenth-century fireplaces.

The actual width of the chimney opening is 7 feet 2 inches, and its height 4 feet 5 inches; while the depth of the embrasure is 2 feet 8 inches. At the time of the purchase of the Manor in 1914 this opening, as has been said, was entirely blocked up, but when cleared of modern obstructions all its original features, many of them of unusual interest, were found intact. The inside is lined with its original Tudor hand-faced stone, and the brickwork of the hearth, set herring-bone fashion, remains almost perfect. The fire, as has been customary from the earliest times, is to this day laid upon the hearth. This 'down-hearth,' as it was called, was used formerly both for cooking and warming, but in kitchens the hearth was generally slightly raised by a step or 'course' of stone or brick.

Wood being the only fuel, for coal was almost unknown, the place for the great slow-burning fire of logs, 'started' with kindling of well-dried sticks, was built wide and deep, and large enough for a seat to be let into the wall on either side for use on wintry nights. When this fireplace was opened up at the restoration in 1920, on the left, notched into the wall, was found a chimney-seat, its back and sides lined with its original smooth cement, with one side hollowed out to form an elbow rest, and its oak seat still in place. Beside the chimney seat is a convenient little cleft or sunk ledge in the stone walling to hold a mug or cup of spiced ale. There is a precisely similar cleft in this position inside the open fireplace in the parlour of the neighbouring Star Inn.

The logs of wood for the fire were supported on fire-dogs to enable a draught of air to pass beneath them. The big heap of wood-ash was never removed, and there would always be enough sparks left from the previous day's fire to be blown into flame with the bellows when fed with dry brushwood in the morning. This plan of raking the ashes together and keeping the embers glowing day in and day out all through the winter months, and in the kitchen all the year round, preserved the warmth of the chimney and so helped to prevent the fire from smoking.

In the wall on the right-hand side of the hearth is set a square oak panel pierced with three upright openings, which serves to ventilate a large cupboard, presumably used to store food, in the thickness of the wall beside the fireplace. Another example of this uncommon arrangement for ventilating a cupboard exists in a room at Dene Park, a Northamptonshire house of the same date.

The back of the fireplace recedes slightly towards the chimney; and fixed across the mouth of the chimney, just behind the chimney beam, are two iron bars or 'ready-poles,' with the original crossbar which can be slid along them. From this crossbar hangs a chain with large twisted links to hold a great pot or kettle over the fire. All this gear is still in perfect order.

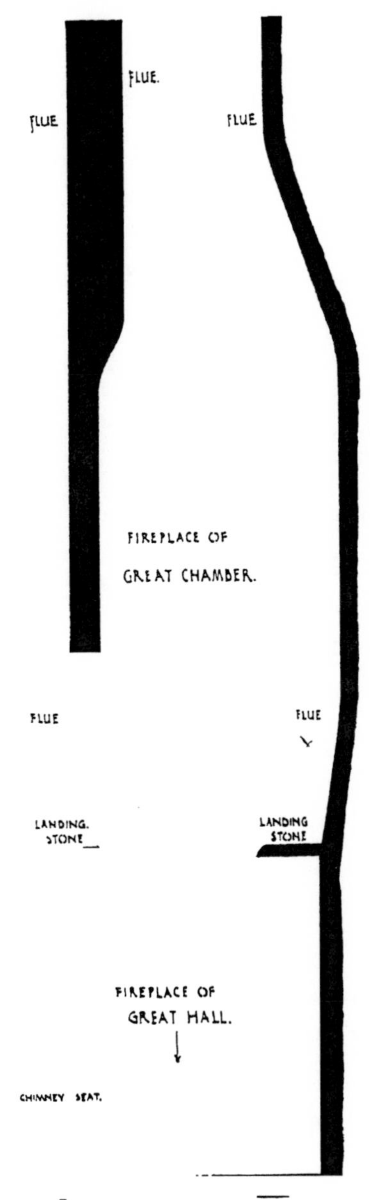

FIG. 9: *Section through Flues of Fireplace of Great Hall and Great Chamber*

The construction of the chimney of this fireplace is very remarkable (Fig. 9). Two independent shafts or 'flues' run outwards, and the shaft of the chimney of the Great Chamber overhead is set between them. At the bottom of each of these flues, some five feet above the hearth, juts a large slab of stone measuring two feet across. These great stones, which were termed 'landing-stones,' served in the past as starting points for the boy chimney-sweep in his journey up the chimney. Sometimes they were actually used as hiding-places; for a fugitive standing upright on either side would be completely hidden from below. The Elizabethan kitchen in Lyveden New Building, also in Northamptonshire – erected by Sir Thomas Tresham of Gunpowder Plot fame about the year 1600 – contains another example of this very curious chimney formation where two large flues run outwards, in each of which a man could hide.[1]

Just inside the fireplace, from a nail in the chimney beam, hangs a curious relic of former days—a chimney scraper (Fig. 10). Discovered a short time ago lodged in a chimney in Sulgrave village this little iron instrument with its much-used wooden handle, brings to mind the long-accepted practice of sending up the flues of chimneys little boys known as 'climbing boys,' to clean away the soot. This ancient method, now almost forgotten, which to-day seems to us utterly inhuman, actually survived until a little over half-a-century ago. Its intense cruelty was first exposed in the year 1785 by the philanthropist, Jonas Hanway (known to posterity as the first man who ever used an umbrella), who showed how orphan and illegitimate children of tender age were sold to chimney-sweeps for twenty shillings or thirty shillings apiece – 'a smaller sum than the value of a terrier' – and forced to crawl up chimneys, 'in a perfectly naked state,' and even to ascend chimneys that were on fire to put them out.

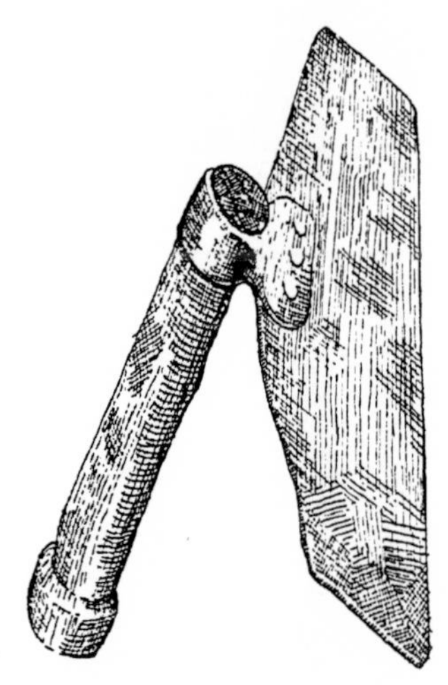

FIG. 10: *Chimney Scraper*

Attempts were made without success to supersede the necessity for climbing boys by encouraging the use of a long jointed chimney brush such as is now universal; and in 1840 a Bill was passed which forbade the apprenticing of any child under sixteen years of age to

[1] A plan of this chimney showing the two flues separated by the flue of the fireplace immediately above it, is illustrated by J. Alfred Gotch in *A Complete Account . . . of the Buildings erected in Northamptonshire by Sir Thomas Tresham between the Years 1575 and 1605*, pp. 35 and 40, and Plate 6.

a chimney-sweep. The Bill had as its chief supporter the Earl of Shaftesbury, the great social reformer; but so deep-rooted was the custom that fines and punishment were useless, and in 1870 Lord Shaftesbury – after some thirty years' untiring effort to enlist public opinion to suppress the evil – drew attention in the House of Lords to the case of 'a poor little chimney-sweeper, seven and a half years old, killed in a flue at Washington[1] in the county of Durham.' Five years later he cited a second terrible case, that of a boy chimney-sweep, fourteen years of age, who had just been suffocated in a flue at Cambridge; and the Bill which he then brought forward to do away with 'one of the greatest reproaches to civilisation known in this country' at length passed into law.[2]

The truth of Lord Shaftesbury's indictment is fully borne out by records which still exist of crimes which the sweeps' boys were forced to commit, and of the cruel severity of their subsequent punishment. Preserved in the London Museum is an eighteenth-century broadsheet which gives an account of a boy of seven, bound to a chimney-sweep in the Borough, who, at the instigation of his parents, deserted from his apprenticeship and was bound by them to a gang of thieves who, promptly availing themselves of his peculiar skill, sent him down a jeweller's chimney in Swallow Street, Piccadilly, to unshutter a shop-window and pass out goods to them through a hole cut in the glass. The noise he made in doing this aroused the house. He alone was taken – his companions escaped – and on being tried at the Old Bailey was found guilty, sentenced, and hanged – at twelve years old.

At the back of the fireplace opening, to protect the stones behind from the fire, stands one of the so-called Armada fire-backs, of cast iron, made in 1588 to commemorate the defeat of the Spanish fleet.

[1] Whence the Washingtons had originally come.

[2] Edwin Hodder, *The Seventh Earl of Shaftesbury*, K.G., *as Social Reformer*.

(a)

(b)

PLATE V

(a) GEORGE WASHINGTON, BY GILBERT STUART, PAINTED ABOUT 1795 FOR CHIEF JUSTICE SHIPPEN AND KNOWN AS THE 'SHIPPEN' PORTRAIT. (See p. 105)

(b) THE GREAT HALL, SHOWING THE OAK CEILING. (See p. 99)

This was purchased and placed here in 1920. The centre panel is decorated with two anchors with spirally coiled ropes. It has a row of fleurs-de-lys above (from the quarterings of the Royal Arms), a row of Tudor roses below, and on either side formal trees hung with large bunches of grapes. In front of the 'Armada' fire-back stand two great fire-dogs, or andirons as they are known in early inventories, which together weigh no less than two and a half hundredweight. They are of cast iron, like the fire-back, but some fifty years earlier, their charming late Gothic ornament pointing to the year of Lawrence Washington's purchase of the manor as their approximate date.

On the wall above the fireplace hangs the greatest treasure of the Manor House, the portrait in oils of George Washington, by Gilbert Stuart, painted for Chief Justice Shippen, the distinguished lawyer, who himself sat to the artist for his portrait. It was purchased from the last member of the Shippen family, and presented to Sulgrave Manor by Miss Faith Moore, sister of Viscountess Lee of Fareham, in 1920. Gilbert Stuart, who was born at North Kingstown, Rhode Island, in 1755, studied in America, Scotland, and England, and became in 1775 a pupil of Benjamin West. He later set up in London, painting portraits there until 1787. He also met with much success in Ireland, which he left in 1793. Returning to America he executed many commissions for portraits of George Washington, including this fine head (Plate v, *a*).

The Sulgrave picture shows a handsome man past middle life with clear blue eyes and ruddy complexion, with his white-powdered wig brushed out over the ears, wearing a dark-blue velvet coat. Round his neck is a cravat of fine white lace, and the black bow of his pigtail is just visible above his shoulder. The dedication and reopening of the Manor House was the occasion of a charming little ceremony, when Mrs. George Harvey, wife of the American

Ambassador, having unlocked the front door of the Manor with the silver key handed to her by Viscountess Lee of Fareham, entered the Great Hall, and drawing aside the American flag with which the frame was draped, revealed this noble portrait of the first President of the United States gazing out serenely from above his ancestral hearth.[1]

The deep cupboard, with its ventilator, on the right-hand side of the fireplace, is lined with oak, divided in half by an oak shelf, and enclosed by a small panelled door with a spring lock. This cupboard was used, amongst other purposes, for storing rush-lights; and on the hearth are two boat-shaped iron pots with long handles and tripod stands, known as 'grisets,' in which the pith of the rushes used for rush-lights were laid to soak in tallow fat or wax melted over the fire. Near by is a rush-light holder, with scissor-like jaws to clasp the rush-light.[2] In the corner of the fireplace is an early 'candle-shade' – a cylinder pierced with holes and fitted with a handle, to guard from draughts the flame of a tallow candle, and prevent danger of fire from an exposed light.

On the left-hand side of the fireplace in the thickness of the wall is a tall cupboard[3] enclosed by a door constructed of upright planks, hung on long iron hinges and fitted with a delicate wrought-iron latch – a beautiful example of native craftsmanship surviving from the days of the Washingtons (Fig. 11). This cupboard was long used as a bacon cupboard by the tenant farmer, but originally there was a doorway here which, when the east wing of the house was still standing, led through the six-foot wall into an Elizabethan parlour which would have been the principal living-room of the

[1] The key was afterwards sent as a gift to the President of the United States, Mr. Warren G. Harding, and is now preserved in the White House at Washington.

[2] Gilbert White, writing in 1775, in *The Natural History of Selborne*, after describing the method of making rush-lights in his day, remarks that a good rush of about four feet in length would burn for upwards of an hour.

[3] This is now used as a cupboard for books. In it are kept books that have been presented to the Manor House; also all the Visitors' Books, dating from 1914.

family – domestic life by this time having assumed greater privacy than could be attained when people lived, ate, and slept together in the great hall.

During the restoration of the Hall in 1920 several relics of great historical value were discovered hidden in a crevice between the ceiling and the floor of the room above, where they must have lain from the time of Lawrence Washington. One of them is a fragment of a late Gothic chest-front carved with a rosette. It dates from about 1540, and would have belonged to the builder of the Manor House (Fig. 12).

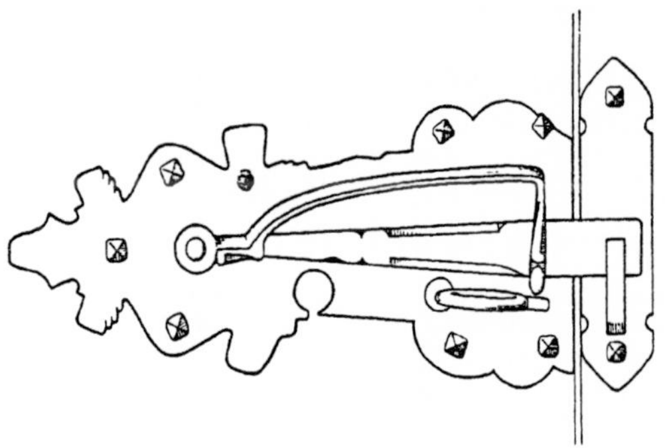

FIG. 11: *Wrought-iron Latch*

A treasure that came to light at the same time is a leather knife-case, tooled and moulded, and fitted on either side with two loops for suspension from a girdle. It dates from the middle of the sixteenth century, and there can be little doubt that in it we have an authentic relic of Lawrence Washington himself (Fig. 13). Its general quality and decoration suggest that it belonged to a man of definite social standing; and as in those days the knives used at table were rare, it was the custom for every one to carry his own table-knife about his person. In Elizabethan days and for long afterwards in England forks were still unknown, and food was helped and conveyed with the fingers from plate to mouth. With the knife-case was a silver sixpence of Queen Elizabeth, dated 1568, and an Elizabethan baby's shoe, which is now preserved in the Great Chamber.[1]

[1] See p. 119.

The panels of heraldic glass, already mentioned, are placed in the top lights of the two windows of the hall, four in one window and two in the other. These are facsimiles of panels of stained glass formerly in the Manor House, five of which are now in Fawsley church, and two at Weston Manor House, three miles distant from Sulgrave. How and when those now at Fawsley left Sulgrave is not known. It is likely that they were obtained from the house by Sir Charles Knightley, who succeeded to Fawsley Manor in 1812 and died in 1864, and was probably the collector of some of the other ancient stained glass of secular origin which is now in Fawsley church.

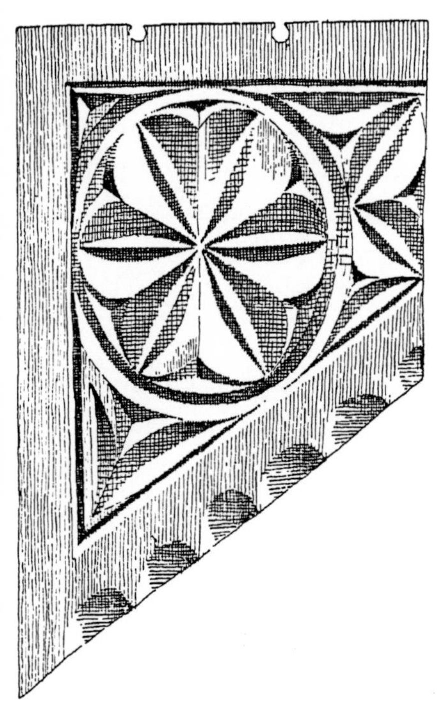

FIG. 12: *Fragment of a Chest Front. About* 1540

The first record we have of these panels is in Henn's manuscript of 1789, in which he says: 'In the Kitchen window are the following Arms finely painted on glass, but, alas! now much injured. These were removed from the part taken down a few years ago.' He then proceeds to describe four of the shields. Further on in his description of the manor he adds: 'In the Rubbish Garret are the following arms among broken

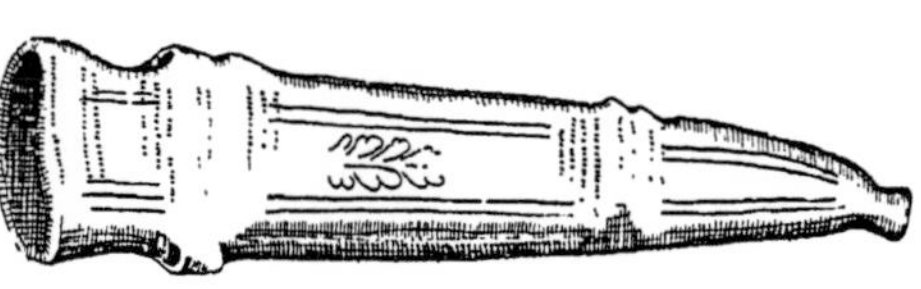

FIG. 13: *Knife Case*

glass: – Wasshington & Lighte, . . . Wasshington & Pargiter, . . . Wasshington [& Crest].' Baker refers to them in 1820, thus: 'Within these few years the arms and alliances of the family [of Washington] ornamented the kitchen window.' Washington Irving, in his *Life of George Washington*, tells us that 'The Washington crest in colored glass, was to be seen in a window of what is now the buttery. A window on which the whole family arms was emblazoned had been removed to the residence of the actual proprietor of the manor.'[1] The then owner of Sulgrave was Colonel the Hon. H. Hely-Hutchinson of Weston Manor, who had acquired the Sulgrave property in 1840.

The seven panels now in existence are probably only a small part of the ancient glass that decorated the windows of the Manor House in the Washingtons' time; for Henn states that he found three of them mixed up with 'broken glass' in the 'rubbish garret.'

The six shields in the windows of the Great Hall represent the coats of arms of Lawrence Washington, the builder; his father; his grandfather; his sons, Robert and Lawrence; and his grandson, Lawrence.[2] Five of them are those of direct ancestors of George Washington, first President of the United States.[3]

The first shield (No. 1), that of Lawrence Washington, the builder, has elaborate mantling of crimson lined with white, the whole surrounded by a border of dark brown. It dates from about 1560, and was probably made at the time that he altered the house and added the south porch. This mantling has a marked

[1] This book was published in 1855, but the actual date of the author's visit to Sulgrave is not stated.

[2] The seventh panel, with the arms of a granddaughter, Amye Wakelyn, is in a window of a room on the first floor.

[3] The respective owners of these seven shields are recorded in the Washington pedigree (p. 23).

resemblance to that on a panel of stained glass[1] in a window of the Stone Hall at Chequers,[2] bearing the arms of William Hawtrey, who is known to have rebuilt Chequers – some forty miles from Sulgrave – in the year 1565.

The remaining six coats of arms (Nos. 2 to 7) which are twenty years later in date, all have borders of identical pattern, composed of a wreath of green foliage adorned at intervals with coloured scrolls and other conventional ornament. The panel with the arms of Lawrence (grandson of the builder) and his wife, Margaret Butler (No. 6), is dated 1588; and it is likely that all six panels were made in 1588 for Robert (second owner of Sulgrave) in celebration of the marriage of his eldest son, Lawrence, to Margaret Butler, which took place in that year.

The panels, from left to right, are arranged as follows (the heraldic description or 'achievement' of each shield is given in full, together with the name of the person to whom it refers)[3] : –

In the large window:

(1) *Argent* [(a)] *two bars* [(b)] *gules* [(c)] *in chief* [(d)] *three mullets*[(e)] *of the second* (*i.e* gules). *In the fesse point* [(f)] *a crescent gules*, for difference. Crest, *out of a crest coronet* [(g)] *or* [(h)], *a demi-raven wings erect sable* [(i)]. Mantling [(j)]: *Gules, doubled* [(k)] *argent.* Under the shield, 'Wasshington.' This is the coat of arms of Robert Washington

[1] This panel is shown in Plate 20 of the *Catalogue of the Principal Works of Art at Chequers*, prepared by the Victoria and Albert Museum, with an Introduction by Viscount Lee of Fareham, and published under the authority of His Majesty's Stationery Office in 1923.

[2] Chequers, in Buckinghamshire, was presented and dedicated as the official country residence of the Prime Minister of Great Britain by Viscount and Viscountess Lee of Fareham in 1921.

[3] Of these seven shields, the originals of Nos. 2 and 6 are at Weston Manor House, and the remaining five at Fawsley Church.

(a) silver. (b) a horizontal band across a shield.
(c) red. (d) the upper part of a shield.
(e) stars of five points, unless otherwise stated. (f) the centre point of a shield.
(g) a crest coronet, generally formed of strawberry leaves, and known as a ducal coronet.
(h) gold. (i) black.
(j) a silk or cloth mantle hung over the helmet. (k) lined with.

of Warton (grandfather of Lawrence Washington, the builder of Sulgrave Manor House), who was the second son of Robert Washington of Warton, Lancs. – hence the crescent indicating a second son (Fig. 14).

This is also Lawrence Washington's own coat of arms. All the other panels of heraldic glass at Sulgrave except his grandson Lawrence's, and his grand-daughter Amye Wakelyn's, have the crescent for 'difference.' His coat of arms carved on the right-hand spandrel of the porch, has, however, no crescent (though the left-hand shield, now defaced, once bore it); nor does the enamelled shield on his tomb in Sulgrave church now show any traces of a crescent.

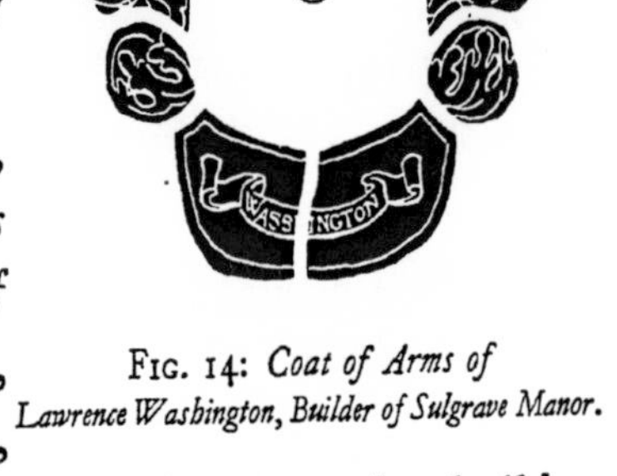

FIG. 14: *Coat of Arms of Lawrence Washington, Builder of Sulgrave Manor.*

(2) Washington as in No. (1), impaling [l] *Sable three trouts or luces hauriant* [m] *in fesse* [n] *argent a chief or*. For John Washington of Warton, Lancs., and his wife, Margaret Kytson, of Warton Hall, parents of Lawrence Washington, the builder (Fig. 15).

(3) Washington as before, impaling, *Barry* [o] *of four pieces or and sable three mascles* [p] *two and one counterchanged* [q]. For

[l] impaled – when two coats are placed side by side in one shield.
[m] said of fishes when displayed upright.
[n] a fesse – a single band drawn horizontally across a shield.
[o] a shield divided horizontally into a stated number of pieces.
[p] a perforated lozenge.
[q] said of an emblem which, when displayed over a field of two colours, has the colours reversed.

FIG. 15: *Washington and Kytson*

FIG. 16: *Washington and Pargiter*

FIG. 17: *Washington and Light*

FIG. 18: *Washington and Newce*

FIG. 19: *Washington and Butler*

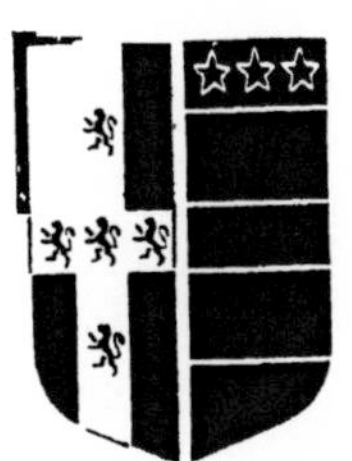

FIG. 20: *Wakelyn and Washington*

Elizabethan Heraldic Panels of Stained Glass showing Marriage Alliances of the Washingtons

Lawrence Washington and his wife, Amee Pargiter, of Greatworth, Northants. (Fig. 16).

(4) Washington as before, impaling *Gules a chevron* [r] *between three swans argent*. For Robert Washington (eldest son of Lawrence Washington, the builder of Sulgrave Manor) and his wife, Elizabeth Light, of Radway, Warwickshire (Fig. 17).

In the small window:

(5) Washington as before, impaling *Sable two pallets* [s] *argent, a canton* [t] *ermine* [u]. For Lawrence Washington of Maidstone (second son of Lawrence Washington, builder of Sulgrave Manor) and his wife Martha Newce, of Great Hadham, Herts. (Fig. 18).

(6) Washington as before, but without the crescent, impaling *Azure* [v] *a chevron between three covered cups or*. For Lawrence Washington (eldest son of Robert Washington of Sulgrave) and his wife Margaret Butler, of Tighes (Ticehurst) Sussex, with the date 1588 (Fig. 19).

In a window in the room above:

(7) *Argent on a cross sable five lions rampant or*, impaling Washington as in No. (6). For Alban Wakelyn of Eydon, Northants, and his wife Amye, daughter of Robert Washington of Sulgrave, and grand-daughter of Lawrence Washington, the builder. It also is dated 1588 (Fig. 20).

The Great Hall and the three rooms above it, which form the existing portion of the Tudor house in which Lawrence Washington and his descendants lived for over a century, are furnished with contemporary examples of Elizabethan and Jacobean oak furniture, chosen with great care to blend with their surroundings and preserve the ancient character and atmosphere of the house.

The centre of the Great Hall is occupied by an oak table 9 feet long and 30 inches wide. This type of table – commonly known as

[r] a gable-shaped heraldic figure. [s] a diminutive of a pale or perpendicular bar.
[t] a square in the dexter corner of a shield rather smaller than a quarter.
[u] a white field powdered over with black ermine spots. [v] blue.

a refectory table, a title derived from monastic times – is really of Elizabethan date, and therefore (like all dining-tables of the kind surviving) actually post-Reformation. Its short bulbous legs are carved with gadroons and acanthus, and the frieze is decorated with a pattern of running scroll-work. Upon it is arranged a collection of wooden table-ware – platters, trenchers, bowls, and salt-cellars of turned wood, or, in the ancient terminology, 'treen,' that is to say, 'of tree.' Beside the platters are early brass and pewter spoons; and the table is further set out with pewter porringers and early glass wine-bottles. At one end of the table stands a tall wassail bowl dating from about 1650 to 1660 – the last few years of the Washington family's occupation of the Manor House. It is of lignum-vitæ, exquisitely turned, and its cover surmounted by a little turned receptacle for spice and nutmeg. At the other end of the table is a three-handled bronze mortar of Elizabethan date.

Although the Manor House can no longer boast of any such treasure as 'the goblet and cover of parcel gilt' which Lawrence Washington bequeathed to his second son and namesake, or the silver 'salt,' to buy which he left him 'four pounds of currant English money,' yet it possesses a rare 'tiger-ware' jug, with contemporary Elizabethan mounts of copper chased and gilt, closely resembling the type of jug which Lawrence would have had beside him as he sat at table (Plate VI, *a*). Accompanying it are two ancient horn cups, stained yellow with use, one of them engraved with intertwined serpents and a sprig of herb within a circle, doubtless a design with some symbolic meaning. With these is a 'standing' cup – that is, a cup with stem and foot – a 'treen' cup, in this instance of pear wood, of unique interest, designed for the use of a man and his wife (Plate VI, *b*). The owner's name – Luke Knee – and the date 1645 are carved upon the foot. On the outside of the bowl are heraldic figures supporting a coat of arms, and around it is the following injunction:—

PLATE VI

(*a*) ELIZABETHAN 'TIGER-WARE' JUG WITH ENGRAVED GILT COPPER MOUNTS ABOUT 1580. (See p. 114)

(*b*) DRINKING CUP OF BEECHWOOD, DATED 1645. (See p. 114)

(*c*) ELIZABETHAN OAK CHEST, THE FRONT AND ENDS CARVED WITH LIONS' MASKS (See p. 116)

(*d*) JACOBEAN OAK STOOL WITH OPEN ENDS. (See p. 127)

[illegible] TRIANGULAR SEAT. (See p. 116)

a refectory table, a title derived from monastic times – is really of Elizabethan date, and therefore (like all dining-tables of the kind surviving) actually post-Reformation. Its short bulbous legs are carved with gadroons and acanthus, and the frieze is decorated with a pattern of running scroll-work. Upon it is arranged a collection of wooden table-ware – platters, trenchers, bowls, and salt-cellars of turned wood, or, in the ancient terminology, 'treen,' that is to say, 'of tree.' Beside the platters are early brass and pewter spoons; and the table is further set out with pewter porringers and early glass wine-bottles. At one end of the table stands a tall wassail bowl dating from about 1650 to 1660 – the last few years of the Washington family's occupation of the Manor House. It is of lignum-vitæ, exquisitely turned, and its cover surmounted by a little turned receptacle for spice and nutmeg. At the other end of the table is a three-handled bronze mortar of Elizabethan date.

Although the Manor House can no longer boast of any such treasure as 'the goblet and cover of parcel gilt' which Lawrence Washington bequeathed to his second son and namesake, or the silver 'salt,' to buy which he left him 'four pounds of currant English money,' yet it possesses a rare 'tiger-ware' jug, with contemporary Elizabethan mounts of copper chased and gilt, closely resembling the type of jug which Lawrence would have had beside him as he sat at table (Plate VI, *a*). Accompanying it are two ancient horn cups, stained yellow with use, one of them engraved with intertwined serpents and a sprig of herb within a circle, doubtless a design with some symbolic meaning. With these is a 'standing' cup – that is, a cup with stem and foot – a 'treen' cup, in this instance of pear wood, of unique interest, designed for the use of a man and his wife (Plate VI, *b*). The owner's name – Luke Knee – and the date 1645 are carved upon the foot. On the outside of the bowl are heraldic figures supporting a coat of arms, and around it is the following injunction:—

'If you bee a goode hussi and youse a good meanes
you muste seeke to keepe youre drincke and youre cupe cleane.'

Rooms in Elizabethan and Jacobean times were still comparatively bare, and besides the table and sideboard, and a cupboard, there were only seats. The joint stool – that is, a joined stool, its framework joined by mortice and tenons – was the usual seat: the chair being a rare article of comfort until early Stuart days. There are good examples here of typical joint stools, and round the room are several Jacobean oak chairs, their panelled backs each carved with a different conventional floral design.

Beside the window stands a long Jacobean oak dresser, its drawer fronts decorated with mitred mouldings; upon it stand a large brass dish and two candlesticks of turned brass. In the drawer of the dresser is preserved a magnificently bound volume containing the names of the thirty-five thousand subscribers to the Endowment Fund presented to the Manor by the National Society of the Colonial Dames of America in 1925; also a volume with the names of those who subscribed to the Restoration Fund presented by the same Society in 1931. Above it, in a beautifully carved and gilt frame – after a design by Paul Revere, a Boston silversmith of the eighteenth century – hangs a portrait of George Washington in British uniform, as Colonel commanding the Virginian Colonial Troops – a copy of the famous picture painted in 1772 by Charles Wilson Peale, now in Washington and Lee University, Lexington, Virginia – which was presented to Sulgrave Manor by the National Society of the Colonial Dames of America in 1915.

On the wall at the other side of the window is an early brass lantern clock, the chased openwork above its dial inscribed: 'William Almond in Louthbury, fecit.' Almond, whose shop was in Lothbury in the City of London, was admitted a member of the ancient Clockmakers' Company of London in 1630.

By the fireplace stands a child's chair of turned ash and elm with a triangular seat. This small chair, which is two feet high and of Tudor date, and is a great rarity, was presented in 1921 by two little boys aged four and five (Plate VI, *e*). Against the wall, at right angles to the fireplace, is a tall oak settle with a panelled back, purchased from Thorpe Mandeville Manor, near Sulgrave, in 1919. On the same wall, between the door and window, hangs a charming Elizabethan oak livery cupboard decorated with carving and geometrical and herring-bone inlay in holly and bog oak – an outstanding specimen of English furniture of its period. This livery cupboard out of which, as its name implies, food was served (*livré*), now forms a receptacle for a collection of Washington relics and small pieces of old American silver-work. It is known as the Eleanor Hope Cupboard, after the name of the donor, the contents being given specially for it by various residents in Virginia.[1]

Under the window stands a small oak table on which lies the Visitors' Book, and beside it a large pewter inkstand. Lastly, from the great cross-beams in the middle of the room hangs a beautiful brass twelve-light chandelier of English seventeenth-century workmanship, fitted with hand-made waxen candles.

[1] These have been temporarily moved for display to the Inner Chamber on the floor above.

Chapter IX

THE GREAT CHAMBER

THE eight-panelled door near the north window of the Great Hall opens on to a handsome oak staircase of two flights, with large, square newel posts, twisted balusters, and solid oak treads, leading up to the Bedchamber floor. It dates from the latter part of the seventeenth century, replacing an earlier, Tudor staircase, probably of spiral construction (Plate IV, *c*).

On the landing at the top of this staircase is a huge, ancient cupboard, with an Elizabethan oak-panelled door, and an early window, now filled in. Various legends have grown up round it. The most persistent – repeated in every history and guide-book – is that Queen Elizabeth hid here as a child. Another relates that Henrietta Maria, consort of Charles I, took refuge in it, together with her pony, after the defeat of the King's army at Edgehill. One can but say with Mr. Henn: 'Antiquarys must not be carried away with every wind of report!'

On the left of the cupboard is the entrance to the Great Chamber, over the Great Hall, a fine, lofty apartment with an open-timbered roof, which occupies the greater part of the upper floor of the Tudor building. It was the principal sleeping apartment in the house, and for many generations served as both bedroom and withdrawing-room of the reigning lord of the manor and his wife (Plate VII).

Here Lawrence and Amee Washington's eleven children, four

sons and seven daughters, are presumed to have been born; and here they played in the picturesque attire in which they are shown upon the two small memorial brasses in Sulgrave church. A souvenir of one of them is an Elizabethan baby's shoe, which was thrown,

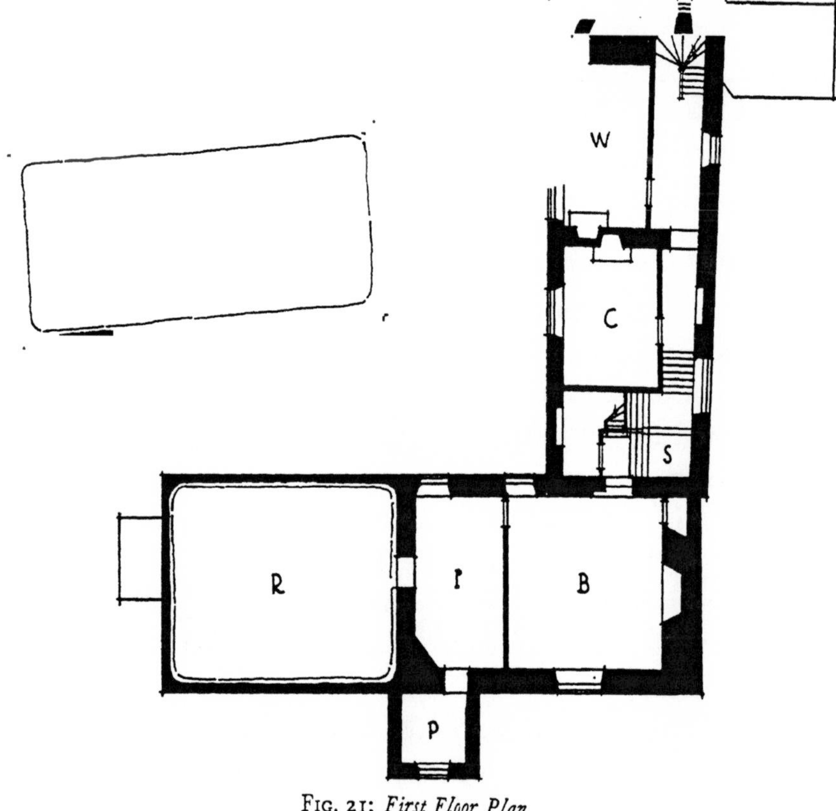

FIG. 21: *First Floor Plan*

S Staircase · *B Great Chamber* · *I Inner Chamber* · *P Porch Room* · *C Chintz Bedroom* · *W White Bedroom* · *R Steward's Residence*

perhaps in a childish prank, behind the skirting of the wall. Here it lay hidden for close on four hundred years, until, in the course of the recent restorations, it slipped through a crevice in the ceiling of the Great Hall. With it Lawrence Washington's knife-case and an Elizabethan silver sixpence fell upon the stone-flagged floor below.

The shoe, with invisible stitchery at its sides and in perfect condition, measures $3\frac{3}{4}$ inches long, and is an exquisite example of the leather-worker's craft, for which the town of Northampton has long enjoyed a world-wide fame (Fig. 22).

The Great Chamber at once strikes the visitor as a singularly bright and cheerful room, owing to the spacious timber-framed window of four lights which overlooks the garden. The window embrasure, owing to the great splay of the solid three-foot walls, is wide and deep; and from the ancient window seat, formed of a single slab of oak, may be obtained a lovely and extensive view, which can have altered little since Amee Washington looked out. In the foreground are smooth spreading green lawns leading to the Tudor orchard, in spring gay with flowering bulbs, and beyond is a wide sweep of timbered country. Beneath the window to the right is 'Madam's Close,' and to the left a delightful prospect of rich valley land, watered by the Tove, which rises from the spring of Holy Well, near the site of the old Grange of St. Andrew's Priory, and flows eastward from Sulgrave to Towcester where it joins the River Ouse on its leisurely course towards the sea.

FIG. 22: *Elizabethan Baby's Shoe*

The room measures eighteen feet long and is almost square. The floor is laid with slabs of polished oak of greater width than was customary even in times when timber was used with the utmost prodigality. In the days of the Washingtons it would have been strewn daily with fresh herbs – an agreeable custom, commented on approvingly by the Dutch traveller, Lemnius, who, in 1560, remarks: 'Their chambers and parlours strawed over with sweet herbes refreshed mee.' Gerard, the Elizabethan herbalist, speaking of meadowsweet, tells us that its 'leaves and flowers farre excelle all other strowing herbes for to decke up houses, to strowe in chambers, halls and banqueting houses in the summer time, for the smell thereof makes the heart merrie and joyful and delighteth the senses.' Of meadowsweet, too, John Parkinson observes that 'Queene Elizabeth of famous memorie did more desire it than any other sweete herbe to strewe her chambers withall.' Still more apposite to the Great Chamber is the declaration of Sir Hugh Platt, who writes in 1603: 'I hold it for a most delicat & pleasing thing to have a faire gallery, great chamber or other lodging, that openeth fully upon the East or West sun, to be inwardly garnished with sweet hearbs and flowers.'

Though the floors are no longer strewn with 'aromatic clippings,' the visitor is greeted by the friendly fragrance of rosemary and lavender which lingers in the air; and the sweet scent of roses brought in from the garden once again fills the ancient Manor House.

The high-pitched roof of the Great Chamber is supported by three pairs of sloping beams or 'principal rafters,' the central pair of which form its chief support, dividing it into two bays of equal size. They are held together at about three-quarters of their height by a cambered 'collar' beam, braced to them by large arch braces – the whole morticed and tenoned, and further held together by stout oak pegs (Fig. 23).

Resting on these three principal rafters are four horizontal beams or 'purlins,' which extend from one end of the roof to the other.[1] Upon these beams, reaching from the apex of the roof to the wall

[1] A roof of this construction with both principal rafters and purlins is known as 'double-framed.' A roof without either, where the common rafters rest only on the ridge purlin and wall-plates, is termed a 'single-framed' roof. The sectional diagram of the room on p. 121 will assist in explaining the details of the roof construction.

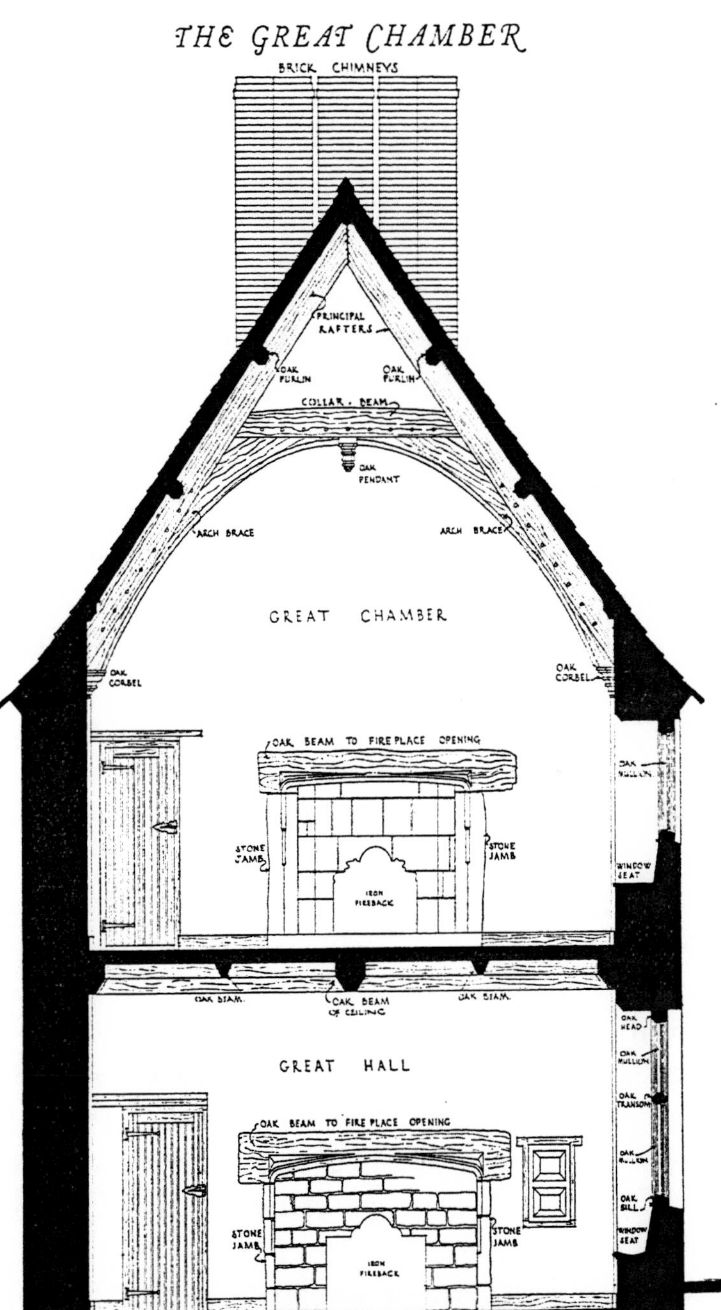

Fig. 23: *Sectional View of Great Hall and Great Chamber*

purlins or wall plates fixed on the tops of the walls, are laid the 'common' rafters – timbers of heavy scantling to support the weight of the stone slates above. These rafters, hidden from view by a covering of plaster-work which intercepts down-draughts from the roof-slates, have stout oak battens nailed to them, to which the slates are fixed by oaken pegs.

The bases of the 'principal rafters,' together with their arch-braces, are supported by richly moulded oak corbels or wall-brackets; while to the centre of the collar-beam above which the arch-braces meet is applied a beautifully shaped pendant ornament of oak, carved, like the corbels, with a series of elaborate mouldings. Outline drawings of the pendant and of the pair of corbels are shown in Fig. 23; and a comparison of the latter shows that the two are not exactly alike, the details of the lower mouldings differing one from the other – an illuminating example of the freedom with which the Tudor craftsmen worked.

The imposing size of the oak 'principals,' together with the Gothic appearance of the wall corbels and moulded pendant, gives them, at first sight, so strong a medieval look that doubts have been expressed as to their precise date. They differ, however, from true medieval work by the great breadth and comparative thinness of their arch-braces. In spite of its apparently early character, the work cannot be of pre-Reformation date, and must have been executed for Lawrence Washington after his purchase of the Manor.

Before the restoration of 1920 the beautiful timberwork of the roof was completely hidden from view by a modern ceiling made of lath and plaster, and its outline can still be clearly traced upon the sides of the oak 'principals.' A large slice of the room, four feet wide, had been cut off by a wooden partition (traces of which are still faintly visible on the floor) built up along one side of it to form a passage-way to the Inner Chamber. The arrangement was doubtless made to suit the views of later occupants who would object to passing through the Great Chamber in order to gain access to the rooms beyond. This inconvenient custom seems to have contented our ancestors until far into the eighteenth century; and we need only look at the long line of bedrooms at Hampton Court or Kensington Palace, leading one out of the other, to see how little regard even the greatest personages had for privacy, less than two hundred years ago.

The oak doorway which gives access to the Great Chamber from the stairs has oak jambs 8 by 7 inches thick. They are stop-chamfered, and of late sixteenth-century date. The threshold board, over which it was customary to step, has long ago been cut away to the level of the oaken floor to avoid the risk of tripping over it.

That considerable alteration took place here in later Elizabethan times is evident, for above the present doorway is an oak beam 5 feet long and 28 inches thick, with a 3-inch splay on the inner side, which is forty or fifty years earlier in date than the door, and must have formed part of a window in Lawrence Washington's building.

Corresponding exactly with it, a little further to the left, is a window looking out on to the Stone Courtyard, which in 1914 was found blocked up, probably since the time of the window-tax. The original lintel of chamfered oak, and the ancient window-seat formed of a wide plank of elm, are still in place, though the oak window-frame has been renewed.

The large open fireplace in the east wall of the Great Chamber is exactly over that of the Great Hall. Previous to 1920 it was entirely filled up, and at the restoration the existence of three successive fireplaces was revealed. Behind a modern grate was a plastered fireplace of Queen Anne date, and behind that the original open Tudor hearth, lined with large blocks of Hornton stone. It now corresponds exactly to the fireplace in the Great Hall, save that its sides are splayed instead of being squared to form a chimney corner, and the hearth-stone is raised a few inches from the floor.

The great cambered oak chimney beam has a four-centred arch and long, shallow, sunk spandrels. Its surface has been hacked to afford a key for the covering of modern plaster-work which completely hid it. It is supported by two stone jambs, each one formed of a single block of Hornton stone, 54 inches high, their angles chamfered, with two small 'stops.'

In the fireplace is a handsome fire-back of cast iron weighing over five hundredweight and decorated with nautical devices. In the centre is an anchor, with a 'fouled' rope forming a pattern above it, and over this the figure of a dove. On either side are grotesque terminal figures.

Beneath the whitewash over the wall above the fireplace are rows of nail-heads which cross one another to form squares. The purpose of these nails, which reach upwards as far as the cross-beam, is uncertain; it is likely that they were used for fixing a decorative painted canvas to the wall.

The opening on the left of the fireplace (now enclosed by an oak door to form a wall cupboard) is surmounted by an early chamfered beam extending as far as the wall. It was once a doorway, and before the east wing was pulled down formed the entrance to a room beyond the Great Bedchamber. The fireplace belonging to this vanished room is of precisely the same size and design as the fireplace of the Great Chamber that backs on to it, its oak chimney-beam and stone jambs, now filled in, being still in position out of doors – built in high up on the face of the present outside wall of the east end of the house (Plate XIII, *a*).

The wall of the Great Chamber facing the fireplace is of timber and plaster construction – commonly known as 'half-timber' – and at every joint the original joiners' marks are visible. These marks were carved on the ends of each joist when the mortices and tenons were cut and fitted together in the workshops, to distinguish the individual timbers at the final re-assembling in their permanent positions. It is rare to meet with so large a series of joiners' marks, and they are worth careful study by students of architecture. Drawings made from some of them are reproduced here (Fig. 24).

The Great Chamber, in Tudor times, always contained the 'best bed,' which was regarded as an heirloom, and here stood the great four-post family bedstead of the Washingtons.[1] We know nothing of its appearance, for though Lawrence Washington left a specific bequest to his second son, Lawrence, of a bedstead in the Gate House and another 'over the Day-House' (*i.e.* the dairy), he makes no mention in his will – as his contemporary Shakespeare does – of his own bedstead, which must have gone, in accordance with the common custom, with the rest of his goods and chattels, to Robert, his eldest son.

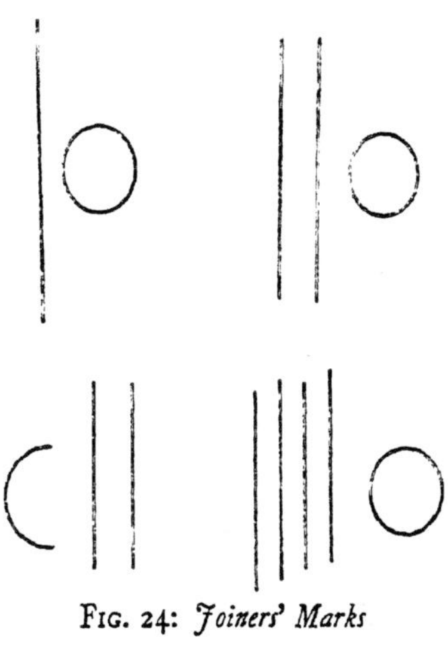

Fig. 24: *Joiners' Marks*

The site of the ancestral bed is now occupied by an Elizabethan four-post canopied bedstead, magnificently carved, which came from Battle Abbey in Sussex, and was purchased for the Manor House in 1921 from a fund presented by the Stars and Stripes Club of Manchester. The back, of particularly elaborate workmanship, is arranged in tiers, the lower having two round-headed arches

[1] Visitors to Sulgrave in former years can well remember the Victorian mahogany four-post bed standing here, which the tenant farmer would point out as the bed in which George Washington was born!

enclosing interlacing strapwork with large rosettes and groups of fruit on either side; the upper, two rectangular panels divided and flanked by grotesque terminal figures wearing fantastic Elizabethan head ornaments. The arches start from a shelf-rail, just wide enough for a single short tallow candle to stand upon it, and marks of burning, the result of this dangerous practice, can be seen on the panels just above this little ledge.[1] The bed-posts supporting the panelled tester with its carved frieze and cornice, rest on square plinths, and are carved with acanthus and with ornaments representing inverted cups. It should be noted here that, as in the case of other very important Elizabethan bedsteads that have survived, the 'bedstock' – the part supporting the mattress – stands clear of the bed-posts.

The curtains and vallance of the bed are of deep rose-red moreen. The quilted bedcover, embroidered with bright silks in the Chinese taste, one would like to fancy was spread over the Elizabethan bedstock a hundred years later by some owner of the Manor House in the time of William and Mary. Presented by Miss Faith Moore, it is a superb example of fine needlework and well repays detailed examination.

In early times the principal article of domestic furniture was the chest or coffer. It was made to serve all kinds of purposes – as a receptacle for storing garments, linen, or valuables, as a bench to sit on, and even as a table. It always stood near the bed; and here, beside the great bedstead, is placed a fine Elizabethan chest – one of the treasures of the Manor House. Its decorative features include a palm-leaf pattern on the four uprights of its framework and on the applied pilasters of its triple arches. Of more distinctive character

[1] It was customary to fix a tallow dip by means of some of its own wax against the walls; and marks of burning thus made can be seen here on the timbers of the half-timber wall, on the door-posts, and elsewhere.

PLATE VII

[…]T CHAMBER, SHOWING TIMBER ROOF, AND ELIZABETHAN FOUR-POST BEDSTEAD. (See p. 11

are the lions' masks boldly carved, affixed to the centre of each sunk panel – a detail common on contemporary French woodwork but rare on Elizabethan furniture (Plate VI, *c*).

On the chest lies a copy of the famous 'Breeches' Bible of the year 1607, complete with concordance, metrical psalms, and prayers, in its original leather binding and brass mounts.

Another chest of particular interest – a type known as a 'None-such' chest – stands at the foot of the bed, though it is not visible in the illustration. The inlay on the front represents Nonesuch, in Surrey, the palace built by Henry VIII and pulled down in the time of Charles II, here conventionalised for the purposes of design. Made of oak and limewood, its distinctive features are its unusually small size (14 inches high and 23 inches long), and the date, 1594, painted upon the lid of the little till inside.

Against the wall beside the window is an interesting example of Jacobean oak furniture – a semi-circular side-table with a hinged semi-circular flap which is supported when open by a movable gate-leg to form a circular top. Upon it stands an early brass basin. Close by is an oak cradle of the same date, its panelled sides carved with volutes. The head is enclosed by an open balustrading, and on either side are knobs for cords to fasten down the bedding. It is completed by an ancient white coverlet quilted in a traditional design. Other attractive small pieces of furniture include a spinning-wheel, a baby's high-backed chair, and an oak 'joynt' stool with open slab ends and a hand-grip on the top – a rare seventeenth-century survival of a fifteenth-century Gothic model (Plate VI, *d*).

Beside the fireplace is a handsome oak arm-chair, presented by Mr. J. Pierpont Morgan in 1919. The panelled back is decorated with conventional lilies and with a many-petalled rose, and has spiral volutes on the cresting and ear-pieces. Its surface possesses a beautiful red-brown patina produced by centuries of rubbing and waxing.

Dating from the time of the Commonwealth, it is of a type which would have been used by the last members of the Washington family at Sulgrave.

Upon the north wall hangs a panel of seventeenth-century tapestry woven with a floral design. Near the doorway leading into the Inner Chamber is a Stuart 'stumpwork' picture embroidered with animals, fruit, and flowers worked in coloured silks, which was presented by Viscountess Lee of Fareham. The upper part of the picture shows a gabled house of the period, and below are figures of Adam and Eve. The back is inscribed in old handwriting: 'This work done by George Washington's twice great-grandmother. Left to Edward Washington, first cousin to George Washington.' The tradition is that it belonged to Elizabeth Light, of Radway, wife of Robert, eldest son of Lawrence Washington, but it actually dates from one generation later.

In the window near by is a beautiful panel of original Elizabethan glass containing the coat of arms of Robert Washington and his wife, Elizabeth Light. It bears the following inscription: –

> 'The Arms of Washington and Light circa 1580, being those of the great-great-great-great-grandparents of George Washington, first President of the United States of America, and other heraldic fragments of old glass from Burton Hall, Leicestershire, were arranged and releaded by the desire of the Duke and Duchess of Somerset, 1915.'

This glass, acquired for Sulgrave Manor in 1933, was discovered in 1915 by the Duke and Duchess of Somerset, stored in the dairy at Burton Hall. It is said to have come from Radway Church in Warwickshire which adjoins Radway Grange, the Lights' ancestral home.

Quartered with the Washington bars and mullets is a coat of arms said to be that of Lawrence; and it is suggested that the shield records a marriage alliance of one of the early Washingtons with a member of the family of Lawrence.[1] If this be so, we have here an explanation of the frequent recurrence of Lawrence as a Christian name among successive generations of the Washingtons – from Lawrence the builder of Sulgrave Manor in 1540 to Lawrence the builder of Mount Vernon in 1743.

[1] 'The Washington Coat of Arms: an Heraldic Puzzle,' by T. Pape, in *The Field*, 29th December 1917.

Chapter X

THE INNER CHAMBER AND THE PORCH ROOM

BEYOND the Great Chamber is a small bedchamber measuring 18 feet by 12 feet, which lies immediately above the 'Screens' passage. It is known by the ancient name of the Inner Chamber, and is entered from the Great Chamber by a door in the half-timbered wall that separates the two rooms. There was once a corresponding doorway at the other end of the wall beyond the great bedstead; this is now closed, but is still recognisable by its stop-chamfered side-posts of the same design as those of the existing doorway. Both are framed in the ancient manner, their oak uprights being morticed into a raised sill or threshold. This raised threshold, inconvenient though it is to cross, may in early times have had a practical as well as a structural purpose in preventing the sweet herbs strewn upon the floor from being dragged from one room to another.

The Inner Chamber has the same wide oak floor-boards as the Great Chamber, but no other features of architectural interest. It serves as a museum and in it are displayed historical records and relics connected with Sulgrave and the early Washingtons, together with autograph letters and personal belongings of George Washington.

The ancient parchment deeds exhibited in this room are chosen

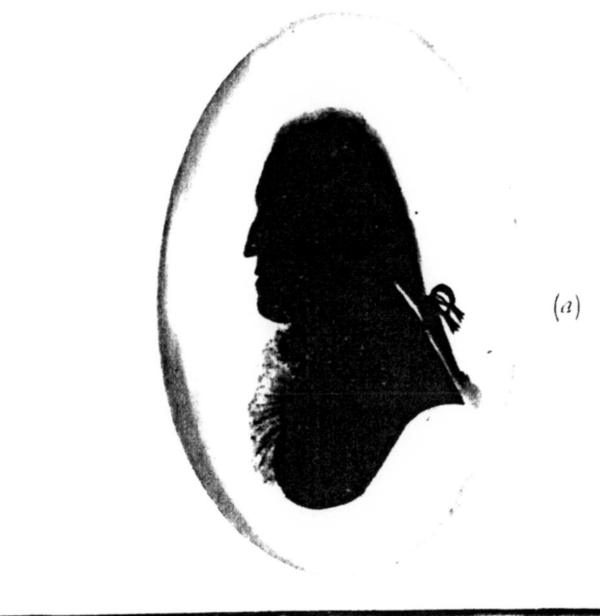

(a)

(b)

PLATE VIII

(a) SILHOUETTE PORTRAIT OF GEORGE WASHINGTON, PAINTED ON PLASTER BY J. THOMASON, ABOUT 1790. (See p. 131)

(b) DEED, DATED 1606, SHOWING SIGNATURES OF ROBERT WASHINGTON (ELDEST SON OF LAWRENCE, THE BUILDER OF SULGRAVE MANOR), AND HIS TWO ELDER SONS, LAWRENCE AND ROBERT. (See p. 131)

from the large and valuable collection in the possession of the Board which has gradually been acquired by gift or purchase.[1] Among the documents shown may be specially mentioned those bearing the signatures of two sons of Lawrence Washington – Robert and Lawrence – of five grandsons – Lawrence, Robert, and Christopher Washington, Lawrence Tomson, and Lawrence Makepeace – and of his great-grandson, Abel Makepeace, the last member of the Washington family to live at Sulgrave Manor. A catalogue of these documents is preserved at the Manor House. The signature of Robert, written in 1606 during his thirty-five years' residence at Sulgrave, together with those of his two elder sons, Lawrence and Robert, is shown in Plate VIII, *b*.

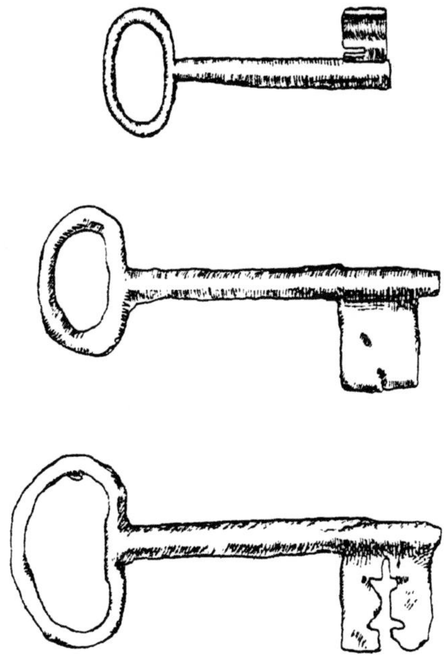

FIG. 25: *Elizabethan Keys*

Relics connected with the Manor House and its Washington owners include coins and tokens, and several wrought iron keys of Elizabethan date which were dug up during the re-planning of the garden and later (Fig. 25).

Amongst the exhibits associated with George Washington the most important is a group of four silhouette portraits which hang upon the wall: two represent Washington himself; one is of Mrs. Washington; and one of Mrs. John Jay, the wife of the American statesman.

Of the two portraits of the President, the larger and more

[1] The title deeds of Sulgrave Manor are deposited at the United States Embassy in London.

important is by J. Thomason of Dublin. It was purchased by the Board in 1933 from the collection of Mrs. F. Nevill Jackson, and was first reproduced in an article by her in the *Connoisseur* of January 1932, entitled 'Contemporary Silhouette Portraits of George Washington.' In it she pointed out that while several hundred oil paintings of him exist, authentic 'shadow portraits' number only fourteen. This one by Thomason is the only example in the 'grand manner,' painted on plaster, by an eighteenth-century master of silhouette. It measures $3\frac{3}{8}$ by $2\frac{5}{8}$ inches, and is in dense black except for the transparencies of the shirt frill in delicate folds which are rendered in thinned black. No body-colour or bronzing 'infringes the shadow tradition.' The portrait, executed between 1790 and 1792, is in its original oval brass frame and has the old convex glass over it (Plate VIII, *a*).

Pasted on the back is the silhouettist's 'trade label,' which has fortunately survived intact, and is sufficiently curious to be worthy of quotation. It runs as follows: –

> 'PERFECT LIKENESSES in Miniature PROFILE taken by *J. Thomaſon*, on a peculiar Plan & reduced to any Size, which preſerves ye most exact Symmetry & animated Expreſsion of ye Features. Superior to any other method. Set in elegant Frames 6s. 6d. only. Likeneſses set in Rings, Lockets, Pins, &c. He keeps ye Original Shades & can ſupply Thoſe he has once taken with any Number of Copies; reduces old ones & dreſses them in y^e preſent TASTE. N.B. Time of ſitting Ten to Two & from Two to Five in the Evening when each perſon is detain'd 2 Minutes only. All orders, Poſt paid, will be duly attended to at No. 25 South Gate, George St.'

The second shadow-portrait of Washington, painted on an oval glass measuring $1\frac{1}{2}$ by $1\frac{1}{16}$ inches, is the work of an unknown

American artist, and, according to the label on the back, dates from 1788. While the head is a dense black, the hair is shaded to grey, as are the President's shirt-frill, his buttons, and the other details of his dress. The likeness is a good one, despite a slight over-emphasis of the sitter's characteristic hawk-like nose. The picture is in its original frame of gilded wood.

The silhouette of Martha Washington, painted in black with touches of gold upon an oval glass, is also the work of an American artist, and suggests an admirable likeness.

The silhouette of Mrs. John Jay, painted on cardboard by an anonymous hand, shows her most fashionably dressed, with an elaborate hat of lace and feathers. She married John Jay in 1774, and is known to have been a friend of Marie Antoinette. John Jay, who was appointed special Minister to Great Britain in 1794, is remembered as the author of the famous 'Jay Treaty,' signed in that year between England and the United States, which brought to a settlement various points outstanding between the two countries at the termination of the American War of Independence. These last three silhouettes formed part of the well-known Wellesley Collection and were presented to the Manor House by Sir Leicester Harmsworth in 1920.

A specially precious relic of the great President is his black velvet coat. It was jointly presented in 1933 by Dr. Alfred Washington Ewing and his sister, Mrs. Maud Janet Wills, fifth in descent from John Augustine, youngest brother of George Washington. The coat, of silk cut-pile velvet, is such as would have been worn by a country gentleman about the year 1775. The tails are full and the sleeves tight, with two velvet buttons on the outside and one on the inside of the cuffs, and two upon the tails. It has a low standing collar and the cut-away front buttons near the neck (Fig. 26).

In a frame close by is a lock of hair which was cut from the head of General Washington soon after his inauguration to the Presidency of the United States. It was presented to the Manor House in 1921 by Mr. William Lanier Washington; its history is given in full upon the label.

Two valuable relics, dating possibly from Washington's campaigning days, are his leather saddle-bags and his iron-bound oak liquor chest, both presented by Colonel Walter Scott of New York in 1924.

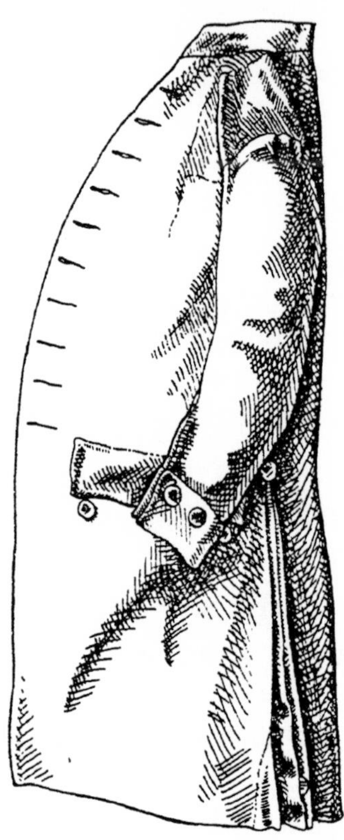

FIG. 26: *George Washington's Velvet Coat*

In a glass case is a piece of the famous elm at Cambridge, Massachusetts, under which Washington stood when he took command of the American army on 3rd July 1773. It was presented by the city of Cambridge, Mass., in 1924. A sapling grown from this same tree, the gift of the Society of the Daughters of the American Revolution, was planted at the Manor House in celebration of the Washington Bicentenary in 1932.[1]

Here also are four autograph letters of George Washington. The first, dated 10th May 1782, and written from 'Headquarters, Newburgh,' to an officer unnamed, was presented by Sir Joseph Lawrence in 1914. The second, dated 11th June 1786, also from 'Headquarters,' and addressed to 'Col. Deyshouse,' was presented by Sir William Mather in 1920. Both deal with military orders. The third letter, written from Mount Vernon on 28th June 1788, and

[1] See pp. 160 and 161.

presented by Lord Wakefield in 1924, is of a more personal nature. It runs as follows: –

'MOUNT VERNON, *28th June*, 1788.

'DEAR SIR,

'When Mrs. Washington was at the Church in Fredericksburg, she perceived the Tomb of her Father, the late John Dandridge Esqr, in a ruinous condition, and being desirous of having it done up again, will you permit me, my dear Sir, to request the favor of you to engage a workman to do this. The cost I will remit as soon as it is known, and you shall inform me of the execution.

'I would thank you for ascertaining the price beforehand, having, from disinclination to dispute accounts, felt, in too many instances, the expansion of Tradesmen's consciences when no previous agreement has been made.

'My best wishes, in which Mrs. Washington joins me, are tendered to Mrs. Carter. With much truth

'I am, dear Sir

'Y^{r} most obed & affect & H^{ble} Ser.

'G^{O} WASHINGTON.'

The fourth letter, written from Philadelphia on 9th March 1787, is addressed to Mrs. Van Berckel, and thanks her for 'good wishes for my health & happiness.' This was presented by Mr. W. A. Cadbury, Lord Mayor of Birmingham in 1921. Preserved in the same case are two cash-vouchers, dated 1796 and 1799, made and signed by George Washington – the gift of Mr. and Mrs. H. S. Perris in 1925; also an autographed copy of *The Life of George Washington*, by President Woodrow Wilson, which was presented by him to the Manor House in 1920. A relic of Mrs. Washington consists of a small fragment of her wedding-dress, presented in 1925 by Mrs. Theodore Bent. It was given to Mrs. Bent when in Florence, in 1878, by Mrs. Bianciardi, whose mother had received it from Mrs. Washington herself.

In this case are also the contents of the Eleanor Hope cupboard in the Great Hall, which have been placed here temporarily for exhibition: an ivory miniature of General George Washington at Valley Forge; a mustard pot, dated 1776, of colonial workmanship in silver and crystal; Martha Washington's ink-well of English silver and rock-crystal; a gold intaglio ring of George and Martha Washington, and a silver teaspoon made in Norfolk, Virginia, in 1795.

Other Washington mementos are described in the rooms in which they are shown.

THE PORCH ROOM

Leading out of the Inner Chamber is a little square room of the same size as the entrance porch which lies below. Now known as the Porch Room, its original title may well have been the 'Porche Chambre' – a name which often occurs in Elizabethan inventories.

The timber-framed doorway has an unusually good Tudor door which repays close examination. Constructed of oak boards, tongued together vertically on the outside and lined with horizontal boarding inside, the whole is fastened together with long wrought-iron nails driven through from the face and clinched on the inner side. The front of the door has a moulded oak handle, and the back is fitted with a spring lock of uncommon construction which is worked from without by a key, and from within by a catch which draws the spring back. The floor has beautifully polished oak boards, and the small oak window-frame is delicately moulded. Above the ceiling, in the apex of the gable, is a tiny chamber entered by a little secret trap-door from the attic beyond, which may have served as a hiding-place.

The walls are hung with pictures; among them is a charming water-colour drawing of Sulgrave Church by a Lichfield artist whose name, by a curious coincidence, was George Washington Smith. Although he showed paintings at a number of public exhibitions in London between 1814 and 1825, he is unrepresented in any of our national collections. Executed about 1810, the drawing forms a valuable record of the original appearance of the church prior to the drastic alterations it underwent soon after that date – alterations partly made good by the restoration of 1885 (Plate xv, *a*).

Chapter XI

THE GREAT KITCHEN

FROM medieval times until nearly the end of the seventeenth century, whether the dwelling was a castle keep or a manor house, the great hall and the kitchen were its most important rooms. So here at Sulgrave the Kitchen, after the Great Hall and the Great Chamber, is the most interesting room in the house. It lies at the north end of the Queen Anne wing. It is of considerable size – nearly seventeen feet long – and its ceiling is supported by a single massive oak beam with chamfered ends. Until 1930 it presented a very forlorn appearance. The great open fireplace was partly blocked up with a modern cooking-stove, and all its original fittings and furniture, except an early eighteenth-century oak dresser, had disappeared.

While the problem was being discussed of how even after long search it might ever be possible to fit up the room so as to present a true picture of a kitchen of a couple of centuries ago, by an almost providential chance news came that an ancient fireplace of exactly the same date and size, complete in every detail and containing every conceivable item of kitchen equipment, which had remained intact for over two hundred years in a manor house at Weston Corbett in the northern part of Hampshire, some eighty miles away, was suddenly for sale. Instead of being dispersed – as would otherwise inevitably have happened – it was purchased as it stood, and trans-

(*a*)

(*b*)

PLATE IX

(*a*) GENERAL VIEW OF THE GREAT KITCHEN. (See p. 139)

(*b*) THE GREAT KITCHEN. THE FIREPLACE, SHOWING CHIMNEY CRANE WITH POT-HANGERS, AND SPIT-DOGS WITH SPIT IN POSITION. (See p. 143)

ferred in its entirety to Sulgrave and, by the aid of drawings and photographs, set up exactly as before. It is worthy, from every aspect, of the closest study and attention, for so singularly perfect is it as a model, in regard both to its fittings and equipment, that nowhere else in the kingdom can a parallel to it be found (Plate IX, *a*).

Valuable as the fittings are, having all been in constant use side by side for two hundred years or more, they possess a peculiar interest and importance from the fact that they are of just the same type as would have been found in the house when the Washingtons lived there, some fifty years before this kitchen was built by John Hodges, their successor; for tradition in kitchen equipment was one of the most persistent features of domestic life in the English country-side. Made of highly durable materials – bronze, iron, brass, copper, steel, pewter, and lead – most carefully designed exactly to fill their purpose by the admirable craftsmen of the day, the same fire-dogs, chimney-back, chimney-crane, pots and pot-hooks as we see assembled together here, would have been used continuously from one century to another, until, under the new conditions that gradually prevailed as the nineteenth century advanced, they were reduced to objects of purely antiquarian and artistic interest and value.

The great square chimney opening, lined with its original blocks of brown Hornton stone, is 10 feet wide and nearly 4 feet deep. The massive oak chimney-beam is 5 feet from the ground, and along the front of it hangs a short frill of material to act as a draught 'sharpener.' Affixed to the chimney-beam and extending beyond it is a long moulded mantelshelf which serves to hold a numerous array of kitchen utensils. The fireplace hearth is 10 inches high – this raising of the hearth above floor-level being not only for convenience in cooking but to secure a better draught.

Inside the chimney corner on the left, is a semi-circular niche, the lower part filled in and forming a charcoal brazier with a wrought-iron top for the heating of flat-irons, and below it is a wrought-iron oven door. In winter-time, when the charcoal fire was not alight, this little niche must have made a very enviable seat. A plan of the fireplace with the niche for the charcoal stove is shown in Fig. 27.

On the right of the chimney opening is the ancient bread oven which extends far into the wall beneath the kitchen stairs. Its arched,

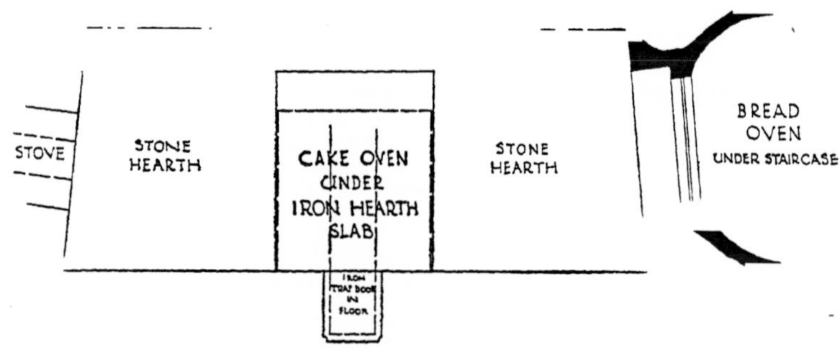

FIG. 27: *Plan of Kitchen Fireplace*

tunnel-like roof has rounded sides, and the whole is lined with fireproof brick. This 'brick' oven, measuring 3 feet deep, 2 feet 10 inches wide, and 18 inches high, has a wrought-iron door with a long-handled latch. In front of it is a ledge on which to rest the 'peel,' or bread-shovel when drawing the loaves out for inspection during baking. As the village baker is gradually superseding the brick oven throughout the country-side, it may be of interest to set on record the traditional method of its use. The fuel for heating it was often of thorns cut from the hedgerow and tied into faggots which were brought into the kitchen on baking day. These were set alight within the oven, and the door closed. When burnt through, the ashes were raked out with the iron peel, the oven mopped out with a rag mop, and the surrounding brick was hot enough to bake the loaves.[1] Round lumps of dough for loaves termed 'batch-cakes' were 'set in' with the wooden peel, a long-handled flat shovel of wood, its name evidently derived from the French *pelle*, the corresponding iron instrument being *fourchon*.[2] Two good examples of wooden peels rest in the rack above the fireplace, their blades of pinewood finely tapered, their handles of ash spliced like a cricket bat.

The 'brick' oven was also used for meat dishes of all kinds, which, with pies, tarts, and patties were placed on the thin iron plates, known then, as now, as 'baking-sheets,' and set in the oven with the wooden peel. The iron peel besides being used for shovelling the wood-ash from the oven was also at times employed for drawing out the 'baking-sheets' and the heavier earthenware dishes.

There is still one more oven, the 'hearth-oven,' which occupies the centre of the raised hearth. It is iron-lined throughout, and is enclosed by a wrought-iron door fitted with long strap-hinges and a small, circular, adjustable vent-hole in the centre. This hearth-oven is covered by a stout iron slab to form a 'hot-plate,' measuring nearly 4 feet long and 3 feet wide, which extends to the back of the hearth. It is supported by the hearth-bricks upon either side, and on it the whole of the kitchen fire is heaped, the ends of the logs resting on a pair of small fire-dogs with an iron bar across them to keep the logs in front from falling forward out of the hearth. The hearth-oven could also be heated from below by means of hot ashes placed in a narrow brick-lined channel which extends from the front of the hearth under the level of the floor to the back of the oven, and opens to the back of the hearth at the base of the chimney. Its entrance is covered by a small iron trap-door set flush into the

[1] Only the older generation at Sulgrave can now remember the mark of the bricks on the underside of the loaf, or the little bits of charcoal found adhering to the crust.

[2] That the functions of the two were practically identical is admirably shown in the French idiom, 'La pelle se moque du fourchon' – a parallel to our familiar phrase, drawn also from the domestic hearth, 'The pot calls the kettle black.'

stone floor of the kitchen, through which the red-hot ashes were put in with the iron peel. The hearth oven, being extremely 'quick,' was used chiefly for pastry; it was also of great service for warming plates or keeping food hot.

Of the many fittings that complete this beautiful and perfectly equipped fireplace the most conspicuous is the spit-jack. In early days the spits were turned by hand by a spit-boy known as a 'turn-spit.' In some districts, notably in Wales, the 'turn-spit' was a dog placed inside a wheel or drum fixed high up on the wall beside the fireplace, which it worked like a treadmill. Another method for turning the spit was by a fan placed in the mouth of the chimney which was ingeniously worked by the draught created by the great open fire. The spit-jack of the kind we see here came into use in Elizabethan times and is an unusually fine example. It is worked by means of a weight at the end of a chain passing over a cylinder joined by a series of cogwheels with another cylinder. This cylinder is connected by a cord to a grooved wooden disc fixed to the end of the spit, which it slowly turns. The weight for ordinary use is of lead beautifully cased in brass. For joints of great size a heavier weight of stone with a ring on the top was available. These weights required winding up at intervals of about ten minutes, and to reach the handle the cook was provided with a low step.

The spit-jack is accompanied by five brightly polished iron meat-spits, or 'broches,' square in section, rounded towards the ends, and tapering to a point. They are graduated in size and length, the greatest being 7 feet 7 inches long, the shortest measuring 4 feet 10 inches. The spits are laid across racks fitted to the backs of the pair of big 'rack andirons,' as the large spit-dogs were called, which stand on the floor before the hearth, their front legs resting on the floor, their short hindlegs on the hearth behind. These racks allowed of the spit being placed nearer to or further from the fire as occasion demanded (Plate IX, *b*). Large joints were pierced by the point of the spit, which was run through them. Poultry or game was roasted on pointed 'stirrups' pushed along the spit by means of a hole in their base. The spare spits rest on the wooden rack above the fireplace. On the floor-level, below the spit, is an iron dripping-pan with a sunk well in the centre.[1]

Instead of a 'ready-pole' or chimney-rod being fixed across the mouth of the wide open chimney for the suspension of cooking-pots, there is here a great iron chimney-crane with an upright bar pivoted on to the wall, so that its arm can swing over the fire. This crane is exactly the same in every respect as the crane that would have hung over Lawrence Washington's kitchen hearth, and it is interesting to know that in the kitchen fireplace at Mount Vernon there still exists an iron chimney-crane of almost the same pattern.

The stout swinging arm is no less than 6 feet long, so that a whole row of pots and kettles arranged on it can feel the heat of the fire at once, each pot being suspended from a pot-hook or from a hanger so adjusted that it can be raised or lowered at will.[2] Here all the boiling took place, and the hot water required for household and domestic purposes was evidently obtained; for, from the ratchet pot-hooks, or 'cotterells' as they were called, hang two water-boilers with spouts and taps, one of copper, one of iron; and beside them hangs a large copper pot with a semicircular swinging handle. In addition to these is a 'girdle iron' – a circular iron plate with a

[1] 'Three yron Drupynge panns' are included among the 'particularyties of the furniture . . . utensyles of household,' etc., belonging to Sir John Petre, afterwards Lord Petre, at Ingatestone Hall, Essex, in 1600. This, perhaps the most complete inventory (unpublished) of an Elizabethan house that has come down to us, includes a number of articles which are identical with those in the Sulgrave kitchen, thus linking the present equipment with that which would have been in use in the Washingtons' day.

[2] Pot-hooks and hangers were an essential part of the domestic hearth, and the phrase, *pendre la crémaillère* ('hang up the pot-hook') is still used in France as the equivalent to our 'house-warming.'

hoop-handle for cooking girdle scones, or oatcakes – a utensil still in common use in Scotland to-day.

On the hearth are other vessels which could be hoisted on to the crane or placed on the tripod stand, a ring with three legs – the simplest form of trivet – and stood over the hot ashes. One of these is a great brass cauldron with ring-handles used for heating the milk used in cheese-making.[1] It came originally from Hever Castle in Kent, and was given to Sulgrave subsequently, being the only article in the fireplace not belonging to the Weston Corbett equipment.

Another cooking-vessel is the skillet, with three legs and long, straight handle, of bronze cast in one piece. This was designed to stand in the burning embers.[2] In the corner of the hearth under the brick oven stands the salt-box, a little oblong chest, 2 feet long, which was placed there to keep the salt dry, and served as a seat in the chimney corner. Finally, at the back of the hearth is a large cast-iron fire-back decorated with Renaissance designs.

Upon the walls on either side of the open fireplace a number of articles of kitchen equipment are hung up. On the right are two pairs of ember tongs, beautiful examples of blacksmith's work, which were used to pick a burning brand from the hearth to light a smoker's pipe, or perhaps even a candle. Beside them is a goffering-iron for 'getting up' ruffles, frills, and flounces, with the bar of iron used to heat its barrel; the crimp being made by holding the linen, damp and starched, in both hands and pressing it over the hot barrel (Plate x, *a*). On the floor beside the hearth stands a large round block of wood, a section of a tree-trunk, with holes bored in its upper surface. In these rest the fire-irons, consisting of steel tongs,

[1] A similar vessel is thus described in the Ingatestone Inventory: 'A great brass caldiron with an yron bande havinge two yron ryngs to carye it.'

[2] 'Two thick brasse Skylletts with large handles, thone bigger then thother' (Ingatestone Inventory).

(a)

(b)

PLATE X

THE GREAT KITCHEN

(a) DETAIL OF THE FIREPLACE, SHOWING OPEN DOOR OF BREAD OVEN. FROM THE CHIMNEY BEAM HANG EMBER TONGS, AND THE HEATING ROD OF THE GOFFERING-IRON SEEN ON SHELF ABOVE. (See p. 144)

(b) CORNER OF OAK TABLE, WITH SPINDLE-BACK ARM-CHAIR, BOOT JACK, AND WOODEN PATTENS. (See p. 147)

shovel, and a large two-pronged fork for moving the burning logs.[1] On the wall on the left-hand side hang a pair of lard-beaters – massive poker-like instruments of polished steel, with hexagonal shafts and long square ends, which were used for pounding lumps of lard. Beside them is the big brass skimmer[2] used to skim the lard after it was boiled down in the copper cauldron. Beyond this hangs a brass basting-ladle for use with the dripping-pan. Near by is a relic of the country-side now obsolete – a wooden flail, universally employed for thrashing corn until supplanted by machinery. Even afterwards, within the memory of older inhabitants of Sulgrave, it was used by labourers to thrash their gleanings and home-grown corn. In this case the handle is of ash, and the blade of crab-apple, the two bound together by a thong of 'whit' leather.

The remainder of this most interesting collection of domestic utensils is arranged upon the long mantelshelf and on the wooden rack above it. Among the various articles brought together from generation to generation which now find a home here is a bronze mortar with an iron pestle, a coffee-mill of turned lignum-vitæ, several iron snuffers and trays, an iron shoe-horn, a hook for jack-boots, a pair of sugar-loaf cutters, two powder-flasks – one of leather, the other of copper – a Queen Anne brass candlestick, two churchwarden pipes, and a fork for roasting small birds, fitted with iron feet to stand on the hearth. The most curious object is a horn sheep-drench, with an iron hook, made of a cow's hoof, for drenching sheep with medicine. Resting on the shelf is a brass warming-pan, the lid engraved with floral designs; and from a nail in the wall beside it hangs a miniature steel-yard, of iron beautifully wrought, which must have been in constant demand for the weighing of the many ingredients used in cooking.

[1] 'A great yron Fire Forke' (Ingatestone Inventory).
[2] 'Two latten Skymmers' (Ingatestone Inventory).

Across the rack, with its large projecting knobs of turned wood, which served originally as a spit rack, where lie the four spare spits, are the two wooden peels[1] for the oven, and a wooden hop-stirrer with a long handle, its open blade resembling a large gridiron, used for stirring or mixing the hops in the beer vat. On the top of the rack are two long duck-guns and below, resting against it, a short blunderbuss and a sword with a long pointed blade, dating from the time of Charles I, of just such a type as would have been used at the battle of Edgehill, not many miles away.

Near the ceiling, and extending in a wide semicircle round the fireplace is an iron rod upon which run curtains reaching to the floor, which, when drawn, enclose the whole hearth and a considerable space beyond it sufficient to contain several seats. This protection from draughts in winter-time must have been very necessary in a kitchen such as the present one, which has two windows, an open staircase, and two doors, one of which – that giving into the Stone Courtyard – is kept constantly ajar to prevent the chimney from smoking.

High up on the left-hand wall not far from the fireplace is a little Queen Anne hanging cupboard of pine – a wood which at that period was seldom used. From the ceiling, suspended from long iron hooks, is a large oak bacon-rack on which formerly the flitches of bacon were stored. On it now rests a remarkably fine pumpkin from the kitchen garden – a reminder to American visitors of the huge orange-coloured pumpkins that in the Eastern States grow between the long rows of Indian corn, and of their celebrated 'pun'kin pie,' made like an English open tart. Suspended from the sides of the bacon-rack are bunches of dried herbs for flavouring or for physic – gathered from the herb garden of the Manor House: –

[1] The 'Pasterye' at Ingatestone in 1600 had 'An yron peele' and 'Three wooden handpeeles'; and there were 'Two wooden peeles' and 'A great yron peele' also in 'The Bakehowse.'

Balm	Sage	Winter Savory
Marjoram	Peppermint	Pennyroyal
Mint	Tarragon	Hyssop
Thyme	Fennel	

Also rosemary and rue, perhaps of all the most familiar, from Shakespeare's lines: –

> 'For you there's rosemary and rue, these keep
> Seeming and savour all the winter long.
> Grace and remembrance to you both.'
>
> *Winter's Tale*, IV, 3.

The furniture of the kitchen, with the exception of the dresser, came from Weston Corbett together with the fireplace and the whole of its equipment, and is all of the same date. In the centre of the room stands a good oak table, 8 feet long and 3 feet 9 inches in width. It has well-turned baluster legs of traditional Tudor type, which survived, as we see here, until the end of the seventeenth century. Between it and the fireplace and occupying the same position which they have always held on either side of the hearth, are two arm-chairs. One of them, with a rounded back formed of turned spindles, has a capacious seat of elm wood no less than 25 inches across, and stands on four hexagonal oak legs, widely splayed (Plate x, *b*). The other, of ash, has a ladder-back, rush seat and turned rails. With the table and the arm-chairs is a large oak settle, 9 feet 3 inches long and 5 feet high, designed to stand against the wall, as can be judged by the rough surface on one side of the back – which is composed of five tall panels.

In a neighbouring corner is a churn with a tapered barrel of oak staves bound with bands of ash – a fine piece of cooper's work. Near by are the remaining two articles from Weston Corbett – a mahogany boot-jack, and, in front of the hearth and to one side, a pair of pattens – clogs with wooden soles, each with a leather toepiece and a thong to tie over the instep, and the sole raised from the ground upon an oval iron ring or frame (Fig. 28). Clogs were commonly used by countrywomen out of doors, not only on their own premises, but further afield, as is shown by the old eighteenth-century notice-board still remaining in the church porch at Walpole St. Peter, Lincolnshire, requesting that 'all persons will take off their pattens at the church door.' So Gay, in *Trivia*, writes: 'Good Housewives . . . safe through the Wet on clinking Pattens tread.'

Fig. 28: *Wooden Patten*

To commemorate the completion of this interesting piece of preservation work, a contemporary model of a kitchen dresser, measuring only 12 inches in height, with its original painted shelves filled with a complete set of more than sixty miniature pieces of original pewter-ware of the early eighteenth century, was presented to the Manor House by Mrs. E. M. Townsend. It stands in a corner of the reinstated kitchen on a beautiful little seventeenth-century joint ('joyned') stool with hexagonal chamfered legs. This stool was found in a cottage in Sulgrave village and may well have belonged to the Manor House in Jacobean times, leaving it when oak furniture was replaced by the more up-to-date walnut and mahogany in the eighteenth century.

Against the wall opposite the doorway leading into the Stone Courtyard stands the elmwood dresser originally made for the kitchen. The top, formed of a single slab of richly grained wood of deep golden colour, rests on two broad, shaped uprights, one at either end, and the back is fitted with three shelves. On it is arranged a large collection of copper vessels of various kinds brought together from houses in the immediate neighbourhood of Sulgrave; they are of interest and peculiarly appropriate here in that they represent local characteristics. These vessels, like the whole of the contents of the fireplace, kept always beautifully bright and polished, bring a pleasant effect of warmth, colour, and brilliance to the room.

The principal part of this collection of copper-ware came from a sale at Apethorpe Hall about 1910. It consists of unusually complete sets of beer-measures and milk-cans. The holding capacity of the beer-jugs ranges from two gallons downwards. With them is a giant funnel for filling barrels. The great two-gallon measure stands on the long kitchen table and formerly would have contained the beer drawn early each morning and served to the members of the household, indoors and out, who gathered in the kitchen at eleven o'clock for a small meal of bread and cheese and beer. The four copper milk-cans, also of graduated sizes, have two handles, one of copper, fixed, for pouring, the other a swinging iron handle for carrying.

The remainder of the vessels, which were also acquired locally, includes amongst other utensils of daily use in the ancient kitchen, an ale-warmer. It is of conical shape with a fairly long handle, and to heat or 'mull' the ale its point was pressed deep into the hot wood-ash, in which it remained upright.

From a hook at the back of the dresser hangs a harvester's wooden 'bottel,' found in Sulgrave – a little one-gallon barrel of oak hooped with iron – which each labourer in the fields during hay-time and harvest had filled three times a day with home-brewed ale. Sulgrave villagers can still remember the hames of the horse-collars hung with these little barrels; also the farm-hand loaded with them when empty, on his way back to the farm where they would be refilled, the bearer being rewarded with an extra 'tot.'

Finally, among other small domestic articles that find a place upon the dresser, is an ancient wooden mouse-trap, made and found in Sulgrave village – a flat, oblong box, measuring 1 foot by 6 inches, fitted with a balanced trap at either end and a hinged door on one side for extracting captured mice.

Chapter XII

THE OAK PARLOUR AND THE WHITE AND CHINTZ BEDROOMS

THE Queen Anne wing to the north of the main Tudor building was built, as has been said, about the year 1700. Though a hundred and fifty years later in date, it is in complete harmony with the earlier work which it adjoins, so much so that certain of its structural features – for instance, the great chamfered oak beams of the kitchen and cellar ceilings – might well date from Lawrence Washington's day. Local tradition in building and in the domestic arts, coupled with fine craftsmanship, held good in the English country-side until the invention of the steam-engine, when the system of mass production which followed on its trail gradually overwhelmed and obliterated both tradition and craftsmanship.

At the foot of the Charles II staircase is the doorway of the Queen Anne oak Parlour, the first ground-floor room of the north wing. This most attractive and sunny little room, measuring 15 feet by 14, is just 8 feet in height, and is panelled in oak from floor to ceiling (Plate XI, *a*). The raised wall-panels, with their projecting mouldings, are divided by the moulded chair-rail which surrounds the room, the tall panels above the rail being a repetition of the smaller ones below, and the whole is surmounted by an elaborate wooden cornice. The mantelpiece is similarly treated, its shelf repeating the moulding of the cornice. Both the doors have their original brass locks and handles, and one of them also has a wrought-iron latch of beautiful design.

Until the restoration, in 1930, when the wood-work was carefully stripped and brought back to its original condition, many layers of paint and wallpaper concealed the ancient panelling of finely figured oak; modern floor-boards, laid over slabs of Hornton stone, hid the fine original elm flooring; and the mantelpiece had undergone considerable alteration.

It has now been charmingly equipped in every detail. In the window, which overlooks the Stone Courtyard, are curtains of green watered moreen completed with a braid and ball fringe in the traditional Queen Anne style. Between them, hanging rather high, is a handsome dome-shaped bird-cage of walnut wood, hexagonal in design, with turned uprights and ivory pinnacles, in which the lady of the manor in Queen Anne's time would have kept her white Java sparrows. The under-side of the base of the cage, which is veneered with figured walnut, has a turned pattern in the centre, and is fitted with six ivory and ebony knobs. Before the window is a circular mahogany tripod tea-table on which are laid out a blue-and-white china tea-set and a small Queen Anne silver teapot.

On the mantelpiece is a beautiful bracket-clock of finely figured kingwood, ornamented with chased ormolu mounts. It has a silvered dial, and the movement, which is fitted with a verge escapement and full repeating action, is the work of Thomas Vernon, who was admitted to the Clockmakers' Company of London in 1708. In the corner beside the fireplace is a grandfather-clock in green-and-gold English lacquer, by Thomas Utting of Yarmouth. On the

(a)

(b)

PLATE XI

(a) THE OAK PARLOUR, SHOWING QUEEN ANNE NEEDLEWORK SETTEE, TEA-TABLE WITH BIRD-CAGE ABOVE, AND DOORWAY LEADING INTO GREAT KITCHEN. (See p. 151)

(b) THE OAK PARLOUR, SHOWING WALNUT SPINET BY THOMAS HITCHCOCK, AND QUEEN ANNE GILT GESSO MIRROR. (See p. 153)

other side stands an early dummy-board figure, about life size, of a little boy in the picturesque costume of about 1690, with lace collar and ruffles, holding a black three-cornered hat in his hand. Original examples of these curious, life-like figures cut out of thin board and painted are of great rarity.

Against the wall opposite the window is a small Queen Anne settee with cabriole walnut legs carved with fluting and terminating with club feet. The cushioned seat, the back, and the arms inside and out, are covered with fine, contemporary petit-point needlework of floral design representing bouquets of gaily coloured flowers intertwined with blue ribbons upon a brown background. Accompanying it is a pair of walnut chairs dating from about 1705, the back of each chair having a vase-shaped splat decorated with a panel of arabesque marquetry.

The wall opposite the fireplace is occupied by a spinet, dating from about 1710, the work of Thomas Hitchcock, one of the most famous of English musical-instrument makers. Its case, of figured walnut of very fine workmanship inlaid with lines of sycamore, rests on the original walnut stand with turned and carved legs. The keyboard has thirty-six ivory full notes and twenty-five sharps and flats of ebony inlaid with ivory. The front has a folding book-rest – a fitting not commonly found in instruments of the time – and upon this is a music-book, published in London in 1747, entitled, *Lessons for the Harpsichord*, 'composed by James Nares, Organist of York Minster.' This volume – originally in the celebrated Lulworth Castle Collection – which is engraved from copperplates throughout, has a handsome title-page of rococo design, and is a fine copy of a very rare work. A long list of distinguished subscribers bound into the volume includes the name of Handel. The author was subsequently organist at the Chapel Royal and was buried in St. Margaret's Church, Westminster (Plate XI, *b*).

Above the spinet hangs a Queen Anne mirror of gilt gesso-work, fitted with brass candle-branches so arranged that the light is reflected in the glass. It came from the Manor House at Baldock in Hertfordshire.

The restoration of the Oak Parlour was undertaken at the expense of Mrs. A. H. Chatfield, of East Walnut Hills, Cincinnati, a member of the Sulgrave Manor Board, and of the House Committee, in memory of her son, Frederick Huntington Chatfield, who accompanied her to Sulgrave on his last visit to England.

THE WHITE AND CHINTZ BEDROOMS

On the first floor of the Queen Anne wing are two most attractive little rooms, known as the White and the Chintz Bedrooms. They are reached from the kitchen by an old stairway with its original elm treads. At the restoration of this wing a small window which had been closed at the time of the window-tax was opened on the landing, its original oak frame and deep window-ledge of elm being found intact.

The floor of the passage leading to the bedrooms is laid with particularly fine oak boards, and the doors of the cupboard set in the wall consist of beautifully moulded Elizabethan oak panels.

The plaster walls of these bedrooms are tinted a warm cream colour, the flooring consists of ancient oak slabs no less than fifteen inches wide, and both rooms have mantelpieces of grey limestone with the customary wide hearthstone as a safeguard against fire. The mantelpiece in the White Bedroom is particularly elaborate, with a bold bolection, or projecting, moulding, and an imposing mantelshelf corresponding in design to the cornice of the Oak Parlour. The door is composed of two oak panels of unusual size, the upper panel being warped in a curious fashion – producing a strange,

(a)

(b)

PLATE XII

(a) THE WHITE BEDROOM, SHOWING CANOPIED BEDSTEAD WITH COLOURED EMBROIDERY, AND DRESSING-TABLE COVERED WITH GREEN MOREEN. (See p. 155)

(b) THE CHINTZ BEDROOM, SHOWING QUEEN ANNE EMBROIDERED BEDSTEAD, AND A HEPPLEWHITE CHAIR ONCE OWNED BY GEORGE WASHINGTON. (See p. 156)

undulating effect. An instance of similar warping in oak is to be found on the staircase of the old library at St. Edmund Hall, Oxford. The rooms are equipped with small typical Queen Anne pieces of furniture, such as the owners of the Manor House at that date would have had in daily use, and the upholstery has been carefully chosen to accord with them.

THE WHITE BEDROOM

In the White Bedroom the curtains are of white wool damask bordered with green floss-silk fringe. The canopied four-post bedstead is covered in ancient material embroidered with a conventional design in shades of soft green, buff, apricot, and blue upon an ivory ground. The coverlet, of antique workmanship, is of green silk very minutely quilted (Plate XI, *a*).

The framework of the dressing-table is covered with leaf-green moreen glued to the surface, and a long green tassel serves as a handle to the drawer. Upon it stands a dressing-glass of black-and-gold lacquer. Close by is a spinning-wheel of mahogany inlaid with satinwood, the driving-wheel and main shaft being of brass beautifully worked, and the bobbin and handle of turned ivory. We know that this was made about 1790 for a certain Mrs. Sherbrooke, of Oxton Hall, Southwell, Nottinghamshire, who had the legs of it hinged so that she could take it with her in her coach. It bears a brass label engraved with the name of the maker: 'S. Thorp, Abberley, inv$^{t.}$' It is worthy of remark that a workman in so small a place as Abberley in Worcestershire – a village of only 750 inhabitants – should have executed so beautiful a piece of craftsmanship. It is still in perfect working order. In the corner of the room is an early winged arm-chair covered with the same white-and-green materials as the curtains.

Before the hearth stands a Queen Anne walnut fire-screen, with a brightly coloured picture in petit-point of a shepherd and shepherdess with sheep and dogs, reposing beneath a tree, and in the distance a cottage with smoke rising from the chimney, and a flight of pigeons overhead. Above the mantelpiece is a small wall-mirror with curious panels of ancient stump-work set into its frame. Near the door hang two needlework samplers, one dated 1817, the other 1819, and both worked by Elinor Louisa Buckley, described as 'a second cousin of George Washington,' when she was respectively thirteen and fifteen years of age. These were sent in 1923 from New Zealand as a present from Mrs. Elizabeth Hambly – the result of a notice in the *Spectator* asking for Washington relics for Sulgrave Manor.

THE CHINTZ BEDROOM

The Chintz Bedroom lies immediately above the Oak Parlour, and, like the White Bedroom, overlooks the Stone Courtyard, with a view of Madam's Close beyond. The windows are curtained with original early chintz, patterned with bright puce and blue flowers upon an ivory ground. The four-post bedstead is upholstered in Queen Anne linen of similar tone, delicately embroidered in crimson and blue; and the finely quilted coverlet is decorated with bright trails of flowers (Plate XII, *b*). The circular dressing-table in the corner of the room has a flounce made from an old ivory silk farthingale, with embroidery which again repeats the colours of the window curtains and bed hangings. Upon it stands a small Queen Anne mirror of inlaid walnut finely figured, and a contemporary embroidered pincushion; while from early summer till late autumn in the vase beside it are freshly gathered roses from the garden – chosen to harmonise with the ancient floral chintz.

Next to the dressing-table is a triangular mahogany basin-stand. On the small Queen Anne writing-table at the other side of the fireplace stands a bust of George Washington in coloured Staffordshire ware; and over the mantelpiece is a Chinese eighteenth-century bird-and-flower picture on fine rice paper. Upon the walnut chest-of-drawers lies a Bible with embroidered binding; and in the corner is a 'tub'-chair covered in a deep pink 'tabinet' piped with yellow.

In the window stands one of the chief treasures of the Manor House, a chair of mahogany, carved and painted, with a shield-shaped back of Hepplewhite design,[1] made about 1790, which was formerly in the possession of George Washington at Mount Vernon. It was presented to Sulgrave Manor by Mr. Robert Washington Dana in 1923.

The second floor, above these bedrooms, is occupied by two attic rooms lighted by dormer windows.

The bedroom passage terminates at the top of the main staircase, by which the visitor returns to the smaller entrance-hall. From the ceiling of the hall hangs an eighteenth-century horn lantern of sheet iron, its conical roof fitted with three rounded gables pierced with holes for ventilation. In the passage-way running from the front entrance-door in the Stone Courtyard to the door leading into the garden, at the head of the Cellar steps underneath the staircase, is an oak door of interesting construction. It is built up of feather-edged boards rabbeted into one another and strengthened behind with horizontal battens fastened with nails clinched over them. Each board slightly overlaps the next, the raised edge of each board being moulded with a 'scratch' beading.[2] It is hung in the doorway by two long iron strap hinges and has its original wrought-iron latch.

THE CELLAR

The Cellar, which lies under the Oak Parlour, is paved with stone, and, before the restoration of the house in 1920, suffered from the

[1] Hepplewhite's *Cabinet Maker and Upholsterer's Guide* was published in London in 1788.

[2] This method of construction is known as clinker-boarding to shipwrights, who use it in boat-building.

general neglected condition of the building, often containing several feet of water. The original purpose of this cellar-room is uncertain, for it presents several features not usually associated with a mere cellar. Thus it has a four-light window with stone mullions, while the ceiling is supported by three large beams with chamfered ends – the centre beam measuring 14 inches in width by 9 in depth – and by smaller cross-rafters. The window is the only stone-mullioned one in the house, the mullions having been apparently a part of the earlier Tudor work used again in their present position.

On the wall of the passage between the courtyard entrance and the garden door hangs a fine hand-coloured copy of Speed's map of the County of Northamptonshire, published in 1610, and engraved with the arms of James I – though unaccompanied by the Lion and by the Scottish unicorn, then introduced, as supporter of the royal coat in place of the Tudor dragon. In the lower left-hand corner, within the Wardon Hundred, can be seen the name SOULGRAVE. In this position it aptly fulfils the purpose described by the famous Elizabethan scholar, Dr. John Dee, who, in 1570, wrote: –

> 'Some to beautify their Halls, Parlers, Studies or Libraries . . . use maps.'

Chapter XIII

THE GARDEN AND ORCHARD

WHEN the Manor House was bought in 1914 all trace of the original flower-garden and pleasaunce of Elizabethan days had disappeared. For no less than a hundred and fifty years the house had been merely a farm homestead, barns and sheds had been built on one side, while elsewhere, save for a small kitchen garden, rough paddocks had encroached to the very walls of the ancient building, and a pig-sty rested against one side of the Elizabethan porch.

Piece by piece, as funds allowed, beginning in 1920 and running concurrently with the work indoors, the re-making of the garden and orchard was undertaken. Like the restoration of the house, the laying out of the whole of the grounds was entrusted to Sir Reginald Blomfield, a recognised authority on the planning of the English formal garden,[1] and gradually a rose garden, herb and flower borders, a grass terrace, lawn and bowling green, an orchard, and thick hedges of close-clipped yew came into being – the right and proper setting for a Tudor dwelling.

On approaching the Manor House from the road the visitor does not at first, however, see the lawns and flower borders which lie to the south and the south-east.

[1] *The Formal Garden in England,* by Reginald Blomfield and F. Inigo Thomas, 1892.

The aspect of the house, facing almost due north and south, is a tribute to the prescience of its builder, Lawrence Washington, for he anticipated the principles of garden-planning laid down by Parkinson, who, some eighty years later, in his *Paradisus*,[1] remarks: –

> '. . . The house should be on the North side of the garden . . . to safeguard it from many injurious cold nights and dayes, which else might spoyle the pride thereof in the bud. . . . Having the fairest buildings of the house facing the garden . . . the roomes abutting thereon, shall have reciprocally the beautiful prospect into it, and have both sight and sent of whatsoever is excellent, and worthy to give content out from it, which is one of the greatest pleasures a garden can yeeld his Master.'

Beside the yew-hedged pathway leading to the house from the entrance drive, which is bordered with white thorn, is a stretch of lawn. Behind this is a long stone wall that connects the ancient brew-house with a small barn at the further end, enclosing what was once the farmyard. Against the wall are planted scarlet-berried cotoneaster and pyracantha, and in summer polygonum covers the coping-stones with its graceful foliage which falls again to the ground, developing in autumn snow-white flower-spikes which rise in tall, fleecy sprays.

The approach has an historical point of interest; for in the centre of the lawn, with the creeper-clad wall for background, stands the 'Washington Elm,' now some eight feet high, an offshoot of the elm tree at Cambridge, Massachusetts, under which Washington stood when he took command of the American army.[2] It bears the following label: –

[1] John Parkinson, *Paradisi in sole Paradisus Terrestris* (1629). It is interesting to note that 'Paradeisos' (Paradise) – a word of Persian origin – is the Greek for a pleasure-ground or garden.

[2] It was sent over by Mrs. James H. Dorsey of Baltimore, Vice-chairman of the National Society of the Daughters of the American Revolution. A similar offshoot of the Washington elm was planted by Mrs. Dorsey in the grounds of the Society's headquarters in Washington in 1926.

Washington
First took command of the American Army under the
grandparent of this elm at Cambridge, Mass:
July 3, 1775.
This tree presented and planted as part of the two
hundredth anniversary of the birth of
George Washington.
1732-1932.

On the further side of the yew hedge, in the paddock known from time immemorial as Little Green, close to the entrance of the Stone Courtyard, stand two giant elms, eighty to ninety feet in height, the sole survivors of an ancient group. Washington Irving, in his *Life of George Washington*, when speaking of his visit to Sulgrave nearly a hundred years ago, refers to 'a rookery in a venerable grove hard by'; and doubtless these trees are a remnant of that grove. The descendants of the rooks, referred to by the same writer as 'those staunch adherents to old family abodes . . . hovering and cawing about their hereditary nests,' are still in evidence to-day (Fig. 29).

The yew hedge bordering the footpath continues in a semicircle in front of the two great elms enclosing an open space before the house (see Plate 1, *a*).

THE STONE COURTYARD

The Courtyard, entered by a little gate in the centre of its low stone wall, is paved throughout with large slabs of local Helmdon stone, save for an oval flower-bed on the left, just beneath the parlour window, filled with pansies – the 'heart's ease' of medieval times – and violas which bloom from early spring to winter.

In its border are set two box-trees clipped to the size and shape of the ball ornaments that surmount the stone piers of the entrance-gates.[1] Beside them is a peacock, also in clipped box.[2] Against the wall of the Queen Anne wing upon the left is an ivy with a heart-shaped leaf, its immense trunk over three feet in girth, and opposite, on the end wall of the brew-house which abuts on to the courtyard is a gnarled and ancient Jargonelle pear which yearly produces a fine crop of fruit (Plate I, *b*).

THE ROSE GARDEN

The Rose Garden, to the south-east of the house, is of geometrical design and follows a Tudor model. Its beds are edged with close-clipped box, and separated by paths of smooth grass of vivid green. Considerable use has been made here, as elsewhere in the Sulgrave garden, of box, as Parkinson recommends: –

> '. . . of the many sorts of herbes and other things, wherewith the beds . . . are bordered to set out the forme of them, . . . Boxe I commend and hold to bee the best and surest herbe to abide faire and greene in all the bitter stormes of the sharpest Winter, and all the great heates and draughts of Summer.'

In the centre of the garden, raised on three circular stone steps, is a sundial,[3] its top set with an ancient square dial-plate of brass engraved with a Tudor rose from which the hour-lines radiate. Beneath this are cut the initials G. N., and a standing deer-hound – the owner's device or crest – with the date 1579.

[1] The stone balls, so frequently used to adorn houses and gate-posts, represent the traditional skull put up in olden times to ward off lightning.

[2] Presented to Sulgrave Manor by the Garden Club of America in commemoration of the visit paid by its Members to the Manor House on 12th June 1929.

[3] The sundial was presented by Mrs. Gilmer S. Adams in memory of her husband, who visited Sulgrave in 1922. It was formally unveiled by Mrs. Joseph R. Lamar on the occasion of her visit to Sulgrave in 1925.

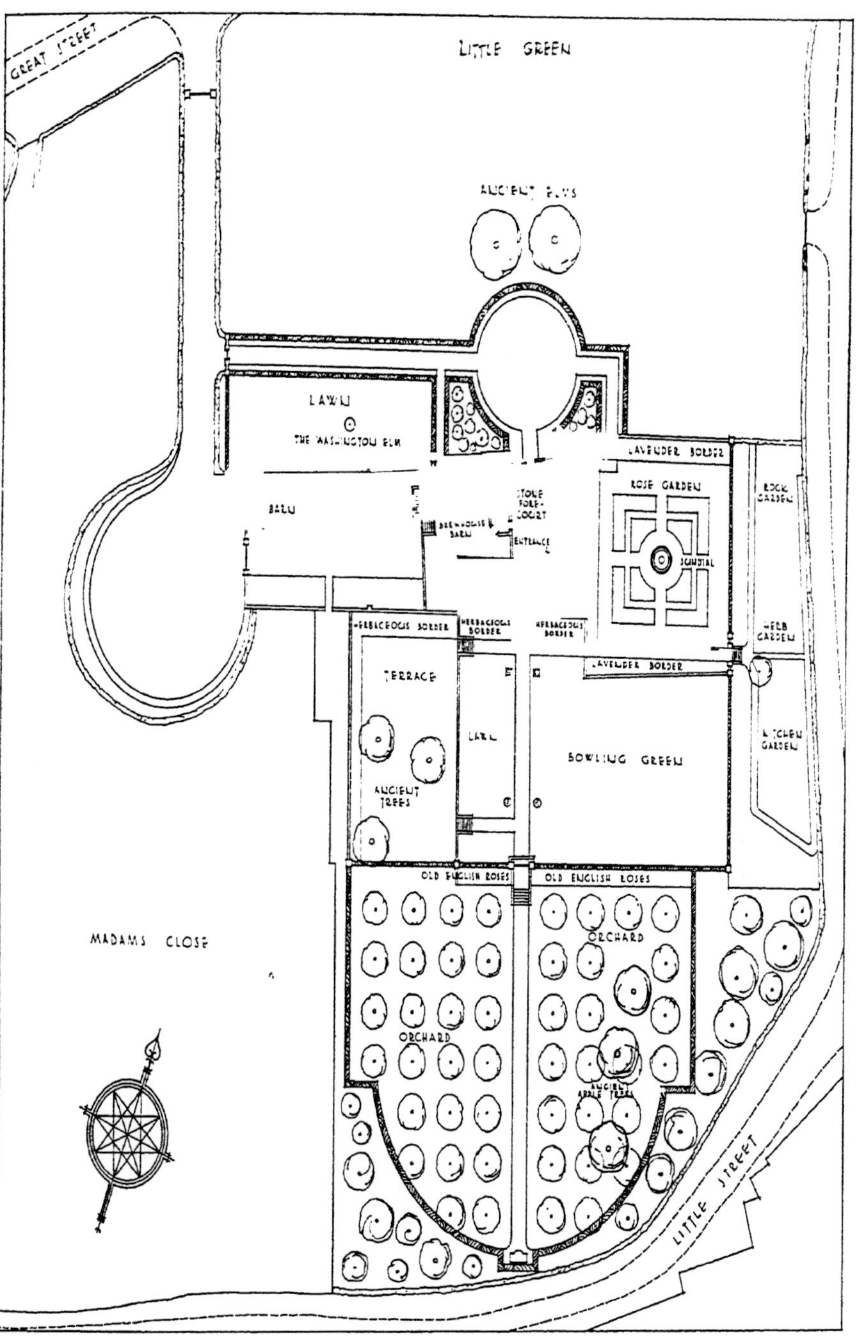

FIG. 29: *Plan of Garden and Orchard*

From crevices between the paving-stones around its base spring tufts of verbena-scented thyme, that –

'Beneath your feet
. . . for all your bruising smells more sweet';

a reminder of a pleasant custom in early times when garden pathways were often planted with sweet-scented camomile in place of grass, and the seats cut in the sides of the green garden banks likewise carpeted with aromatic herbs.

Of the rose, a thirteenth-century writer, Bartholomew the Englishman, observes: –

> 'Among all flowers of the world the flower of the rose is chief and beareth the prize. And by cause of virtues and sweet smell and savour. For by fairness they feed the sight; and pleaseth the smell, by odour, the touch by soft handling.'[1]

In the garden at Sulgrave most of the older roses thrive – the white rose of England, the red rose of England, the damask rose (the 'Rose of Damascus,' which is said to have come to this country through the Crusaders); the *Rosa gallica* with its varieties, the red and white roses of York and Lancaster, and the striped or particoloured rose – the *Rosa mundi*, called perhaps after Fair Rosamond – also the musk rose, and the sweet briar or eglantine.

The formal rose garden is, however, planted with a number of the newer roses, specially chosen for their beauty and for the sweetness of their perfume, to provide a succession of bloom during their long flowering season (Plate XIII, *a*).

Beside the low stone walls to the north and south of the Rose

[1] The original Latin of this quotation from *De Proprietatibus Rerum*, by Bartholomæus Anglicus, together with a translation of it, printed in the fifteenth century, is given in *The Scented Garden*, by Miss Eleanour Sinclair Rohde.

PLATE XIII

(*a*) THE ROSE GARDEN, SHOWING OUTLINE OF ANCIENT FIRE-PLACE ON END WALL OF THE TUDOR BUILDING. (See pp. 87 and 164)

(*b*) FLOWER BORDER BESIDE THE TUDOR PORCH, AND ENTRANCE TO THE ROSE GARDEN. (See p. 166)

Garden run wide borders edged with box and filled with lavender, its silvery foliage serving as a foil to the gay colouring of the roses. Since its planting in 1920 this sweet smelling herb has flourished exceedingly, yielding each year a richer harvest.[1]

THE HERB AND VEGETABLE GARDEN

On the east side, facing the Queen Anne wing, a tall yew hedge separates the Rose Garden from the Kitchen Garden which lies below it, and is reached by a short flight of stone steps. At the head of the steps is a stone balustrading, and trailing across it are sprays of the beautiful Nellie Custis rose, with its myriads of blossoms and clusters of aromatic buds.[2]

From the foot of the stone steps, across the kitchen garden runs a grass path bordered on one side by a row of hollyhocks 'both single and double, of many and sundry colours,' which 'yeeld out their flowers like Roses on their tall branches, like Trees, to sute you with flowers, when almost you have no other to grace out your Garden.'[3]

Facing the hollyhocks are wide herb beds, where many of the herbs known to the Tudor gardener – balm, chives, borage, fennel, horehound, hyssop, lavender, pennyroyal, peppermint, rue, marjoram, sage, savory, sorrel, tansy, tarragon, common thyme and lemon thyme – are found. The borders of the Kitchen Garden are outlined with stone tiles, which 'keepe up the edge of the beds in a pretty comely manner.' The bank under the yew hedge, planted with primroses, arabis, rock-cistus and narcissus, presents a charming

[1] In 1921 Her Majesty Queen Mary and the Princess Royal – then Princess Mary – accepted a gift from the first year's crop; and since, countless bags of lavender have been sold to visitors. In 1928 no less than eight hundred were carried away as souvenirs.

[2] It was grown from a cutting taken from the rose-tree planted by General George Washington for his stepdaughter, Nellie Custis, at Mount Vernon, and it was brought over in 1923 as a gift to Sulgrave by a young girl who planted it here with her own hands.

[3] Parkinson's *Paradisus*.

appearance in early spring; while a little later in the year, along the top of the bank, grow foxgloves and groups of columbines: 'flowers of that respect,' says Parkinson, 'as that no Garden would willingly bee without them, that could tell how to have them.'

THE LAWNS AND FLOWER BORDERS

On returning to the Rose Garden and passing through a gateway in the low wall at the opposite corner, the visitor arrives at the south or principal front of the Manor House. Previous to the restoration this wall was continued beyond the Elizabethan porch to act as a barrier to the cattle grazing in the meadow that lay before it. There are now deep borders on either side of the porch filled with many of the old-fashioned flowers – sweet William and sweet John, crane's bill, marigolds and lupins, sweet rocket, gilliflower, 'sops in wine,' and lilies white and red – that Gerard, Parkinson, and other great Elizabethan and Jacobean gardeners knew and loved three and four centuries ago. Here as elsewhere in the garden the general scheme followed is to maintain a succession of flowers in bloom through the greater part of the year; it has been said that 'no matter what month of the year you walk in Sulgrave garden it is looking its best!' – and indeed in every corner, from early spring until late autumn, when the frost finally cuts the blossoms from the herbaceous plants, flowers are to be found[1] (Plate XIII, *b*).

The garden not only aspires to beauty, but provides adornment for the interior of the house. Every room is decked with freshly gathered sprays and blossoms, and visitors in passing through the Manor House may echo the words of Lemnius, who, writing of the English in Elizabethan times, observed: –

[1] The Sulgrave garden owes much of its brightness and beauty to the generosity of donors who have contributed plants and seeds from their own gardens. Not least are those presented by the Regent and Vice-Regents of the Mount Vernon Ladies' Association of the Union – the Regent of the Association being herself a trustee, *ex officio*, of the Manor House.

'. . . their nosegays finely intermingled with sundry sorts of fragraunte flowers, in their bed-chambers and privy rooms, with comfortable smell cheered me up, and entirely delighted all my senses.'[1]

Amongst the plants growing in the borders of the south front there is in one angle of the porch, near the window of the Great Hall, a bush of rosemary now no less than 12 feet high. It is of great beauty in early spring when covered with a cloud of grey-blue flowers, and perfumes the whole house with its aromatic fragrance wafted through the open windows of the Great Hall and the Great Chamber. Lawrence Washington no doubt had rosemary in his garden, possibly growing in this very spot, for it is known to have been a very favourite herb in Tudor times. Sir Thomas More says: –

'As for rosemarie I lette it runne all over my garden walls, not onlie because my bees love it, but because it is the herb sacred to remembrance and to friendship.'

Hentzner, the German traveller, who visited England in the reign of Queen Elizabeth, reports that the custom of planting rosemary against walls was 'exceedingly common,' and at Hampton Court it was 'so planted and nailed to the walls as to cover them entirely.'

A wide expanse of smooth, well-kept lawn is divided by a straight path which leads from the porch to the orchard. Set at the corners nearest to the house are two fine examples of topiary work, birds standing on broad bases, in clipped yew.[2] Two smaller birds on

[1] From *The Story of the Garden* (1932), by Eleanour Sinclair Rohde – the most comprehensive work on the subject that has yet been published.

[2] The 'bird' on the left was planted in 1924 by ex-President Taft, that on the right by Ambassador Harvey.

taller bases stand at the other end of the path near the orchard gate[1] (Plate XIV *a*).

The lawns are enclosed on the east and south by thick yew hedges. These hedges, planted in 1921, have attained to a uniform height of 6 feet and a width of 4 feet throughout their length. It is worthy of note that the total length of yew hedges round about the Manor House is no less than 1166 feet; to keep them clipped is no inconsiderable task, and their excellent condition is a tribute to the gardeners.

To the west is a wall 3 feet 6 inches in height, interesting on account of the material used in its construction. It consists of stones from the former farm buildings which, in their turn, had been built up of ancient materials obtained from the portions of the original Tudor house dismantled during the eighteenth century. The importance of the buildings destroyed at that time is shown by the quality and size of these stones, all of which are hand dressed, and measure, some of them, as much as two feet across.

The wide grass terrace which this wall supports is approached at either end by a short flight of stone steps, at the head of which stand tall flag-staffs, one displaying the Stars and Stripes, the other the Union Jack.[2] It is shaded by a fine walnut tree and two wide-spreading horse-chestnuts, and has been the scene of many notable gatherings.[3]

[1] These were planted in 1925 to celebrate the endowment of the Manor House by the National Society of the Colonial Dames of America, the one on the right by Mrs. Joseph R. Lamar, the president, the one on the left by Mrs. William Adams Brown, the treasurer of the society.

[2] The American flag is endowed by a fund provided by the late Mr. F. T. King of New York, in 1924.

[3] Here in 1921 the re-opening of the Manor House by the late Marquess of Cambridge, brother of Her Majesty Queen Mary, took place. Also, in 1932, the celebration of the George Washington Bicentenary, at which the American Ambassador, Mr. Andrew Mellon, presided.

MADAM'S CLOSE

Beyond the terrace, with a frontage on Great Street to the north and on Little Street to the south, is a large five-acre meadow bearing the picturesque traditional title, 'Madam's Close' – a name by which it has, no doubt, been known since Tudor times. Even as far back as the days of Chaucer, the style 'Madam' was commonly applied to a married woman of position, such as the squire's wife; a spinster being more commonly addressed as 'Mistress.' 'Close' designates an enclosed piece of ground, and is a term still used in the Midlands. Madam's Close, therefore, was the part of the pleasaunce or flower garden more especially reserved for the lady of the house; and we might well suppose that the title was first given to this enclosure by Lawrence Washington in honour of his wife.

It was, doubtless, in those days a true country housewife's garden, not only a pleasaunce but a garden where healing herbs and pot herbs were grown, the whole close surrounded with a hedge or stone wall – a garden full of the quiet colours and fragrance of old-fashioned flowers. It would have been laid out on formal lines – straight paths, rectangular raised beds (supported by flat stones or tiles or boards) or beds surrounded with rails painted in colours copied from the owner's coat of arms, in this case white and red. For 'Madam's' pleasure there would have been charming privy walks, either pleached alleys or walks beside the enclosing walls with plants trained to make a screen against the sun and an archway overhead. At intervals there would have been apertures through which she and her companions 'might the more fully view and have delight of the whole beautie of the garden.' It is most likely there would have been an arbour, possibly an elaborate construction with a tower and chimneys, or a humbler structure 'where honeysuckles ripen'd with the sun forbid the sun to enter'; or covered in summer with scarlet runners – then only recently introduced, for Parkinson, in his *Paradisus*, states that this plant was used to adorn arbours and banqueting-houses.

The garden would certainly have contained specimens of topiary work, cut not only in yew and box but also in rosemary, for William Lawson, in his *New Orchard and Garden* (1618), tells us that rosemary was commonly 'sette by women for their pleasure to grow in sundry proportions as in the fashion of a cat, peacock, or such things as they fancy.' Possibly there was also a dwarf maze, set in hyssop, lavender cotton, or thyme, and a knot garden in which the design would have been laid out in some evergreen herb and the interstices planted with flowers. And the pleasure-garden would probably have been adorned with a fountain or a pool 'whose shaking crystal was a perfect mirror to all the other beauties.' Nor would the pleasant music of bees have been lacking, for bees were universally kept in those days when sugar was a luxury only the wealthiest could afford. 'And I will not account her,' says Lawson, 'any of my good Housewives that wanteth either Bees or skilfulnesse about them.'

THE ORCHARD

The gateway into the Orchard has tall stone piers surmounted by ornamental balls.[1]

In laying out his garden Lawrence Washington may well have had in his mind the instructive work of Dr. Andrew Borde, published in 1500, entitled *A Boke for to lerne a man to be wyse in buylding of his house*, wherein he says: 'It is a commodious and pleasant thing in a mansyon to have an orcharde of sundrye fruytes.' It is more than probable that when the monks of St. Andrew's of Northampton owned the property they had an orchard on this spot. All that now

[1] The ivy that grows round the base of these was brought from Mount Vernon and planted here in 1924 in pious memory of the great General by the Daughters of the American Revolution.

(a)

(b)

PLATE XIV

(a) THE LAWN AND BOWLING GREEN FROM THE TERRACE, SHOWING PATH LEADING FROM ENTRANCE-PORCH TO ORCHARD. (See p. 167)

(b) THE ORCHARD IN SPRINGTIME, SHOWING ANCIENT APPLE TREES. (See p. 170)

FRONTISPIECE

SULGRAVE MANOR HOUSE. THE SOUTH FRONT.

remains here of earlier orchards are a few apple-trees of great age. Two of them – a 'Hanwell Souring' (one of the finest cooking-apples known in the Midlands) which has attained the great girth of 6 feet 7 inches; and an 'Annie Elizabeth' (one of the best of dessert apples) which measures no less than 6 feet 5 inches in circumference – still bear heavy crops of fruit (Plate XIV, *b*).

Except for these few fruit trees, the acre of ground lying to the south of the lawns had remained a rough field until the year 1927, when it was decided to lay out the whole of it once more as an Elizabethan orchard.[1] On the wooden bench at the end of the orchard, placed so as to command a direct view of the Manor House, is a touching inscription: –

'This Orchard was given in memory of Thomas Sherrerd,
1908-1924.
beloved son of William Dusenbery and Mary Eva Moore
Sherrerd.

"A spirit that knew not December,
That brightened the sunshine of May." '

The aim in planting the orchard was to maintain it as a definite part of the pleasure-garden as was customary in medieval and Tudor times, the ground beneath the trees resembling a flowery mead, its 'grass of the deepest green, starred with a thousand various flowers.'

Between the formal rows of fruit trees, chosen as much for the beauty of their blossom as for the quality of their fruit, appear in the springtime masses of daffodils and narcissi, jacinths and muscari, snowdrops and crocuses – 'the Medowe Saffron of the Spring.'

[1] The laying-out and re-planting of the orchard with fruit trees and spring flowers was a gift to Sulgrave from Mr. and Mrs. Sherrerd – the latter President of the Colonial Dames of New Jersey – in memory of their young son.

Mingled with them are varied wild flowers growing freely in the grass – primroses, cowslips, 'lady's smock' or 'cuckoo flower,' and yellow celandine.

As the summer advances the delicate scent of the apple-blossom and spring flowers gives way to the delicious perfume of the old English roses in the wide borders facing the orchard upon the south.

Beyond the ancient apple trees a group of hedgerow trees screen it from Little Street, which forms a boundary upon two sides. The group includes an elm of similar height and size to that of the two giant elms on the north side of the house.[1]

When the Manor House was purchased in 1914, the land surrounding it, including Madam's Close and Little Green, together with the present lawns, flower-gardens, and orchard, amounted in all to nine acres. In 1930 the property was extended to twenty-two acres by the fortunate acquisition of an adjoining meadow, known as Great Green, which had originally formed a part of the Tudor estate. This thirteen-acre meadow is bounded on the north by the bridle-path to Weston, with Cobb's Close across the way, on the south by a field known as Dean's Leys, and on the east by Great Green Spinney. It is of the same width as the Manor House property from north to south, and extends eastwards in a parallelogram, being only separated from it by Little Street (see Fig. 30 on p. 175).

Here, in Great Green, on the edge of the lane and immediately facing the Manor House, a red asbestos-roofed residence, completely out of harmony with the prevailing stone buildings of the countryside, had been constructed by the farmer, formerly the tenant of the Manor House. Efforts to hide it by the planting of a row of

[1] From one of these great trees a sapling was obtained which was taken over to America in 1922 and planted at Mount Vernon. In the same year an oak tree was also sent from Sulgrave, and was planted by the British Ambassador at Mount Vernon.

poplar trees only further obscured the outlook. Happily, it is no more. Cattle now graze where it once stood, and a delightful and far-reaching prospect from the Manor House eastwards over the country-side, with a distant view of Weston woods, has been regained.[1]

About the same time another danger to the landscape was averted. A row of lofty 'pylons' for carrying electricity to the village was on the point of being erected along the road around the Manor House. Negotiations, however, were successful and the wires were taken underground – the cost being defrayed by the Sulgrave Manor Board.

An earlier event was the diversion of a footpath and right-of-way in front of the Manor House which crossed Little Green. An exchange was effected, and a sharp corner of the field rounded off and thrown into the road, improving the Manor property while adding to the safety of the highway.

[1] It was owing to the energy and enterprise of Mrs. E. M. Townsend, a Colonial Dame and a member of the Sulgrave Manor Board, that the purchase of this piece of meadow land was rendered possible; and to commemorate this event Great Green in 1930 was re-named Townsend Close.

Chapter XIV

THE VILLAGE OF SULGRAVE

AFTER the Manor House, the parish church next claims attention, and the way to it takes one through the greater part of the village, in which will be found many points of interest.

Immediately facing the entrance-gates of the Manor House is the picturesque Thatched House, erected about the year 1700 by John Hodges. Its walls of dressed grey stone are good examples of local masonry; and the well-proportioned stone chimney-stacks of traditional Northamptonshire design are identical with those of the north wing of the Manor House. High up on the face of one of them is just visible a small square sundial. This house differs from most others in the village in that it is set back from the road, from which it is separated by a garden with a lawn and wide borders of flowers.

Next to the Thatched House is the Manor Cottage. It is slightly earlier in date, is also thatched, and has a smaller flower-filled garden. Its rough grey walls of Helmdon stone are inset with bands of red-brown Eydon stone. As part of the Manor House property, it is under the control of the Sulgrave Manor Board, and is familiar to all visitors to Sulgrave as an agreeable halt for luncheon or tea.

As the plan of Sulgrave village shows, just opposite the entrance to the meadow known as Madam's Close is a field bearing the old

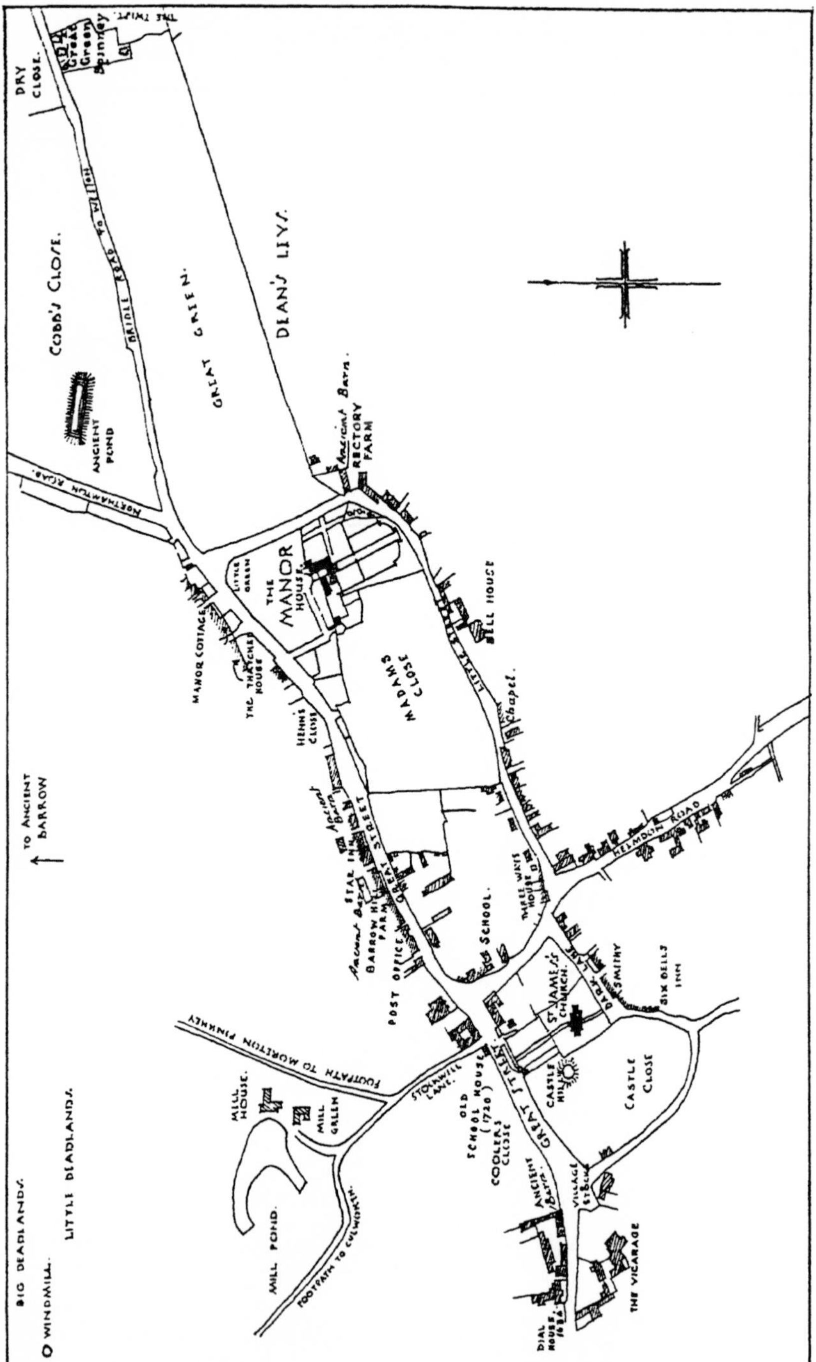

Fig. 30: *Plan of Sulgrave Village*

title of Henn's Close. A little further along Great Street is the Star Inn, its tall sign-post decorated with wrought-iron work made by the village blacksmith in 1839 – a striking example of local craftmanship. In the yard behind is a fine lofty barn with a high-pitched roof of early date.

Adjoining the Star Inn is Barrow Hill Farm, a good stone house with mullioned windows still existing at the back, which takes its name from Barrow Hill to which its lands extend. It possesses one of the finest barns in the village, a noble building, 66 feet long, many of the large jamb stones of its great doorway bearing inscriptions of names and dates of former owners, extending from 1670 to 1840.

Of Barrow Hill, Henn says: 'There is a high hill about a mile northward from the town called Barrow Hill, from whence is such an extensive prospect, that it is said, Nine Counties may from thence be seen, viz. Northampton, Warwick, Worcester, Oxford, Gloucester, Berks, Bucks, Bedford & Hertford, & 'tis thought, on a very clear day, some parts of Hamps, & Wiltshire may also be seen: whether this is absolutely so, or not, I will not take upon myself to determine, but methinks 'tis a wonderful, &, as it were, an almost unbounded prospect. On this Hill is a Tumulus or Barrow, which gives name to the hill, on the top of which grows a large Ash Tree, called Barrow Hill Tree.'

This tree was a famous witchhaunt, and the story goes that the people of Sulgrave wished to cut it down. But after they had climbed the hill, and had begun their work, they saw their village to all appearance in flames, and returned home in haste. Meanwhile the witches repaired the injury done to their tree, and so it was preserved. The old tree has long since gone, and the spot where once it stood is now a haunt of foxes.

Another of the older buildings that line Great Street is the present post office, until recent years an inn, known as the Compasses, or, as Henn describes it: 'a little petty Alehouse, the Scale and Compasses.'

Just beyond the post office, Great Street, which here runs in a gentle ascent, divides; the lesser road, known as Little Street, passes southwards and winds round to meet Great Street again on the east of the Manor. A view of Great Street is shown in the accompanying sketch (Fig. 31).

A little further to the west is Stockwell Lane at the corner of

FIG. 31: *View of Great Street, Sulgrave*

which stands the ancient School House, a small stone building bearing on its eastern gable a tablet inscribed:

H.
I. M.
1720

These three initials are those of John Hodges and Mary his wife. John Hodges, who was then lord of the manor, and, as we have seen, played so important a part in the Sulgrave story, built this house as a charity school for ten poor boys, endowing it with an income of £4 per annum, which, Henn in 1789 tells us 'the late Mr Robert Gardiner about 1777 augmented with 5£ p^{r} annum, adding six more boys, which have each a coat and hat annually.' It is now used as a recreation room, and is entered by a doorway with handsome Queen Anne mouldings, on either side of which is a stone-mullioned window. The following description of the state of this old school-house so lately as 1890, before its recent restoration, appeared in the *English Illustrated Magazine*: –

> 'It is now deserted and ruinous. You can crane your neck in at the aperture and see the master's desk at the wall, a scholars' desk running along one side, and rows of pegs, while lying about in the dust of the floor are the Royal Arms and the tablets containing the Creed. . . . Ruinous steps lead from the outside to a sort of loft above the school.'[1]

Stockwell Lane runs along the east side of Cooler's Close, a large field bordering on Great Street, and from this point a windmill can be seen standing on rising ground against the skyline, gaunt and sail-less, though still serving as a landmark for many miles.

From Stockwell Lane, branch two footpaths, one leading to Moreton Pinkney, the other to the village of Culworth; the lane itself continuing to a water-mill. The water for the mill is provided by a large mill-pool fed by a spring known in former times as Holy Well Spring, and by another spring called Vigo Spring, near by, said to have medicinal properties. The overflow of the pool from this double source forms a stream, the Tow or Tove, which winds eastwards to Towcester.[2] Between this water-mill and the

[1] The Royal Arms would be the 'tolerable painting of the Arms of George the Second,' referred to by Henn in his description of the church, and must have been thrown here, together with the wooden tablets, at the restoration of the church in 1885. Both have long since vanished.

[2] The name Tove is derived from the word *tof*, meaning 'dilatory' – a reference to its winding course (*Place-Names of Northamptonshire* (1933), p. 4).

windmill stood the medieval grange belonging to the monks of St. Andrew's, but, as Henn remarks: 'There are not the least traces of this Grange now.'

The story of these mills can be followed over a period of at least a hundred and fifty years in the collection of ancient deeds now brought together at the Manor House, affording an instance of the value, if this were needed, of the preservation of such documents for the study of local history. These mills – focal-points of the material well-being of the community, for they supplied it with the first necessity of life – were probably included in the 'messuages, mills, etc., in the towns or parishes of Sulgrave and Woodford' which were granted to Lawrence Washington with the Manor of Sulgrave in 1539.

The first allusion to the mills in the Manor House deeds is in 1646, when Abel Makepeace, great-grandson of Lawrence Washington, was living at the Manor House, and from them it appears that both had already passed out of the hands of the family. The next reference to them is in 1666, when Thomas Whitton of Sulgrave sells for £50 to Edward Brockliss of Coaton Mill, Culworth, for 999 years at peppercorn rent, a watermill (described as a 'water-round' mill) and windmill in Sulgrave.

A century later, in 1761, another Edward Brockliss is named in the 'Award of the Parish of Sulgrave' under the Enclosure Act, as owner of the mills. The next reference to the owner of the mills appears two years later in an acknowledgment of a debt of £7, 14s. 6d. owing to Edward Brockliss, miller of Sulgrave, by Francis Blencowe, labourer, of Culworth, 'for bread, fflower, and other Goods by him Sold and Delivered.' As security the debtor gives a lien on 'all his household goods and the tools and implements belonging to his labouring business.'

The inventory of his goods, which is unusually complete, supplies us with valuable information concerning the contents of a well-to-do labourer's cottage in the early years of George III's reign. Among the items mentioned are 'three pewter dishes, eight pewter plates, and thirteen Delft plates,' and among the various articles of furniture are 'seven fflagon chairs' (otherwise 'flagen,' that is, flag- or rush-bottom chairs). Other entries are 'one Jersey wheel' and 'one Linen wheel,' which gives us an interesting clue to cottage industries of the day.[1]

Another document of very special interest is an agreement, dated 1788, between John Brockliss of Sulgrave Mill, and Boulton and Watt, the famous engineers of Birmingham, to erect a steam engine of eight horse-power 'for the purpose of grinding wheat and other grain into meal and pressing the same into flower, and for performing such other service as it may be capable of for the use of the same mill.'

It says much for the enterprise of John Brockliss that he should have set up in so remote a spot as Sulgrave a machine which at that date must have been a great novelty. Amongst the Boulton and Watt Collection in the Public Library in Birmingham, some fifty miles distant from Sulgrave, is a letter addressed to John Brockliss containing a complete specification for this engine and the estimate for its erection. A similar engine of exactly the same date, set up by Boulton and Watt at the Soho Works, Birmingham, is now in the Science Museum, London.

The invaluable chronicler, Mr. Henn, again supplies us with a comment on this event, and in a vivid picture he writes: –

[1] The Jersey wheel, which spun a single thread of cotton, was a hand-driven spinning-wheel. The Linen wheel was, in all probability, worked by a treadle and was used for spinning flax. This flax would have been grown locally, for, in an agreement dated 1762, we read that one Thomas Jarvis, labourer, took of Edward Brockliss and Edward Haycock nineteen acres (odd) of land, 'to afflax for one proper flax season,' at £3, 10s. an acre.

'Mr J. Brockliss's Mill and pond.

Steam Mill

The present proprietor of this spot, has a Water mill, with a neat premises, a good Fish pond whereon is a boat, and walk around the pond; also a *Steam* Engine for grinding corn is now erecting; indeed, this sequester'd rural spot has been of late years much improved by it's present owner.'

Boulton and Watt in their letter of 1788 to Edward Brockliss on the subject of the proposed engine, 'working by the force of steam,' remark: 'Such an engine will consume about 80 pounds weight of *good* coals per hour when working.' Here Henn, once again, makes an illuminating observation. Informing us of how the new fuel was already procurable in Sulgrave, he writes: –

> 'Wood is very scarce; but since the canal to Banbury, about six miles distant, has been completed, there is a plentiful supply of coal, at about fifteenpence to eighteenpence per hundred-weight, brought home.'

After passing the water-mill the footpath to Culworth skirts a ploughed field known as 'Windmill Ground,' in the corner of which stands the dilapidated windmill. Further on are two meadows bearing the striking titles of Big and Little Deadlands – names which confirm an ancient tradition that the village graveyard once lay here. Bridges, in his *History of Northamptonshire*, compiled between 1719 and 1724, writes: –

> 'In the midway between Culworth and this town (Sulgrave) is about an acre of ground, fenced in with an hedge, called the *Old Church-yard*, where the church is supposed to have stood. Stones and bones are often dug up here, and it is preserved as consecrated ground though never used, unless privately by *Roman Catholics*.'

Henn, in quoting from Bridges' account of the Old Churchyard, adds his own marginal notes: 'This hedge is now grubb'd up'; and beside the remark, 'unless privately by *Roman Catholics*,' inquires, 'Qy. if ever used within memory?'

At the further end of Cooler's Close, and just where the road from Banbury enters the village, is the Dial House, a beautiful little farmhouse with a stone porch and mullioned windows, so called from the sun-dial on its gable. Above the doorway is a stone bearing the initials of the original owner and his wife, together with the date 1636 – when Lawrence Washington's descendants were still in possession of the Manor House. Attached to the Dial House is an extensive range of farm buildings, including a large ancient barn.

On the opposite side of the road is the Vicarage, the present house dating, according to Henn, from about 1770, having been rebuilt by the Rev. Richard Wykham, then vicar of the parish, to whom he dedicated his manuscript.

Just outside the Vicarage gate, on a triangular grass plot, are the original Elizabethan village stocks. They were formerly upon the village green to the south of the churchyard and in front of the smithy, in what is still known as Dark Lane; but in 1850 the bit of ground on which they stood was thrown into the churchyard and they were taken down. The village carpenter and wheelwright, Richard Taylor by name, who was instructed to remove them, left them lying outside his workshop. Here they remained for fifty years, until 1905, when his son, George Taylor, put them in his loft, and here they were discovered nearly thirty years later by the author of this book, and, after being carefully repaired, were set up in their present position.[1] As vivid reminders of public correction in Elizabethan days they are of special interest, for they are actually

[1] The cost of their restoration and erection was borne by Lieutenant-Colonel P. Lester Reid of Thorpe Mandeville Manor, a member of the Sulgrave Manor Board.

contemporary with Lawrence Washington, the builder of the Manor House. Made for two malefactors seated side by side, they could also accommodate a couple of standing miscreants, whose wrists would be inserted into the iron hasps on either side of the oak uprights.

From the village stocks runs Dark Lane, a narrow road, which leads to the 'Six Bells,' an ancient inn, with a painted sign framed in handsome scrolled iron-work wrought on the anvil of the smithy (Fig. 32). About the middle of the nineteenth century it was occupied by one Thomas Jones, described as 'victualler and ropemaker' – apparently the last to carry on a local industry no longer in existence. His 'Rope-Walk,' now occupied by a row of cottages, lay alongside the ancient barn of Dial House Farm in Cooler's (*i.e.* School House) Close.

FIG. 32: *Sulgrave Church from The Six Bells*

In the field known as Castle Close is a mount called Castle Hill. A Norman castle, built by Ghilo de Pinkeney in the time of William the Conqueror and for many years the stronghold of the

Pinkeney family, is said to have stood here, but all trace of this building has long since vanished.

Adjoining it is the Parish Church, dedicated to St. James, with a massive thirteenth-century tower buttressed at the angles. The church and its history and a description of the Washington pew, and Washington memorials, form the subject of the following chapter.

Chapter XV

SULGRAVE CHURCH AND THE WASHINGTON MEMORIALS

THE parish church of Sulgrave is situated barely a quarter of a mile from the Manor House, and, standing in the shade of the chestnut and walnut trees of the garden terrace and looking westward over Madam's Close, one sees its battlemented tower outlined against the sky above the trees and buildings that lie between it and the Manor.

The route by which the Washingtons would have reached it was probably by the narrow lane – the present Little Street, then doubtless a private field-path – which leads from the porch on the south front of the Manor House and bending to the west meets Dark Lane which runs along the south side of the church.

The majority of visitors to Sulgrave now approach the church from the north by a straight path with a stone archway on the main road, which leads up to the north porch, replacing, since 1925, the ancient stone-flagged way which ran diagonally from the porch to the little Queen Anne school-house across the road. This north porch was probably the most-used entrance in medieval times, as being the nearest to the castle which once stood upon the Castle Hill close by.

It would be by the south porch, however, that Lawrence Washington and his family entered each Sunday to seat themselves in the Manor House pew which was within a few paces of the south door, and through it five of his daughters passed to their weddings.

This porch, dated 1564, is of special importance, for Elizabethan structural work in churches is excessively rare, and it was probably built by Lawrence Washington. The outer doorway has the flattened Tudor arch, like that of the Manor House, under a square head. In the spandrels are the sacred monogram, the Latin 'IHS' on the one side, and the Greek 'XRS' on the other. Beneath these are the letters I.R. (which may stand for 'Jesus Rex'). Above the arch is a stone shield inscribed with the date 1564, with the initials E.R. (Elizabeth Regina) and a single fleur-de-lys, from the Royal Arms, beneath it. Across the centre of the shield, between the numerals and the royal monogram, can be faintly seen the inscription, 'MARCH 17.'

The date is significant, for it was the year in which Lawrence's wife, Amee, mother of his eleven children, died; and it is more than likely that he built this beautiful porch to her memory. The date recorded on her tomb is 6th October 1564 – five months previous to the erection of the porch; for before the adoption by England of the Gregorian Calendar in 1751 the New Year started on 25th March.

The presence of a fourteenth-century apex stone in the gable of the porch has given rise to the theory that it replaced an earlier one, but as there is no other evidence, it is possible that the only original porch was that on the north side, and that Lawrence erected this Tudor addition to the doorway by which he and his wife were accustomed to enter the church together.

The single fleur-de-lys above the archway is likewise significant, for it also appears on the gable of the Manor House porch. In using this emblem, the golden lily of France, which appears in the first

PLATE XV

(*a*) SULGRAVE CHURCH, SHOWING SOUTH PORCH BUILT BY LAWRENCE WASHINGTON IN 1564. FROM AN OLD WATER-COLOUR DRAWING. (See pp. 137 and 187)

(*b*) and (*c*) ENGRAVED BRASSES (1564) OF THE ELEVEN CHILDREN OF LAWRENCE AND AMEE WASHINGTON IN SULGRAVE CHURCH. (See p. 190)

quartering of the Royal Arms of Queen Elizabeth, Lawrence Washington was but signifying his devotion to the Crown at a time when it was a constant custom for loyal subjects to adorn their buildings with the Royal Arms. The French fleurs-de-lys, it will be remembered, were added to the Royal Arms of England in 1327 by Edward III, son of Isabella, heiress to the throne of France, and here for five hundred years they remained until after the signing of the Treaty of Amiens in 1802, when they were at length removed.

The outward appearance of this south side of the church, which it must have retained since the Washingtons' day, may be gathered from the charming water-colour by George Washington Smith, of Lichfield, painted about the year 1810, which now hangs in the Manor House (Plate XV, *a*). We also possess a picture of the north side of the church, for Henn in his history, written some twenty years before, gives a rough sepia sketch of it, drawn presumably by his own hand. A somewhat indifferent drawing of the church from almost the same aspect was engraved for the *Gentleman's Magazine* of May 1799.

These pictures, which are valuable records of the church as it appeared towards the close of the eighteenth century, show a building of three clearly defined periods – a tower of late thirteenth-century work, a nave and south aisle dating from the middle of the fourteenth century, and a late fourteenth-century chancel. Soon after these drawings were made, the church seems to have suffered severe alterations, for Baker, writing of it in his History of the County of Northampton (1822-30) remarks: 'Most of the windows are despoiled of the tracery.'

There is no documentary evidence of the date of the actual building of the church, but we do know that quite early in the thirteenth century it was in the possession of the Cluniac monks of St. Andrew at Northampton, who were likewise the owners of the

Manor of Sulgrave, and we possess a record that a certain Robert de Northampton was vicar of Sulgrave in 1222.[1]

The tower is, architecturally, the most interesting feature of the church. The west doorway is undoubtedly Saxon; its stones, according to a local tradition, were brought in the thirteenth century from the earlier church, already referred to, as having stood in what was called the Old Churchyard, near the present disused windmill. This doorway, which probably dates from the end of the tenth century, has a straight-pointed arch formed by two stones inclined to meet each other in the way usual at that date. It would seem probable that originally the tower was lower than at present and crowned by a spire. Towards the end of the fourteenth century this may have collapsed or been struck by lightning, and instead of rebuilding it, the tower was partly reconstructed, somewhat higher, with the old material, and a new west window inserted. Finally, at the beginning of the fifteenth century, it seems to have been completed by perpendicular battlements, though without pinnacles.

The north aisle is an addition made in 1885, the wall and windows being largely constructed out of the original material of the older north wall. The handsome fourteenth-century north porch, with its moulded archway decorated with ball-flower ornament, and its inner doorway, were taken down stone by stone and built up again in the same position on the north side of the church, but further out. In the eastern wall of this porch is a small unglazed window with a trefoiled head and transome, the sill being formed of part of a thirteenth-century stone slab with an incised cross.

To the majority of visitors to the church the chief point of interest will be the Washington memorials, which are situated at the east end of the south aisle. In pre-Reformation times an altar stood under the window, and in the south wall beside it there remains

[1] A list of the vicars of Sulgrave is given at the end of this chapter.

the trefoil-arched recess, or piscina, in which the priest rinsed his hands and the chalice. It has a small outlet by which the water passed away into consecrated ground. The actual position of this early altar is now occupied by the pew in which the Washingtons sat, and immediately in front of it, beneath a large slab of Hornton stone, lie Lawrence Washington, his wife Amee Pargiter, and Robert, their eldest son.

The stone, which is six feet long, originally held six brass plates. At the head of the stone is a shield bearing – though now very indistinctly – the coat of arms of Lawrence Washington in enamel, but not the crest, nor, curiously enough, the arms of his wife. Below the shield is the figure of Washington, now, alas! headless, and beside it the indent which once contained the effigy of his wife; the effigy of Lawrence Washington, when complete, was about nineteen inches high, and that of his wife somewhat less. The head of the husband and the effigy of the wife were already missing when Henn described these brasses in 1789. At their feet is a brass plate inscribed with their names and the date of the wife's death; below this are two groups, each measuring 6½ inches in height, representing their children – four sons and seven daughters; the sons below their father's figure, the daughters below that of their mother.

Lawrence Washington, with his hands in an attitude of prayer, is represented in the dress of a well-to-do Tudor gentleman – a close-fitting doublet and over it a loose fur-edged gown with hanging sleeves, and broad-toed shoes. The ground on which he stands is engraved with flowerlets. The inscription, in black letter, reads: –

> 'Here lyeth buried ye bodies of Laurence Wasshingtō Gent & Amee his wyf by whome he had issue iiij sons & vij daughts Wc laurence Dyed ye day of ao 15 & Amee deceassed the vj day of October ao Dnī 1564.'

The brass was obviously made at the death of Amee Washington, spaces being left for the date of her husband's death. These were never filled in by his successor, an omission not uncommonly met with in the case of monumental inscriptions. Lawrence, as we know, survived his wife for twenty years, and died in 1584.[1]

The four sons – the eldest of whom is aged twenty – are represented wearing long-sleeved, high-necked jerkins, long hose and square-toed shoes, and each one carries a gipcière, or purse, at his belt. The seven daughters are shown with close-fitting Tudor coifs and long-sleeved gowns secured round the waist with a girdle; the bodices are cut square to reveal a chemisette The sixth daughter, Mary, it will be remembered, married Abel Makepeace, and it was her son, Lawrence Makepeace, who purchased the Sulgrave estate from his uncle, Robert Washington, in 1610 (Plate xv, *b* and *c*).

In August 1889 the monument was sacrilegiously despoiled of the two little brasses of the children – the only contemporary portraits that we possess of the Washingtons of Sulgrave. When missed from Sulgrave church a hue-and-cry was raised throughout this country and also in America, so that it was impossible for the thief to dispose of them as Washington relics. The police were satisfied, however, that the thief was someone who knew the village well and were confident that the brasses had never left the country. In 1923, thirty-four years later, they reappeared in the possession of an individual, a former resident in Sulgrave, who sought an interview one day with Mr. Francis Thacker of the Public Library at Birmingham, confided to him that he was their owner, and subsequently produced them, stating that he had bought one from a labourer who had found it in a ditch near Sulgrave, and that he himself had found the other in a bush near by. After much negotiation he agreed to return them, accepting for them the sum of £15, which

[1] See p. 57.

was paid by Dr. J. R. Ratcliffe of Moseley, Birmingham, and in the following year they were refixed in their places on the Washington tomb.[1]

Beneath this same slab – though there is no memorial to him – Lawrence Washington's eldest son, Robert, was buried forty years later, in accordance with his own instructions. For in his will, made on 7th February 1619 and proved on 3rd January 1620 he wrote: 'My body to be buried in the South Aisle of the church before my seat where I usually sit under the same stone that my father lieth buried under' – words almost identical with those used by his father, Lawrence, in his will written in October 1581.

The seat mentioned in both cases is the ancient pew belonging, by custom, to the owners of the Manor House, which has long been known as the Washington pew. This famous pew has undergone vicissitudes almost as strange as the Washington brasses. At the restoration of the church in 1885, together with the Georgian pulpit, gallery, and altar rails, it was thrown out of the church by the contractor, and was rescued by Mr. W. T. Peareth of Thorpe Mandeville Manor, where it was stored until his death in 1917, when it was purchased by the Rev. W. G. Cruft, Rector of Greatworth. In 1924 it was acquired by Sir Charles Wakefield, now Lord Wakefield, who restored it to its original position in the church, and on 25th July of that year in the presence of a large congregation the ceremony of unveiling, presenting, and dedicating the pew was held in Sulgrave church (Fig. 33).

It is constructed of small oak panels with characteristic Elizabethan mouldings, set in a moulded framework, and was very likely two or three feet higher originally. Below the window, beside the

[1] The story was told to the present writer by Mr. Thacker in 1932, shortly before his death. Further details of the episode are given by Mr. Thacker in a letter published in *The Times*, 12th April 1924.

FIG. 33: *The Washington Pew*

pew, is a brass plate engraved with the Washington arms and a copy of the inscription on the slab below, which was placed here in 1890 by the children of Admiral John Washington, as English representatives of the Washington family.

On the south wall behind the pew are three marble tablets to the memory of members of the Hodges family, who followed the Washingtons as owners of the Manor House and occupied their pew. The central tablet is to the memory of John Hodges and his brother the Rev. Moses Hodges, Rector of Harvington, Worcestershire, both of whom died in 1724. Framed in coloured marble, ornamented with Ionic columns and by flaming urns, and surmounted by the coat of arms and crest of the Hodges, it is an admirable example of the decorative style of the early Georgian period. John Hodges, who has already been spoken of as lord of the manor of Sulgrave and builder of the north wing of the Manor House, was perhaps, as has been said, the most outstanding figure among the Washingtons' successors. The elaborate epitaph, set out in accordance with the fashion of the time, enumerating his virtues, concludes with his benefactions to Sulgrave; stating that in addition to having built and endowed the Charity School, he also gave '4£ p^r^ Ann to be distributed in Bread at 18^d^ p^r^ Day every Lord's Day to twelve poor Families, but such only as attend Divine Service.'

The smaller tablets on either side, also of architectural design, are to the memory of Martha, wife of the Rev. Moses Hodges, and to Theodosia, their daughter; both bear the arms of Hodges. Theodosia was one of four daughters who divided during their lifetime the Manor of Sulgrave.[1] Of these, Anne, who married the Rev. John Lord and died in 1762, is commemorated with her husband on a marble tablet on the north wall.

It is probable that all the members of the Hodges family were

[1] See p. 73.

buried in the Washington vault; for here, during the restoration of the church in 1885, the coffin-plate of Lydia Jackson, a grand-daughter of Moses Hodges, was found.

The entry of the death of Martha, the wife of Moses Hodges, in the church books, includes a note which runs as follows: –

> 'Martha Hodges of Sulgrave died December the 27th 1741 & was buried in Linnen contrary to Act of Parliam[t], for which the penalty of five pounds was pay[d] upon the information of Mary King, one half of wc[h] went to the Informer, the other half to the Poor of Sulgrave distributed at the discretion of the officers.'

This curious entry recalls an ancient law entitled the 'Burying in Woollen Act,' passed in 1678 and repealed a hundred and twenty years later, which enacted that everyone must be buried in a woollen shroud. It was designed to encourage the wool trade, and would have a special bearing in a district where wool was the staple industry, and also that from which the Washington fortune was originally derived. Evidence of this industry at Sulgrave is preserved at the Manor House in a deed of 1647, recording the sale of a parcel of land by Mr. John Crewe of Steane (father of the first Lord Crewe and then owner of part of the Manor of Sulgrave) to one Richard Spiers, of Sulgrave, whose occupation is given as 'wool-winder.'

At the corner of the Washington pew, in the wall between the window above it and the chancel arch, is an oblique aperture, commonly known as a squint, the purpose of which was to allow of the high altar being seen by the celebrant in this chapel. In post-Reformation days these openings were frequently blocked up, and the one here was restored to its original condition when the church was repaired in 1885.

Having examined this corner of the church so rich in associations with the Washingtons, and with their successors at the Manor House, the visitor will note the more outstanding features of the interior of the building. One which will be immediately apparent is that the archway of the tower is not in line with the centre of the nave and chancel. The cause of this peculiarity may perhaps be that the tower, which dates from the end of the thirteenth century, was added to an existing Norman nave, with which it was then in proper alignment. When, about the middle of the fourteenth century, the south aisle was added, its arcade was built *inside* the line of the old south wall, thereby narrowing the nave and shifting its centre northwards, and a little later the chancel was rebuilt with its centre in line, not with the tower and the old nave, but with the new and narrower nave.

The date suggested for the chancel is indicated by the two carved stone heads on either wall, forming the corbels or brackets that supported the wall-posts of the central truss of the fourteenth-century roof. That on the south side represents a bearded king, and is probably intended for Edward III; that on the north his Queen, Philippa of Hainault. Unfortunately the whole chancel was very largely altered in 1885. The floor was raised and steps added at the east end in such a manner that the piscina is now only six inches above the floor of the sanctuary. The east end was reconstructed to suit the level of the new floor, the east window being entirely re-designed. The easternmost window in the south wall retains its fourteenth-century tracery; the other window on this side is Perpendicular, of about 1400, and is a rare instance of the carving of the whole tracery from a single block of stone. Under this window is a 'low-side' window with a trefoil under a square head. In the splay of this window is the squint already mentioned as being beside the Washington pew.

A will preserved in the Archdeaconry of Northampton, dated

1557, is of twofold interest in that it not only mentions the name of Lawrence Washington, but affords information concerning the furnishing of the altar of the church at that time. In it Lawrence is named as overseer of the will of Thomas Plumer, a husbandman of Sulgrave, who gave 'to the highe Altar in Sulgrave Church iij yards of lynnen clothe, at xiid. the yard to make an altar clothe.'

In the Middle Ages, before their destruction at the Reformation, every church, even the smallest, possessed a certain number of valuables such as plate, vestments, and ornaments for the altar. These were often stored in the great oaken chests of which there was at least one in every church, together with valuable documents, belonging to the church or deposited for safety by parishioners. A usual place for such a chest was not far from the altar, against the north wall.

Sulgrave is fortunate in still possessing its original chest, of the same date as the church itself, which now stands beside the pulpit. Until the recent alterations it stood in the chancel, and here Henn saw it and described it in the following words:

> 'In the Chancel stands an old iron-cased Chest, wherein are the Parish Books. . . . This Chest had once three Locks and, as one may imagine must have been made some hundred years ago; it is now very rotten and much broken.'

It was just two years before this account of it was written, that the chest was put to the strangest of uses by William Abbott, parish clerk and highwayman, who made of it a receptacle for his ill-gotten spoil.[1] After its removal from the chancel in 1885, the chest was relegated to a dark corner near the tower where it was again put to base purposes, being used for storing coal. In 1920 it was transferred to the honourable position that it now occupies (Fig. 34).

[1] See page 73, *ante*.

In spite of what Henn says as to its condition, this great oak chest, considering its age and the vicissitudes that it has undergone, is in a wonderful state of preservation, and is one of the most striking examples of its kind in existence. Of the type known as a 'dug-out,' it is hollowed from a single tree trunk.[1] The tree must have been a huge one, for the chest stands 1 foot 8 inches from the ground, measures 2 feet 2 inches from front to back, and is nearly 6 feet long. An unusual feature here, and one that must have added enormously to the labour of its making, is that the interior is hollowed into two squared parts with a solid section of the oak four inches thick – the same thickness as the walls of the chest – left between them. The lid, on account of its great weight, is sawn in half, each half covering one of the cavities and overlapping the partition.

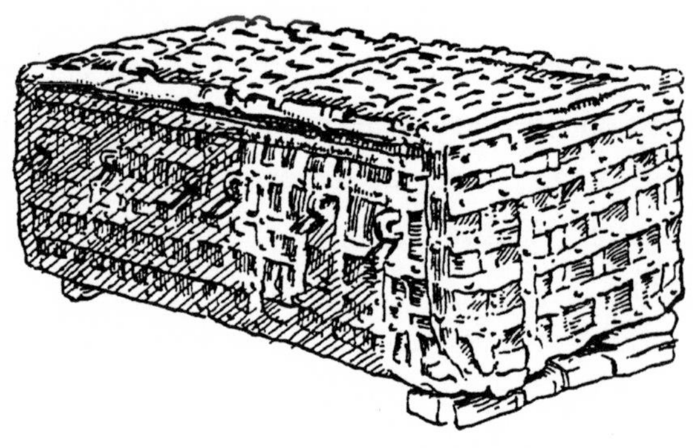

FIG. 34: *Fourteenth Century Iron-bound Chest*

The chest is heavily bound and clamped with iron bands placed so close together that little of the wood is visible; each lid has five hinges terminating in massive iron hasps. From the iron-work we may judge the chest to be of the fourteenth century, though the primitive character of the woodwork suggests a much earlier date.

Most of the pews in the body of the church are Elizabethan, and, most fortunately, were only slightly altered during the restorations of 1885. Their ends terminate in boldly carved finials. Elizabethan seating in churches is rare, and it is not unreasonable to suppose that

[1] Hence the origin of the term 'trunk,' as commonly used to-day.

these pews were given to the church by Lawrence Washington in 1564 when, as we believe, he built the south porch. This suggestion is borne out by the close resemblance between the mouldings of the finials and those of the wooden corbels supporting the timber roof of the Great Chamber of the Manor House.

The font stands beside a pillar near the south door. The bowl dates from the time of Charles II and is carved with a conventional leaf decoration in the manner of the period. The octagonal stem and base date from the fifteenth century. The original bowl was no doubt destroyed during the Commonwealth, when the use of fonts was forbidden, and their place taken by any household basin. The present bowl is a very interesting and rare example of a seventeenth-century restoration on semi-Gothic lines.

On the wall close by, fixed in such a way that both front and back are visible, is the fourteenth-century lock, now in perfect working order, which originally belonged to the west door. When the old door was replaced by a new one, in 1885, the lock was thrown aside, and, in 1932, was discovered in the village carpenter's shop by the present writer, who acquired it on condition that it was returned to the church. Formed of a massive block of chestnut wood, it measures 16 inches in length, 9 inches in width, and is no less than 2½ inches thick. The enormous key, 10 inches long, dates from about 1750, the original key having been presumably worn out or lost. It now hangs from the wall by an ancient chain which allows of its being inserted in the lock and turned.

Sulgrave church possesses a fine peal of six inscribed bells, and also a small Sanctus or Priest's bell, which is medieval, but bears no inscription.

In connection with the bells there is an interesting document in the Public Record Office, dated 1552. It is an inventory of the goods belonging to Sulgrave church. From it we learn that the church then possessed four bells and a Sanctus bell – evidently the one that is still there. They are described as: 'Item iiij bells in the Steple and a Sauncts bell whereof one is sold as appereth in the defauts.'

With regard to the bell referred to as sold, the document goes on to state that the churchwardens, John Humfrey and John Mayo, had disposed of it to Thomas Stuttesbury and Lawrence Washington for £16, that the purchasers had already paid £6 of this, which had been spent on repairing 'highe wayes and fordes,' and that it was intended to use the remaining £10 in the same way. In the meantime the bell was still hanging in the steeple.

The two oldest bells of the present peal are of the time of James I, when the Washington family still occupied the Manor House; one is dated 1610, the other 1612, and both bear the following inscription: –

'Be yt knowne to all that doth me see
that Newcombe of Leicester made mee.'

Of the remainder, two date from the eighteenth century and two are modern. The sixth, the treble bell, was given to complete the peal in 1932.

In 1929 the base of the tower was enclosed by a screen to form a vestry. This screen, which was executed by craftsmen at Broadway in Worcestershire, is constructed of oak, its carving being decorated in blue and red. It was presented to the church by the Women's Committee of the George Washington Sulgrave Institute of America. Above is the belfry floor, the railing in front of it being draped with the British and American flags. Another gift to the church from donors in the United States is the organ, presented by the Society of Colonial Dames of America in 1930.

VICARS OF SULGRAVE

1222. Robert de Northampton.
1264. . . . Thorald.
—— Robert de Wardington (date missing).
1284. Henry de Aston.
1302. Robert de Middleton.
—— John de Bocton (date missing).
1325. Hugh Paine.
1347. Henry Warren de Buckingham.
1363. William Wycock.
1369. John Wyberd.
1391. John Ward.
1423. Thomas Bythebrook.
1428. William Jewster.
1429. William Goneld.
1430. John Irby.
1438. Henry Hopton.
1441. Thomas Hastings.
1448. Walter Blade.
1451. John Edwin.
1452. Robert Cornwall.
1453. Richard Monmouth.
—— William Andrew (date missing).
1464. John Baldwin.
1475. Edward Fox.
1489. John Alysander.
1496. Richard Wright.
1510. John Hogeson.
1511. John Hynton.

1540. William Marshall.
1547. Ralph Greenhall.
1561. Hugh Charnock.
1655. Richard Fisher. (The next by record.)
1686. George Fisher.
1725. John Loggin.
1741. Richard Lydiat.
1750. Thomas Lydiat.
1753. James Wilmot.
1760. Richard Wykham.
1804. William Harding.
1826. James Harding.
1829. William Harding.
1882. James William Harding (Ardenne).
1922. William S. Pakenham-Walsh.

Chapter XVI

THE PURCHASE AND RESTORATION OF THE MANOR HOUSE

On Christmas Eve 1814 was signed at Ghent the Treaty of Peace between England and America, of which a century later Sulgrave Manor became a permanent memorial.

Late in the summer of that year five envoys from the United States met, at Ghent, three envoys from Great Britain in order to conclude a peace between the two countries. The British mission consisted of Admiral Lord Gambier, Henry Goulburn, and William Adams, with Anthony John Baker as secretary. The American Commissioners were John Quincy Adams, United States Minister to Russia; Jonathan Russell, Minister to Sweden; James Bayard, Senator; Henry Clay, Member of Congress; and Albert Gallatin, Financial Secretary to the Treasury. It was almost entirely due to the tact, forbearance, and diplomacy of Albert Gallatin that the object of the mission was at last successfully achieved.

He was accompanied by his son, James, a lad of seventeen, who acted as his secretary throughout the negotiations, and kept a private diary in which he gave a lively first-hand account of incidents as they occurred, his impressions of the discussions which preceded the signing of the Treaty and of the celebrations that followed it. This diary was published in 1914, under the title of *A Great Peacemaker*, by Count Gallatin, grandson of the diarist.

The American delegates reached Ghent on 7th July and were lodged in the Hôtel d'Alcantara, a fine old family mansion situated at the corner of Rue des Champs. Here for a month they awaited the arrival of the British Mission, who were housed in the Carthusian monastery, and nearly five months later, in its refectory, the Treaty was signed and sealed. So complicated and delicate were the preliminary negotiations that they were often in danger of breaking down. Indeed, the diary shows that, despite all Gallatin's efforts, this would most probably have happened, had it not been for the intervention of the Duke of Wellington, then British Ambassador in Paris.

Under the date 28th November the young Gallatin records: 'To-day father received a private despatch from the Duke of Wellington. . . . It is marked "Strictly confidential." It is couched in the most friendly terms, assuring father he has brought all his weight to bear to ensure peace.' He adds significantly: 'Father burnt this dispatch and does not even know that I have recorded it. I wanted to copy it, and was doing so when he took it off the table and burned it.'

The signing of the Treaty was followed by a thanksgiving service in the cathedral, and the Christmas Day festivities, which brought all parties together, are described by James Gallatin, who writes: –

> 'The British delegates very civilly asked us to dinner. The roast beef and plum pudding was from England, and everybody drank everybody else's health. The band played first "God Save the King," to the toast of the King, and "Yankee Doodle,"

to the toast of the President. Congratulations on all sides and a general atmosphere of serenity; it was a scene to be remembered. . . . I never saw father so cheerful; he was in high spirits, and his witty conversation was much appreciated.'

The ratification of the Treaty two weeks later was celebrated by a gala performance at the theatre, and on the evening of 8th January 1815 the municipality of Ghent gave a splendid banquet to the Commissioners in what is now the Hall of Archives in the Hôtel de Ville. 'The banquet,' so the diarist tells us, 'was very fine, lasting over five hours – speeches, nothing but speeches and toasts.'

Towards 1911, as the Centenary of the Treaty of Ghent drew near, discussions began, both in England and America, as to the most suitable means of celebrating it. It was in America, during the closing year of Mr. Roosevelt's administration, that the idea of an international celebration of its signing was suggested, and in 1911 the American Peace Centenary Committee was constituted, Mr. Roosevelt being its Honorary Chairman, Mr. Andrew Carnegie its acting-Chairman, and Mr. William B. Howland Chairman of the Committee on International Conference and Organisation, while among its prominent members were Mr. Joseph Choate and Mr. Elihu Root, the latter having already formulated the project with Mr. Mackenzie King, afterwards Premier of Canada.

In June 1912 a Canadian National Association was organised to join with the kindred associations in Great Britain and America; and in October 1911 Earl Grey, on his retirement from the Governor-Generalship of Canada, consented to become President of a British body to be formed for the conduct of the celebrations. On 21st February 1912 the first meeting of the Executive Committee took place; private meetings were held in London at which

Mr. Howland, the American representative, Mr. (afterwards Sir) Robert Donald, editor of the *Daily Chronicle*, and Mr. (now Sir) Harry Brittain, secretary of the Pilgrims' Club, took part; and in due course the British branch of the Peace Centenary Committee was completed by the appointment of Lord Revelstoke and Lord Rothschild as honorary treasurers; Lord Cowdray as chairman of the Finance Committee; Mr. (afterwards Lord) Plender as honorary auditor; and Sir Arthur Conan Doyle as honorary secretary. The Committee included Mr. Ramsay MacDonald, Lord Weardale, Lord Crawford and Balcarres, and Mr. Arthur Lee, now Viscount Lee of Fareham, appointed chairman of the Sulgrave Manor Board in 1925. Later in the year Mr. Howland, with Mr. Brittain and Mr. H. S. Perris, secretary of the British Committee, visited Ghent to arrange for the organisation of the centenary celebrations to take place there in December 1914.

The proposals of the British Committee were first put before the public at an inaugural meeting in London held on 18th December 1912 at the Mansion House; the Lord Mayor presided, and among those present was M. Emile Braun, the Burgomaster of Ghent. Earl Grey, who made the principal address, before outlining the plans for the celebration which had already taken shape, read the following message from Mr. Theodore Roosevelt:

'My heartiest congratulations to those assembled at the historic Mansion House, and my earnest wishes for success in the effort to secure adequate celebration of the centenary of peace between the great English-speaking Empire of Britain on the one hand and the great English-speaking Republic of America on the other.'

Earl Grey then proceeded to set out the three chief proposals, which were as follows: –

(1) The erection of a monument to George Washington in London.

(2) The purchase of Sulgrave Manor.

(3) The promotion, by well-considered educational methods, of a better knowledge and understanding of Anglo-American relations, past, present, and future.

This last suggestion resulted, in 1919, in the foundation and endowment by Sir George Watson of the Watson Chair of American History, Literature, and Institutions, which is administered by the Sulgrave Manor Board.[1]

To the first suggestion effect was given in 1921 by the placing in Trafalgar Square of Washington's statue – a gift to Great Britain from Virginia, his native state.

At the meeting the Burgomaster of Ghent stated that he was charged by his municipality to say that they were disposed to participate in the celebrations by giving in the same chamber in their Town Hall on 5th January 1915 a fête which should be, as far as possible, a repetition of the function held there a hundred years before. Unhappily, this kindly intention was not to be fulfilled, for by 5th January 1915 Ghent was in the hands of the invader.

The remaining and most important project – the purchase of Sulgrave Manor – had already been discussed in many quarters and had received very warm support, and in his opening speech Earl Grey announced that an option upon the property had been secured, and that to complete the purchase and to provide for its maintenance a sum of from £25,000 to £30,000 would be required.

Early in 1913 Mr. Harry Brittain, as chairman of the Dominions and Overseas Committee, paid a preliminary visit to the United States and Canada to discuss the whole project with the United States and the Canadian Committees. In April it was announced that a large and representative delegation would proceed to America

[1] The history and scope of this Foundation, together with the names of the lecturers and the subject of their addresses from 1921, when the Inaugural Lecture was given at the Mansion House by Viscount Bryce, will be found in Appendix v.

to confer with the American Peace Centenary Committees. The delegation, which, previous to its departure, was received by the King at Buckingham Palace, was headed by Lord Weardale, with Sir Arthur Lawley, afterwards Lord Wenlock, as deputy leader. Together with corresponding delegations from the United States, the Dominion of Canada, and the municipality of Ghent, a tour was made of many of the great American cities where the meaning and purpose of the impending celebrations were explained, the British Committee dwelling more especially upon the commemorative purchase of the ancestral home of George Washington – Sulgrave Manor.

During 1913 this project made much progress, and by October sufficient money had been raised by subscription to justify the appointment of a Committee of Management of Sulgrave Manor, formed of members of the British Peace Centenary Committee. These were: –

The American Ambassador
Earl Grey
Mr. Andrew Carnegie
Lord Shaw of Dunfermline
Lord Weardale
The Rt. Hon. James Bryce
Lord Cowdray
Lord Spencer
Mr. William B. Howland (of New York)
Mr. John A. Stewart (of New York)
Mr. Robert Donald
Mr. Harry E. Brittain

Towards the end of the year Earl Grey, owing to ill health, resigned the Presidency, and the post was accepted by His Highness the Duke of Teck, afterwards Marquess of Cambridge, brother of Her Majesty Queen Mary.

On 22nd January 1914 the purchase of Sulgrave Manor was completed, the price paid being £8400. This event was announced by Mr. Asquith,[1] the Prime Minister, at a second and even more important meeting at the Mansion House; the distinguished persons on the platform included the Duke of Teck, who occupied the chair, the American Ambassador (Mr. Walter Hines Page), the Archbishop of Canterbury, and Viscount Bryce, formerly British Ambassador at Washington.

Towards the end of February the United States Ambasador presided at the American Embassy at the first meeting of the Board of Management of Sulgrave Manor, and on the following day the Duke of Teck paid a visit to the Manor House in company with Sir Reginald Blomfield, R.A., the consulting architect to the Board, to decide upon the necessary repair of the building.

Up to this time no less than £12,000 had been collected from British contributors, and out of this sum Sulgrave Manor had been purchased. More funds being now needed for the execution of the British programme for the centenary celebrations, further public subscription lists were opened and met with a generous response.[2]

A singularly successful effort on the part of the organisers of the fund was the Anglo-American Peace Centenary Ball, held in London at the Albert Hall on 10th June 1914, of which the chief feature was a historical pageant. This great social event received such support that the very substantial profit of £1700 was realised.

Towards the end of July the Duke of Teck, the American Ambassador, and a large party of distinguished people paid a visit of ceremony to Sulgrave, 'in honour of the memory of George Washington and his ancestors who once resided there.' Amongst the guests of the Committee were Mr. Lanier Washington, the leading representative of the Washington family in America, and

[1] Afterwards, Earl of Oxford and Asquith.

[2] The names of some of the principal subscribers to the Centenary Fund between the years 1912 and 1917 will serve to show the widespread interest aroused. They will be found in Appendix I.

Mrs. T. Harrison Garrett, representing the National Society of the Colonial Dames of America, which was later destined to play so vital a part in the affairs of the Manor House.

Within ten days of this visit the European War broke out, and all the elaborate arrangements for the celebration of the Peace Centenary in either England or America were of necessity abandoned. The Peace Centenary Committee, however, remained in being until October 1918, when it handed over its work to the Management Committee of Sulgrave Manor.

At a meeting of the Sulgrave Board of Governors at the American Embassy on 1st April 1919, it was announced that Viscount Burnham, a member of the Board and proprietor of the *Daily Telegraph*, proposed to open a public appeal in the columns of that paper for the restoration of the Manor House. The first subscription list, published on 25th April, was headed by His Majesty the King, who contributed £100. His name was followed by that of H.R.H. the Prince of Wales. The total sum recorded on the opening day was nearly £3000, the amount finally realised being upwards of £6000.[1]

By means of this Fund – supplemented in 1920 by a gift of £2500 from the Sulgrave Institution of America – it was at last possible to begin the work, so long delayed, of restoring the Manor House and laying out the garden. Full details of the repairs carried out are given in the descriptive account of each portion of the building and need not be further outlined here. While this restoration was proceeding, preliminary steps were taken towards the furnishing of the house. It was begun by Lady Paget, who died in 1920, and was completed by Lady Lee of Fareham.

The Manor House was formally opened and dedicated on 21st

[1] The names of the principal subscribers to the *Daily Telegraph* Fund will be found in Appendix II.

June 1921. The ceremony at the Manor, which followed a service in the parish church, was presided over by the Marquess of Cambridge. The Bishop of Peterborough, in whose diocese Sulgrave lies, dedicated the building; and the main entrance-door of the house was unlocked by Mrs. George Harvey, wife of the American Ambassador. A sense of historical continuity was lent to the proceedings by the presence of the Mayor of Northampton – successor in office to Lawrence Washington, the builder of the Manor House. Preceded by the Borough mace-bearer and the beadle, and followed by the members of the council, the mayor was a striking figure, his traditional crimson fur-trimmed robe and gold chain of office vividly recalling his predecessor of four hundred years before.

The words with which the Marquess of Cambridge ended his speech of welcome eloquently expressed the inspiration underlying the project for the preservation of the Manor House. He said:

'In effecting this restoration we have had one idea in mind. We want this house to be a shrine for all Americans who visit the old country and a centre from which sentiments of friendship and goodwill between the British and American peoples will for ever radiate; and these sentiments we believe to be the greatest security for the world's peace.'

In July 1924 a number of members of the American Bar Association, then in England, visited Sulgrave as guests of the Board and witnessed the unveiling of the Washington pew. The duties of host were performed by Sir Charles Wakefield (now Lord Wakefield), a former Lord Mayor of London, who was then honorary treasurer of the Sulgrave Manor Board, and had himself purchased and restored the pew to the parish church. On its way the party was accorded an official welcome at the Town Hall, Northampton, by the Mayor and Corporation, who, for the second time, entertained distinguished visitors to Sulgrave; the former occasion having been in 1914, on the first official visit to the Manor House of the Duke of Teck (Marquess of Cambridge), the American Ambassador, Mr. Page, and the chief organisers and supporters of the movement for the acquisition of the Manor House.

Fig. 35: *Coat of Arms of Northampton*

Chapter XVII

THE ENDOWMENT OF THE MANOR HOUSE BY THE NATIONAL SOCIETY OF THE COLONIAL DAMES OF AMERICA

IN the account already given of the first public visit to Sulgrave, in 1914, of the committee who were responsible for its purchase, mention has been made of the presence of a representative of the National Society of the Colonial Dames of America. The purpose of this society, inaugurated in 1891, is (in the words of its president, Mrs. Joseph R. Lamar), 'to preserve the records and the relics of the Colonial period of American history, and to teach, by these object lessons, the meaning of patriotism.'

Its members are the descendants of the men of the Colonies, *i.e.* the thirteen Colonial States, who 'shaped the foundation upon which the Nation was built, and determined its character and its institutions.' Since only these thirteen States have historic houses and sites to be preserved, the Associate Societies in the non-Colonial States have had to find other, widely diversified, patriotic objects, extending from the replacing of milestones on pioneer trails to the translation and printing of unpublished diaries of historic interest and value. Above all the Colonial Dames seek to preserve the Colonial traditions brought by their fathers to the non-Colonial States.[1]

The Biennial Council, held in Washington, is composed of delegates from the forty-one State Societies; at each meeting reports are made of the varied work individually accomplished, and every few years some national project is launched in which all the State Societies can share. In 1914, while the Biennial Council was actually in session in Washington, news came that a number of public-spirited English men and women – members of the British Peace Centenary Committee – had bought Sulgrave Manor and had presented it jointly to the peoples of England and the United States as a memento of their common inheritance; also that it was proposed to restore it.

The delegates were quick to recognise the historic value of Sulgrave Manor, the ancestral home of the Washingtons in England, and that its acquisition had a very special interest for their Society, in that it represented one of the definitely stated objects of their constitution – to preserve and restore buildings connected with the early history of their country. The National Council forthwith decided to present to the Washington Manor House in Northamptonshire a copy of the portrait, by Charles Wilson Peale, of George Washington in the uniform of a Colonel of Provincial (British) Forces, bequeathed to Washington and Lee University in Virginia by a descendant of his wife.

The gift was but a preliminary token of the Society's great personal interest in the Manor and their realisation of its significance to the citizens of the United States. Soon afterwards the members set to work to collect money for 'immediate repairs,' and a cheque

[1] *The National Society of the Colonial Dames of America: its Beginnings, its Purpose, and a Record of its Work, 1891-1913*. A copy of this publication is preserved at the Manor House.

for $1000 (£200) was acknowledged by the English Committee on 15th April 1915, as 'the first contribution received from American sources.'

During the Great War, and in the years immediately following, the patriotic efforts of the Colonial Dames were wholly directed towards the equipment of hospital ships and other essential war services, but, notwithstanding this, in 1917 they sent a second cheque for $2000 'for further urgent repairs.'

Six years later, in 1923, it was reported to the General Meeting of the Council that except for the re-building of the west wing, the Manor House was now restored. It was thereupon determined to raise, as a gift from the people of the United States, an Endowment Fund of not less than $100,000 (£20,000), the income of which was to be devoted to the general maintenance of Sulgrave Manor.

The Colonial Dames at this time numbered 9000 members,[1] and each member was asked to collect $10 in subscriptions of $1 and upwards from the people of her State. The Society undertook to bear all expenses and guaranteed that every dollar subscribed would go to the Endowment Fund without diminution, each donor's name being entered in a book to be deposited at the Manor House.

Fired by the indomitable spirit of their forefathers, these patriotic ladies, working on their own initiative and without outside assistance or co-operation, began the task of raising this great sum of money. Each member was supplied with copies of an Appeal, written by the President of the Society, Mrs. Joseph R. Lamar, giving a history of Sulgrave Manor and the reasons why its future upkeep should be undertaken by the citizens of the United States.

The Appeal, statesmanlike in its simplicity and breadth and most eloquent in its wording, so inspired the members who carried out the scheme and so stirred the imagination of the public that the

[1] The membership of this society is now about 11,500.

amount necessary to carry out this project, lying though it did, beyond the geographical confines of their own country, was over-subscribed within the next twelve months, the actual sum received from the thirty-five thousand contributors being $112,000 – a result the more remarkable since, to judge by the history of the Society's former national undertakings, it would normally have taken some five or six years to achieve.

The Appeal opened by explaining that with the exception of certain early contributions towards its restoration, the English Committee alone had purchased, restored, and furnished the Manor House, and maintained it for ten years – from 1914 to 1924.

It continued:

'The English Committee have employed the best skill in making these restorations; everything is as nearly as it was when the Washingtons lived there, as possible. They have planted the old-fashioned garden, with its box-wood and hollyhocks – one of the most beautiful features of the place – and they have done it all with the loving and painstaking attention to detail that the English understand so well, and with an appreciation of the character of Washington that is only second to our own. Except for the American Embassy, it is the only spot in England where the American Flag flies; and in all this lovely Island there are few places more full of charm.

*

'We hope through this friendly gift to make a great many Americans interested in Sulgrave and in what we call the Sulgrave Spirit – which is one of goodwill and helpfulness among people of one language, and through them, among all mankind; and also to relieve the British Committee of the burden of maintaining the Manor House and grounds.

'We feel that this duty should be ours. We share with England all of her history before the American Revolution. Shakespeare is ours, as well as England's; Oxford and Westminster are ours. They are – until the signing of the Declaration of Independence – a part of our common heritage. But Sulgrave Manor is wholly ours; the name that lends it lustre is our own; and the place should be our care for all time to come.

*

'Americans are not wanting in national pride or in a sense of moral obligation; and certainly not in their appreciation of those places endeared to them by their connection with the early history of their country. "America has no Crown jewels nor palaces; but simple spots made sacred to her children by hallowed association with the great men of her destiny"; and there are few buildings more intimately connected with our Colonial history than Sulgrave Manor. For, with few exceptions, they were Englishmen who planted the Colonies from which our Nation grew; who founded this Great Republic and brought, from England, the Institutions, Laws, Customs and Traditions which lie at its foundation. They were Englishmen who established our first representative, legislative assembly, in 1619; who signed the Mayflower Compact in 1620; who wrote our Constitution in 1787. "Our flower of liberty grew from seed brought from English soil."

*

'The place is knitted into our history with many strands. . . . When the present English Committee has passed away, it is a question whether there will be other Englishmen to take their places and to care for Sulgrave as sympathetically and intelligently as they have done. Surely it would be a disgrace to this country if the place were to fall into neglect because we were too indifferent or too parsimonious to continue its preservation.'

*

The magnificent sum of money resulting from this great patriotic effort on the part of the Colonial Dames, invested in a United States Trust Company, provides an annual income of £1000 for the perpetual care and upkeep of Sulgrave Manor, thus fulfilling the desire and intention of its promoters.

The Endowment of Sulgrave Manor, which formed the second great landmark in its history – following its opening and dedication four years before – was marked by a special ceremony; and in June 1925 Mrs. Joseph R. Lamar and Mrs. William Adams Brown, representing the National Society, visited the Manor House, by invitation of the Sulgrave Manor Board, to present formally to the Manor, as 'a record of friendship,' the handsome folio volume entitled *The Sulgrave Endowment Record.* It contains the thirty-five thousand names, arranged by States, of those who had contributed to the Endowment Fund, together with the number of members of the Society and the sum collected in each State.[1] The Chairman of the National Committee to raise the Endowment Fund was Mrs. William Adams Brown, and the Chairman of the Committee on this Record of Contributors was Mrs. Edward Mitchell Townsend of New York.

The book is a beautiful specimen of the finest American craftsmanship. It is bound in brown morocco leather stamped with the coat of arms of the Colonial Dames on the cover, in gold; the arms being again repeated on the title-page with their motto, *Virtutes majorum filiæ conservant* ('The daughters preserve the virtues of their ancestors') words which aptly sum up the pious aim of each one of its members.

The Preface to the volume, signed 'Clarinda Pendleton Lamar,' having clearly set out the underlying purpose of the Colonial Dames in endowing Sulgrave Manor, continues thus: –

[1] The names of the members of the Committee who raised the Endowment Fund are recorded in Appendix III.

'The Society sought to interest as many Americans as possible in the Manor and its history, and to this end the Endowment Fund of one hundred thousand dollars was divided among the States in which there are Societies of Colonial Dames, in proportion to the comparative wealth of those States; each Society was asked to collect from the citizens of the State its share of the fund. These "quotas" ranged from several thousand dollars in the larger and wealthier States, to a few hundreds in the smaller and less prosperous communities. But almost without exception, each State gave the share that was asked of it; some of them giving more.'

A limited edition, numbered '1' to '48,' was printed.[1] A copy was given to the British Museum and to the Congressional Library in Washington. The volume numbered '1' was presented to Sulgrave and is kept in the Great Hall of the Manor House for the inspection of visitors. Each State Society of Colonial Dames bought a copy, and the few remaining volumes were disposed of at steadily increasing prices to American Libraries – the last realising no less than $150 (£30).

In grateful recognition of their great achievement, the Sulgrave Manor Board expressed the wish that two members of the National Society of the Colonial Dames of America should accept seats upon the Board. The national president, Mrs. Joseph R. Lamar, accordingly nominated Mrs. Edward M. Townsend and Mrs. Albert H. Chatfield, the former representing a Colonial or Ancestral State Society (New York), the latter a non-Colonial or Associate State Society (Ohio).

At the next Council Meeting of the National Society of the

[1] The printing was done by D. B. Updike, The Merrymount Press, Boston, in the month of June 1925. The binding was executed by Stikeman and Co., New York.

Colonial Dames in the following year, it was decided to make a grant to set up a replica of the Manor House at the Exposition held in Philadelphia to commemorate the hundred-and-fiftieth anniversary of the founding of the United States of America; and a Building Committee of Dames from a number of State Societies, under the chairmanship of Mrs. James Starr, was constituted. The beautifully executed facsimile of the Tudor Manor House, erected from photographs and carefully measured architectural drawings supplied by the Sulgrave Manor Board, was visited by many thousands of enthusiastic sightseers – most of whom would have had but little prospect of ever seeing the original – and was awarded the gold medal as the best exhibit.

A large committee of Pennsylvania Dames acted not only as custodians of the building, but as hostesses, showing the interior to visitors, selling pictures of it, and serving tea; the whole of the fifteen thousand dollars taken in entrance-fees being presented to the Sulgrave Manor Board towards the Restoration Fund. After the closing of the Exposition the replica was bought and moved to St. Martin's, a suburb of Philadelphia, where it was re-erected as a private residence.[1] A memento of this most successful project was sent to the Manor House in the form of a vellum document bound in gold-tooled leather with the arms of the Society upon its cover. It is illuminated in gold and colours with a record of the event and with the names of the Executive Committee: Mrs. James Starr (chairman), Mrs. Arthur H. Lea, Mrs. George H. Earle, Jr., Mrs. John C. Groome, Mrs. Alvin A. Parker, Mrs. Nathaniel S.

[1] In this connection it may be recorded that a wing of Virginia House, Richmond, Virginia, the residence of Mr. and Mrs. Alexander Weddell, is a careful and beautiful reproduction of Sulgrave Manor. Virginia House is the headquarters of the Virginia Historical Society, and contains a valuable collection of books and manuscripts relating to the Colonial period of Virginian history; also portraits and relics of early Colonists and other prominent figures in the history of the State.

Reay, Mrs. William E. Lingelbach, Mrs. John Gribbel, Mrs. William McK. Morris, Mrs. Christopher L. Ward, and Mrs. Alexander Laughlin.

Mrs. E. M. Townsend and Mrs. A. H. Chatfield – the representatives of the National Society of the Colonial Dames on the Sulgrave Manor Board – finding on their first official visit to the Manor House that much work remained to be done, including the re-building of the west wing, requested the permission of the National Society to raise personally a further Restoration Fund. With the help of many of the State Societies and with generous gifts from friends outside the organisation, \$58,936 (approximately £10,000) was obtained between the years 1926 and 1931. A record of the names of the two hundred and seventy-five contributors, bound in leather and signed by the two ladies who were primarily responsible for the collection of this large sum, is preserved at Sulgrave.[1]

FIG. 36: *Coat of Arms of the National Society of the Colonial Dames of America*

Another handsome and welcome gift of \$16,000 was received almost at the same time; and it was with this money, given through Mrs. Townsend by a small body of donors, some of whom had already subscribed to the Restoration Fund, that the thirteen acres of beautiful meadow-land known as Great Green were secured.

By means of these restoration funds so successfully created by the National Society of the Colonial Dames, augmented by a personal gift of \$1500 from Mrs. Chatfield, the west wing of the

[1] The names of the subscribers are recorded in Appendix IV.

Manor House was re-built, and spacious and well-appointed cloak-rooms were accommodated in what had been a disused barn. The north wing containing, amongst other rooms the oak-panelled Parlour and ancient Kitchen, was also restored and furnished in time for the Celebrations in honour of the Two-Hundredth Anniversary of the birth of George Washington, which took place at Sulgrave in July 1932 under the presidency of Mr. Andrew Mellon, the United States Ambassador.

APPENDIX I

PRINCIPAL SUBSCRIBERS TO THE BRITISH PEACE CENTENARY FUND FOR THE PURCHASE OF SULGRAVE MANOR

1912-1917

	£	S.	D.
Mrs. Woodhull Martin	1000	0	0
Lord Rothschild	500	0	0
Anglo-American Oil Co.	500	0	0
Sir John Brunner	500	0	0
Lord Cowdray	500	0	0
Imperial Tobacco Co.	262	10	0
Lord Burnham	400	0	0
Sir Ernest Cassel	250	0	0
The Rhodes Trust	250	0	0
Messrs. Speyer Bros.	250	0	0
Frank Lloyd	200	0	0
Lord Revelstoke	200	0	0
Washington Singer	157	10	0
Sir Henry Wellcome	105	0	0
Lord Ashton of Hyde	100	0	0
Sir John Barker	100	0	0
Lord Beaverbrook	100	0	0
Sir Otto Beit	100	0	0
Lord Blyth	100	0	0
Lord Brassey	100	0	0
Barrow Cadbury	100	0	0
George Cadbury	100	0	0
Lord Cadogan	100	0	0
Thomas Cook and Son	100	0	0
Cunard S.S. Co.	100	0	0
Daily Telegraph	100	0	0

	£	S.	D.
Sir Robert Donald	100	0	0
Emile Erlanger and Co.	100	0	0
Sir Algernon Firth	100	0	0
Robert Fleming	100	0	0
Lord Glencoats	100	0	0
Lord Glenconner	100	0	0
Sir Robert Hadfield	100	0	0
Lord Iveagh	100	0	0
Lazard Bros.	100	0	0
Sir William Mather	100	0	0
Walter Morrison	100	0	0
Lord Northcliffe	100	0	0
C. S. Ralli	100	0	0
Lord Rosebery	100	0	0
Lord Rothermere	100	0	0
Joseph Rowntree	100	0	0
Sir Clement Royds	100	0	0
Gordon Selfridge	100	0	0
Lord Weardale	100	0	0
Lord Wakefield	100	0	0
White Star Line	100	0	0
Lord Shaw	95	0	0
Sir Percy Alden	80	0	0
Lord Queenborough	75	0	0
Lord Courtenay	70	0	0
Western Union Telegraph Co.	53	0	0
Willis Faber and Co.	52	10	0
L. McCormick Goodhart	52	10	0
Lord Joicey	50	0	0
Sir Robert Perks	50	0	0
Lord Plymouth	50	0	0
W. Ferens	50	0	0
Canon Charles	50	0	0
Lord Rhondda	50	0	0
Balfour Williamson and Co.	50	0	0
Proprietors of the *Statist*	50	0	0
Sir Edward Bowden	50	0	0

APPENDIX I

	£	S.	D.
Sir Charles Henry	50	0	0
A. Morley	50	0	0
Proprietors of the *Connoisseur*	36	0	0
Lord Aberconway	25	0	0
Earl of Balfour	25	0	0
Booth S.S. Co.	25	0	0
A. Booth and Co.	25	0	0
Cunard Steamship Co.	25	0	0
Lord Harcourt	25	0	0
Lord Hambledon	25	0	0
Lord Kinnaird	25	0	0
T. K. Laidlaw	25	0	0
Arnold Morley	25	0	0
Lord Melchett	25	0	0
Sir Robert Mond	25	0	0
Lord Stanhope	25	0	0
W. Hazell	25	0	0
Horlick's Malted Milk Co.	25	0	0
Miss A. Peckover	25	0	0
J. G. White and Co.	25	0	0
A. Norton	25	0	0
Sir George Alexander	25	0	0
William Young	21	0	0
Sir Joseph Lawrence	21	0	0
Lord Reading	21	0	0
Moreton Frewen	20	0	0
E. Sassoon and Co.	20	0	0
Sir Thomas Barlow	20	0	0
Earl Grey	20	0	0
Lord Lee of Fareham	20	0	0
J. Francis Mason	20	0	0
J. R. Kinnell	15	15	0
Lord Kintore	15	0	0
Sir H. B. Marshall	15	0	0
Sir J. H. D. Berridge	10	10	0
Sir H. Spicer	10	10	0
W. Burdett-Coutts	10	10	0

	£	S.	D.
J. D. Cross	10	10	0
Louis Forsheim	10	10	0
A. L. Reckitt	10	10	0
Arnold Rowntree	10	10	0
Sir Richard Stapley	10	10	0
Bishop of St. Albans	10	0	0
Lord Astor	10	0	0
Sir Arthur Crosfield	10	0	0
Sir W. Morgan	10	0	0
S. V. Morgan	10	0	0
Rev. W. Moore Ede	10	0	0
Sir G. O. Trevelyan	10	0	0
Mrs. W. Arbuthnot	10	0	0
William A. Cadbury	10	0	0
William Gillett	10	0	0
H. W. C. Carr-Gomm	10	0	0
J. J. Lloyd	10	0	0
Lord Meath	5	5	0
Sir William Anson	5	5	0
Sir Victor Horsley	5	0	0
James F. Muirhead	5	0	0
John Galsworthy	3	3	0
Lord Sydenham	2	0	0

APPENDIX II

PRINCIPAL SUBSCRIBERS TO THE *DAILY TELEGRAPH* FUND FOR THE RESTORATION OF SULGRAVE MANOR

1919-1920

	£	S.	D.
His Majesty the King	100	0	0
H.R.H. the Prince of Wales	10	0	0
Proprietors of the *Daily Telegraph*	500	0	0
Anglo-American Oil Co., Ltd.	500	0	0
Selfridge and Co., Ltd.	500	0	0
Stars and Stripes Club of Manchester	500	0	0
Lord Wakefield	250	0	0
Lord Mount Stephen	200	0	0
Sir Thomas Lipton	200	0	0
Andrew Carnegie	200	0	0
Northampton Mercury and Daily Echo	134	2	0
Bank of Liverpool and Martin's Bank	105	0	0
Midland Bank	105	0	0
National Provincial Bank	105	0	0
N. M. Rothschild and Sons	105	0	0
Lord Queenborough	100	0	0
Alderman Sir Marcus Samuel	100	0	0
Sir Horace Marshall, Lord Mayor of London	100	0	0
Sir Algernon Firth	100	0	0
Armour and Co., Ltd.	100	0	0
Lord Duveen	100	0	0
Clarence H. Mackay	100	0	0
Colonel Isaac C. Lewis	100	0	0
Samuel Samuel	100	0	0
Louis S. Swift, Chicago	100	0	0

	£	S.	D.
Lord Furness	52	10	0
W. and A. Gilbey, Ltd.	52	10	0
Lloyd's Bank	52	10	0
Anonymous	52	10	0
Viscount Hambleden	50	0	0
Lord Leverhulme	50	0	0
Sir Robert Hadfield	50	0	0
Hadfields, Ltd., Sheffield	50	0	0
James Speyer	50	0	0
Lord and Lady Lee of Fareham	26	0	0
G. J. Gribble	25	0	0
Pynchon and Co.	25	0	0
L. G. Sloan, Ltd.	25	0	0
H. A. Titcomb	25	0	0
Lord Reading	21	0	0
J. W. Hope	21	0	0
Miss Mabel Lyman, Waltham, Mass.	21	0	0
Vicars Bros.	21	0	0
Hon. John W. Davis, American Ambassador	20	0	0
Lord Blyth	20	0	0
C. K. Crane, Dalton, Mass.	20	0	0
Charles E. Hughes	20	0	0
Henry Fairfield Osborn	20	0	0
Sir Roderick Jones	15	15	0
Mrs. D. M. Rawcliffe	15	0	0
The English-Speaking Union	10	10	0
J. B. Kennedy	10	10	0
J. B. MacAfee	10	10	0
National Cash Register, Ltd.	10	10	0
Henderson, Craig and Co.	10	10	0
Frank Partridge	10	10	0
Alfred Wigglesworth	10	10	0
Lord Swaythling	10	0	0
Sir Sam Fay	10	0	0
Sir Charles Henry	10	0	0
Mrs. W. Reierson Arbuthnot	10	0	0
Carreras, Ltd.	10	0	0

	£	s.	d.
The Clothworkers' Co.	10	0	0
Colonel Alfred Gilbey	10	0	0
Major Louis Livington Seaman, New York	10	0	0
Mrs. J. R. Tremenheere	10	0	0
Warner M. Van Norden, New York	10	0	0
Sir William Osler	5	5	0
Major-General Sir H. W. Thornton	5	5	0
Lieutenant-General Sir Hubert Gough	5	5	0
H. E. Davies, Mayor of Gravesend	5	5	0
W. Hislop	5	5	0
Algernon Maudslay	5	0	0
A. C. Rogers, Mayor of Buckingham	5	5	0
Mrs. W. P. Ward	5	5	0
Lord Fitzmaurice	5	0	0
Lady Musgrave	5	0	0
Sir Robert Perks	5	0	0
Lieutenant-General Sir W. P. Pulteney	5	0	0
George Cadbury	5	0	0
James Colquhoun	5	0	0
Robert B. Skinner, American Consul-General	5	0	0
Sir Anthony Hope Hawkins	3	3	0
Lord Downham of Fulham	2	2	0
A. C. R. Carter	2	2	0
Victor Rienaecker	2	2	0
Lord Channing of Wellingborough	1	1	0
Horace Aldridge	1	1	0
W. Hobart Bird	1	1	0
Robert Gladstone	1	1	0
Major-General Sir J. Headlam	1	1	0
Cecil Headlam	1	1	0
F. Paul Impey	1	1	0

APPENDIX III

MEMBERS OF THE COMMITTEE OF THE NATIONAL SOCIETY OF THE COLONIAL DAMES OF AMERICA WHO RAISED THE ENDOWMENT FUND FOR SULGRAVE MANOR

1923-1925

Mrs. Joseph R. Lamar, National President.

Mrs. William Adams Brown, National Chairman	New York.
Mrs. Gilmer Speed Adams, Vice-Chairman	Kentucky.

Central Committee

Mrs. John F. Bransford	Georgia.
Mrs. Holmes Forsythe	Illinois.
Miss Margaret Foster	California.
Mrs. Joseph B. Hutchinson	Pennsylvania.
Mrs. John Lowell	Massachusetts.
Mrs. George J. Schleicher	Texas.
Mrs. Edward S. Shoemaker	Maryland.
Mrs. Robert J. Johnson	Iowa.

State Chairmen

Mrs. Thomas Allen	Massachusetts.
Miss Sarah R. Anderson	Georgia.
Mrs. S. Thruston Ballard	Kentucky.
Mrs. S. Godwin Boykin	Virginia.
Mrs. Thomas Casady	Nebraska.
Mrs. Lewis W. Cherry	Arkansas.
Mrs. Edwin L. Dana	Wyoming.
Mrs. Charles W. Dempster	Illinois.

Mrs. Edgar H. Evans	Indiana.
Miss Anita Furness	Minnesota.
Miss Mary S. Goggin	Texas.
Mrs. Ben F. Gray	Missouri.
Mrs. Harris Hancock	Ohio.
Mrs. Charles Henderson	Alabama.
Mrs. William Pegram Hamilton	Michigan.
Mrs. A. Barton Hepburn	New York.
Mrs. Frederick Hewlett	California.
Mrs. I. K. Heyward	South Carolina.
Miss May Houghton	Wisconsin.
Mrs. Joseph Huckins	Oklahoma.
Miss Edith D. Kingsbury	Connecticut.
Mrs. Charles W. D. Ligon	Maryland.
Mrs. W. E. Lingelbach	Pennsylvania.
Mrs. Sumpter De Leon Lowry	Florida.
Mrs. W. A. Maurer	Iowa.
Mrs. John Morris Morgan	Mississippi.
Mrs. Henry McAllister, Jr.	Colorado.
Mrs. John P. Nields	Delaware.
Mrs. C. C. Nottingham	Tennessee.
Miss Agnes Peters	District of Columbia.
Mrs. David W. Pipes	Louisiana.
Miss Jennie Stuart Price	West Virginia.
Mrs. John Ewing Price	Washington.
Miss Josephine Rohrer	Vermont.
Mrs. William Dusenbery Sherrerd	New Jersey.
Mrs. E. C. Shevlin	Oregon.
Mrs. Frank S. Spruill	North Carolina.
Mrs. Frank L. Vance	Michigan.
Mrs. Maurice King Washburn	Rhode Island.
Mrs. Richard Webb	Maine.
Mrs. Bennet R. Wheeler	Kansas.
Mrs. Gordon Woodbury	New Hampshire.

The Committee appointed to prepare the List of Contributors to the Endowment Fund

Mrs. Edward Mitchell Townsend (Chairman)	New York.
Mrs. Morris B. Belknap	Kentucky.
Mrs. Elihu Chauncey	New York.
Mrs. Joshua Green	Washington.
Mrs. L. Dean Holden	New York.
Mrs. Walter Jennings	New York.
Mrs. Arthur H. Lea	Pennsylvania.
Mrs. Osgood Putnam	California.
Mrs. James Starr, Jr.	Pennsylvania.
Mrs. Joseph Ioor Waring	South Carolina.
Miss Alice Delano Weekes	New York.
Mrs. Barrett Wendell	Massachusetts.

APPENDIX IV

SUBSCRIBERS TO THE FUND RAISED BY THE TWO REPRESENTATIVES OF THE NATIONAL SOCIETY OF THE COLONIAL DAMES OF AMERICA ON THE SULGRAVE MANOR BOARD FOR THE FURTHER RESTORATION OF SULGRAVE MANOR

1926-1931

Mrs. Gilmer Speed Adams, C.D.	Kentucky.
Mrs. Lewis Adams	New York.
Miss Aldrich, C.D.	New York.
Mrs. Charles L. Anderson	Ohio.
Mrs. David C. Anderson, C.D.	Ohio.
(In memory of Mrs. Herman Groesbeck.)	
Mrs. E. L. Anderson	Ohio.
Mrs. Lars Anderson, C.D.	Ohio.
Mrs. William P. Anderson	Ohio.
Mrs. Edgar S. Auchincloss, C.D.	New York.
Mrs. Hugh D. Auchincloss, C.D.	New York.
Mrs. L. A. Ault	Ohio.
George F. Baker, Jr.	New York.
Rudolph F. Balke	Ohio.
O. T. Bannard	New York.
Alexander C. Barker	New York.
Mrs. George D. Barron, C.D.	New York.
Mrs. S. Westray Battle, C.D.	North Carolina.
Mrs. George B. Beecher, C.D.	Ohio.
Mrs. Morris B. Belknap, C.D.	Kentucky.
Mrs. Sanford Bissell, C.D.	New York.
Mrs. Charles S. Blake	Ohio.
Mrs. Edward C. Bodman, C.D.	New York.
Mrs. Edward Bok	Pennsylvania.
Mrs. Benjamin P. Bole	Ohio.

Mrs. Stephen Bonsal, C.D.S.N.Y.	Washington, D.C.
Mrs. C. C. Bovey, C.D.	Minnesota.
Mrs. Robert B. Bowler, C.D.	Ohio.
Mrs. Frederick F. Brewster, C.D.	Connecticut.
Mrs. Samuel Dwight Brewster, C.D.	New York.
Mrs. Henry D. Bruns, C.D.	Louisiana.
Mrs. Henry W. J. Bucknall	New York.
Miss Rowena Buell, C.D.	Ohio.
Mrs. B. F. Bullard, C.D.	Georgia.
General R. L. Bullard	New York.
C. H. Burton	Ohio.
Mrs. James Byrne, C.D.	New York.
Mrs. J. N. Camden, C.D.	Kentucky.
Miss Campbell, C.D.	Texas.
Mrs. Elbert L. Carpenter, C.D.	Minnesota.
Mrs. Edward V. Carey, C.D.	New Jersey.
Mrs. E. Crane Chadbourne	New York.
Miss Catherine H. Chambers, C.D.	New Jersey.
Mrs. J. W. Chapman, C.D.	New Hampshire.
Miss Ann Chatfield	Ohio.
Mrs. A. H. Chatfield, C.D.	Ohio.
Charles Wolcott Chatfield	Ohio.
Frederick H. Chatfield (second)	Ohio.
Miss Helen H. Chatfield	Ohio.
Henry H. Chatfield	Ohio.
Miss Marion Chatfield	Ohio.
Robert Bruce Wallace Chatfield	Ohio.
Frederick Huntington Chatfield	Ohio.
Mr. and Mrs. William Hayden Chatfield	Ohio.
Mrs. Elihu Chauncey, C.D.	New York.
Mrs. George Chase Christian, C.D.	Minnesota.
Percy Chubb	New York.
Miss Blanche M. Clough, C.D.	Minnesota.
Samuel P. Cochran	Texas.
Mrs. Tucker Skipworth Cole, C.D.	Pennsylvania.
Edward Colston	Ohio.
Mrs. W. O. Connor	Texas.
Mrs. George Rea Cook (third), C.D.	New Jersey.

Mrs. Jacob Dobson Cox, C.D.	Ohio.
Mrs. Joseph H. Crane	Ohio.
Mrs. E. M. Cravath, C.D.	New York.
Paul D. Cravath	New York.
Miss Sarah W. Cresswell, C.D.	New York.
Mrs. George A. Crocker	New York.
Mrs. James S. Cushman	New York.
R. Fulton Cutting	New York.
George F. Dana	Ohio.
Miss M. E. Danbridge, C.D. (In memory of Mrs. Herman Groesbeck.)	Ohio.
Mrs. William Henry Davis, C.D.	Ohio.
Mrs. Marius de Brabant	New York.
Mrs. Henry W. de Forest, C.D.	New York.
Mrs. Robert W. de Forest, C.D.	New York.
Mrs. William L. Dickson, C.D.	Ohio.
Mrs. Robert L. Dodge	New York.
Julius Doolittle	New York.
Mrs. W. S. Doolittle	New York.
Mr. and Mrs. F. N. Doubleday	New York.
Mrs. Henry P. Drought, C.D.	Texas.
Mrs. Samuel Drury	New Hamsphire.
Miss Anne Deas Duane, C.D.	New York.
Mrs. T. Coleman du Pont	Delaware.
E. W. Edwards	Ohio.
Miss Isabel Ellison	Ohio.
Mrs. Edward S. Ellwanger, C.D.	New York.
Mrs. T. J. Emery, C.D.	Ohio.
Mrs. John C. English, C.D.	Connecticut.
Mrs. Lewis H. English, C.D.	Connecticut.
Paul Esselborn	Ohio.
Mrs. Thomas Ewing, C.D.	New York.
Miss Mary Failing, C.D.	Oregon.
Miss Farwell, C.D.	Louisiana.
Mrs. Chiles M. Ferrell, C.D.	Virginia.
Mrs. Charles H. Ferry	New York.
Miss Margaret Field, C.D.	Maryland.
Mrs. Harry H. Flagler, C.D.	New York.

Miss Clara B. Fletcher	Ohio.
Mrs. B. W. Foley	Ohio.
Mrs. Joseph B. Foraker	Ohio.
Mrs. Frances Forschheimer (In memory of Mrs. Groesbeck.)	Ohio.
Mrs. Joseph C. Foster, C.D.	Maine.
Mrs. P. A. S. Frankoin, C.D.	New York.
Mrs. Walter J. Freeman, C.D.	Pennsylvania.
Mrs. A. H. Freiberg	Ohio.
Maurice J. Freiberg	Ohio.
Hollis French	Massachusetts.
Mrs. William Gaston	Massachusetts.
Francis Gilbert	New York.
Mrs. J. G. M. Glessner, C.D.	New Hampshire.
Miss Blanche Goodhue, C.D.	Ohio.
Mrs. Joshua Green, C.D.	Washington.
Mrs. Charles Theodore Greve, C.D.	Ohio.
William Groesbeck	Pennsylvania.
Mrs. F. E. Haight, C.D.	New York.
Mrs. J. K. Hamilton, C.D.	Ohio.
Mrs. John Henry Hammond	New York.
Miss Mary Hanna	Ohio.
Mrs. Richard Hardy	Tennessee.
Mrs. Edward S. Harkness, C.D.	New York.
Mrs. William L. Harkness, C.D.	New York.
Mrs. E. P. Harrison, C.D.	Ohio.
Mrs. Charles Henry, C.D.	Pennsylvania.
Mrs. Louis W. Hill	Minnesota.
Mrs. A. H. Hinkle, C.D.	Ohio.
Mrs. Frederick W. Hinkle	Ohio.
Mrs. George Hoadly, C.D. (In memory of Mrs. Groesbeck.)	Ohio.
Anton G. Hodenpyl	New York.
Charles F. Hofer	Ohio.
Mrs. L. Dean Holden, C.D.	New York.
Mrs. Eustis L. Hopkins, C.D.	New York.
Miss Isabella F. Hopkins	Ohio.
Mrs. Henry S. Hunnewall, C.D.	Massachusetts.

Illinois Society of Colonial Dames	Illinois.
Mr. and Mrs. C. Oliver Iselin	New York.
Mrs. C. L. Jackson, C.D.	Oregon.
Henry A. James	New York.
Mrs. Walter B. James, C.D.	New York.
Mrs. Frank D. Jamison	Ohio.
Mrs. Silvanus F. Jenkins, C.D.	New York.
Mrs. Herbert Jenney (In memory of Mrs. Herman Groesbeck.)	Ohio.
Miss Annie Burr Jennings, C.D.	Connecticut.
Mrs. Frank E. Jennings, C.D.	Florida.
Mr. and Mrs. Oliver G. Jennings	New York.
Walter Jennings	New York.
Mrs. Chauncey Keep, C.D.	Illinois.
Mrs. Frederick J. Kingsbury, C.D.	Connecticut.
Mrs. Harry Kearsearge Knapp, C.D.	New York.
Mr. and Mrs. Rudolph Koehler	Ohio.
Mrs. Lewis H. Lapham, C.D.	New York.
Mrs. Arthur H. Lea, C.D.	Pennsylvania.
Miss Fanny B. Lehmer, C.D. (In memory of Mrs. Groesbeck.)	Ohio.
Miss Anna K. Lewis, C.D.	Ohio.
Adolph Lewisohn	New York.
Mrs. Charles J. Livingood, C.D.	Ohio.
Luke Vincent Lockwood	New York.
Louisiana Society of Colonial Dames	Louisiana.
Mr. and Mrs. Howard Luther	Ohio.
Mrs. E. B. McCagg, C.D.	Washington, D.C.
Miss Petrea McClintock, C.D.	Ohio.
Cyrus McCormick	Illinois.
Mrs. Howard Townsend Martin, C.D.	New York.
Massachusetts Society of Colonial Dames	Massachusetts.
William J. Matheson	New York.
Mrs. Florence Foraker Mathews, C.D.	Ohio.
Mrs. Frederick Mead, C.D.	New Jersey.
Mrs. George Metcalf, C.D.	Minnesota.
Otto Meyer	New York.
Mrs. Charles S. Millard, C.D.	Ohio.

Mrs. Bellinger Mills, C.D.	Texas.
Mrs. Sidney Z. Mitchell	New York.
Mrs. William H. Moore, C.D.	New York.
Mrs. Dave Hennen Morris	New York.
Mrs. Thomas F. Moxey, C.D.	Texas.
New Hampshire Society of Colonial Dames	New Hampshire.
Mrs. Edward Norris	New York.
Mrs. C. C. Nottingham, C.D.	Tennessee.
James A. Noyes	Massachusetts.
Mrs. Clinton Ogilvy, C.D.	New York.
Ohio Society of Colonial Dames	Ohio.
Ohio Society of Colonial Wars	Ohio.
Mrs. Nelson B. Oliphant, C.D.	New Jersey.
Mrs. Walter M. Parker, C.D.	New Hampshire.
Miss Katharine de B. Parsons, C.D.A.	New York.
Miss M. A. Parsons, C.D.	Ohio.
Mrs. Z. C. Patten, C.D.	Tennessee.
Miss Jessie Patterson, C.D.	New York.
Mrs. Charles A. Pauley, C.D.	Ohio.
Mrs. John Carroll Payne, C.D.	Georgia.
Rev. Endicott Peabody	Massachusetts.
Mrs. James H. Perkins, C.D.	Ohio.
William R. Peters	New York.
Mrs. Edmund J. Phelps, C.D.	Minnesota.
Miss Ruth Shepard Phelps, C.D.	Minnesota.
Miss Lina Phipps, C.D.	Connecticut.
Mrs. Robert Lowe Pierrepont, C.D.	New York.
Mrs. Charles S. Pillsbury, C.D.	Minnesota.
Mrs. D. W. Pipes, C.D.	Lousiana.
Julian A. Pollak	Ohio.
Mrs. Joseph K. Pollock, C.D.	Ohio.
Mrs. Frederic B. Pratt, C.D.	New York.
Mrs. Harold Irving Pratt	New York.
Mrs. John T. Pratt	New York.
Mr. and Mrs. William Cooper Procter	Ohio.
Mrs. Moses Taylor Pyne, C.D.	New York.
Mrs. Joseph Ransohoff	Ohio.
Dr. Charles A. L. Reed	Ohio.

Mrs. Charles C. Richardson	Ohio.
Mrs. Charles L. Riker, C.D.A.	New York.
Mrs. Henry M. Robinson	California.
John D. Rockefeller, Jr.	New York.
William S. Rowe	Ohio.
Mrs. R. M. Saltonstall	Massachusetts.
Mrs. Henry B. Sargent, C.D.	Connecticut.
Mortimer L. Schiff	New York.
Mrs. Frank P. Shepard, C.D.	Minnesota.
Mrs. W. D. Sherrerd, C.D.	New Jersey.
Mrs. John Sherwin	Ohio.
Mrs. Edward Shoemaker, C.D.	Maryland.
Mrs. Joyce Shonnard	New York.
Mrs. S. W. Skinner, C.D.	Ohio.
Mrs. Samuel Sloan, C.D.	New York.
Miss Dora N. Spalding, C.D.	New Hampshire.
Charles S. Stephens, Jr.	Ohio.
Rt. Rev. Ernest M. Stires	New York.
Mrs. James Storrow, C.D.	Massachusetts.
Albert Strauss	New York.
Mrs. Edward W. Strong	Ohio.
Mrs. Samuel T. Taft	Ohio.
Hon. William H. Taft	Washington, D.C.
Mrs. Magnus Tate, C.D.	Ohio.
Myron C. Taylor	New York.
William Ambrose Taylor	New York.
Mrs. William Ambrose Taylor, C.D.	New York.
Tennessee Society of Colonial Dames	Tennessee.
Mrs. John Van B. Thayer, C.D.	New York.
Mrs. B. F. Thomas, C.D.	Tennessee.
Mrs. Peter G. Thomson	Ohio.
Mrs. Edwin Thorne, C.D.	New York.
Mrs. Harry Toulmin	California.
Miss Helen Mae Townsend, C.D.	Ohio.
Mrs. R. C. Townsend, C.D.	New York.
Mrs. H. C. Truesdale, C.D.	Minnesota.
Mrs. H. Peters Wallace	Ohio.
Miss Lucy Carlile Watson, C.D.	New York.

Mrs. Stephen M. Weld, C.D.	Massachusetts.
Mrs. Barrett Wendell, C.D.	Massachusetts.
Mrs. C. A. Weyerhaeuser	Minnesota.
Mrs. Richard Wheatland, C.D.	Massachusetts.
Mrs. Arthur M. Wheeler, C.D.	Connecticut.
Miles White, Jr.	Maryland.
Mrs. M. Morris White, C.D. (In memory of Mrs. John Gates.)	Ohio.
Miss Anna P. Williams, C.D.	Illinois.
Mrs. Aras T. Williams	New York.
Charles Wilson	Ohio.
Mrs. John F. Winslow, C.D.	Ohio.
Miss Beatrice Woods	Ohio.
Harry F. Woods	Ohio.
Mrs. H. F. Woods, C.D.	Ohio.
Mr. and Mrs. H. A. Worcester	Ohio.
Mrs. David J. Workum	Ohio.
Miss Julia Worthington, C.D.	Ohio.
Mrs. Clifford B. Wright	Ohio.
Mrs. Clifford R. Wright, C.D. (In memory of Mrs. Perin Langdon.)	Ohio.
Mrs. Lucien Wulsin	France.

APPENDIX V

THE SIR GEORGE WATSON CHAIR OF AMERICAN HISTORY, LITERATURE, AND INSTITUTIONS, ADMINISTERED BY THE SULGRAVE MANOR BOARD

The Watson Chair was founded in November 1919, on the return of the Prince of Wales from his American tour, by a gift from the late Sir George Watson, to the Anglo-American Society (now merged in the Sulgrave Manor Board). At that time there was no university in the British Isles which had either a Chair or Lectureship of American History.

The scope of the Chair is sufficiently indicated in its title: 'Watson Chair of American History, Literature, and Institutions,' and it has been the aim of the Sulgrave Manor Board to draw upon a wide variety of eminent lecturers, capable of interpreting American life and history, in its broadest aspects, to the British people. It is not attached to any one university, but is intended to stimulate interest in and study of America in all British universities. The lecturers, chosen annually by the Board, are, alternately, of American and British nationality, thus drawing upon the best intellectual resources of the two countries, and securing a variety of treatment of the subjects dealt with. Each course consists of six lectures, which are usually delivered during the Michaelmas term, and are afterwards published in book form.

The inaugural lecture of the series was given at the Mansion House, London, on 27th June 1921, by Viscount Bryce, on 'The History of the United States in relation to Anglo-American Ideals of Peace.' Subsequent lecturers have been:

1922. President Hadley, of Yale University.
Subject: 'Economic Problems of Democracy.'

1923. President Nicholas Murray Butler, of Columbia University.
Subject: 'Building the American Nation.'

1924. Professor A. F. Pollard, of University College, London.
Subject: 'Factors in American History.'

1925. Sir Robert Falconer, President of Toronto University.
Subject: 'The United States as a Neighbour.'

1926. Dr. Robert McElroy, Harmsworth Professor of American History at Oxford University.
Subject: 'Some British-American Crises.'

1927. Professor C. H. Van Tyne, of Michigan University.
Subject: 'The struggle for the Truth about the American Revolution.'

1928. Professor Reginald Coupland, Beit Professor of Colonial History in the University of Oxford.
Subject: 'The After Effects of the American Revolution on British Policy.'

1929. Dr. John H. Finley, Associate-Editor of the *New York Times*.
Subject: 'The Predestinating of America.'

1930. Dr. G. S. Gordon, President of Magdalen College, Oxford.
Subject: 'The Literary Relations, Past and Present, of England and the United States.'

1932. Hon. James Montgomery Beck, Member of Congress, Solicitor-General of United States, 1921-5.
Subject: 'The United States Constitution as an Experiment in Democracy.'

1933. Sir John Squire, Editor of the *London Mercury*.
Subject: 'American Poetry and its Relations with English Poetry.'

APPENDIX VI

THE SULGRAVE MANOR BOARD, SOLE AUTHORITY FOR THE MAINTENANCE, CARE, AND CONTROL OF SULGRAVE MANOR AND THE ADMINISTRATION OF THE 'WATSON' CHAIR OF AMERICAN HISTORY, LITERATURE, AND INSTITUTIONS

Board of Governors

Chairman: The Viscount Lee of Fareham, P.C., G.C.B., G.C.S.I., G.B.E.
Vice-Chairman: The Earl Spencer.
Hon. Treasurer: Sir Percy Alden.

The Marquess of Crewe, K.G., P.C.
The Marquess of Northampton, D.S.O.
The Countess of Sandwich.
The Viscount Burnham, C.H.
The Viscountess Lee of Fareham.
The Right Hon. H. A. L. Fisher, P.C., F.R.S.
Lady (Arthur) Herbert.
Sir Reginald Blomfield, R.A.
Sir Harry Brittain, K.B.E, C.M.G.
Sir Sam Fay.
The American Consul-General in London (*ex officio*).
The Mayor of Northampton (*ex officio*).
Mr. J. L. Garvin.
Lt.-Col. P. Lester Reid, O.B.E.
Mr. H. Clifford Smith, F.S.A.
Mr. J. Howard Whitehouse.
Sir Evelyn Wrench, C.M.G.

*Mrs. Edward M. Townsend.
*Mrs. Albert H. Chatfield.
Hon. Mrs. Alfred Lyttleton, G.B.E.

Trustees (ex officio) *of Sulgrave Manor*

H.E. The American Ambassador in London.
H.E. The British Ambassador in Washington.
The Regent of the Mount Vernon Ladies' Association of the Union.

House Committee

The Viscountess Lee of Fareham.
Lady Hudson, G.B.E.
*Mrs. E. M. Townsend.
*Mrs. A. H. Chatfield.
Hon. Mrs. Alfred Lyttleton, G.B.E.
Mr. H. Clifford Smith, F.S.A.

Secretary: Miss D. K. Palmer, 1 Central Buildings, Westminster, London, S.W.1.

Resident Steward and Caretaker at Sulgrave Manor: Mr. Frederick Carter.

* Nominated by the National Society of the Colonial Dames of America.

BIBLIOGRAPHY

ANDREWS, HERBERT C. MS. Catalogue of Deeds and Documents, the property of the Sulgrave Manor Board. 1933.

Award of the Parish of Sulgrave under the Enclosure Act (manuscript). 1761.

BAKER, GEORGE. *History of the County of Northampton.* 1820-30.

BLOMFIELD, SIR REGINALD, R.A. *Memoirs of an Architect.* 1932.

BRIDGES, JOHN. *History and Antiquities of Northamptonshire*, 2 vols. 1791.

CONWAY, MONCURE D. 'The English Ancestry of Washington,' *Harper's Magazine*, 1891, p. 877.

Country Life, 23rd December 1911, 'The Peace Centenary and the Home of the Washingtons.'

CREWE, MARQUESS OF. 'The Sulgrave Institution and the Anglo-American Society,' *The Nineteenth Century and After.* January 1922.

DODGE, HARRISON HOWELL. *Mount Vernon: Its Owner and Its Story.* 1932.

DRYDEN, ALICE. *Memorials of Old Northamptonshire.* Edited by Alice Dryden. 1903.

DRYDEN, SIR HENRY. 'The Washingtons,' *Northamptonshire Notes and Queries.* January 1885.

—— 'The Washington Manor House at Sulgrave,' *Northamptonshire Notes and Queries.* April 1885.

DUGDALE, SIR W. *Monasticum Anglicanum*, Vol. v. 1817-30.

Gentleman's Magazine for May, August, and September 1789. Contributions by Jeremiah Henn on the History of Sulgrave.

HENN, JEREMIAH. 'History of Sulgrave, Northamptonshire' (manuscript). 1789.

HOPPIN, CHARLES ARTHUR. *The Washington Ancestry, and Records of the McClain, Johnson, and Forty other Colonial American Families.* Prepared for Edward Lee McClain by C. A. Hoppin. 3 vols. Greenfield, Ohio. (Privately printed) 1932.

Illustrated Handbook of Mount Vernon, the Home of Washington. Printed for the Mount Vernon Ladies' Association of the Union. 1921.

LONGDEN, H. ISHAM. *The History of the Washington Family*. 1927.

MUIRHEAD, J. F. *American Shrines on English Soil*, with an Introduction by the Earl of Birkenhead. 1924.

MURRAY'S *Handbook for Travellers in Northamptonshire and Rutland*. Second Edition. Edited by H. M. Cundall. 1901.

National Society of the Colonial Dames of America: Its Beginnings, Its Purpose, and a Record of Its Work, 1891-1913. 1913.

NORDEN, JOHN. *Speculi Britanniæ Pars Altera: or, A Delineation of Northamptonshire*. 1720.

PAPE, T. 'Heraldic Glass Memorials of the Sulgrave Washingtons.' *Connoisseur*, July 1919.

—— *Sulgrave Manor and the Washington Family*. 1921.

—— 'The Washington Coat of Arms.' *Connoisseur*, February 1932.

—— 'Washington's Arms and "Old Glory."' *Connoisseur*, March 1932.

Public Record Office. Calendar of State Papers *temp*. Henry VIII. 'Rental of St. Andrew's Priory.' (1538.)

SMITH, H. CLIFFORD. 'Sulgrave Manor and the Washington Bicentenary.' The *Landmark*, May 1932.

—— 'The George Washington Bicentenary: Sulgrave Manor, Northamptonshire.' *Country Life*, 25th June 1932.

The Place-Names of Northamptonshire. Edited by J. E. B. Gover, A. Mawer, and F. M. Stenton. English Place-Name Society, Vol. x. 1933.

Washington, George, Letters and Recollections of. Being Letters to Tobias Lear and Others between 1790 and 1799. 1906.

WATERS, HENRY F. An Examination of the English Ancestry of George Washington. Printed for the New England Historic Geological Society. Boston, 1889.

TECHNICAL WORKS CONSULTED

BLOMFIELD, SIR REGINALD, R.A. *The Formal Garden in England.* 1892.

CESCINSKY, HERBERT, and GRIBBLE, ERNEST. *Early English Furniture and Woodwork*, 2 vols. 1922.

DAWBER, E. GUY, A.R.A. *Old Cottages, Farm-houses, and Other Stone Buildings in the Cotswold District, Examples of Minor Domestic Architecture in . . . Northants* . . . etc. 1905.

HOWARD, F. E., and CROSSLEY, F. H. *English Church Furniture and Woodwork.* 1917.

JACKSON, MRS. F. NEVILL. 'Contemporary Silhouette Portraits of George Washington.' *Connoisseur*, January 1932.

JEKYLL, GERTRUDE. *Old English Household Life: Some Account of Cottage Objects and Country Folk.* 1925.

LAWSON, WILLIAM. *New Orchard and Garden.* 1618.

LINDSAY, J. SEYMOUR. *Iron and Brass Implements of the English House.* 1927.

MACQUOID, PERCY, and EDWARDS, RALPH. *The Dictionary of English Furniture*, 3 vols. 1924-7.

NORTH, THOMAS. *The Church Bells of Northamptonshire.* 1878.

PARKINSON, JOHN. *Paradisi in Sole Paradisus Terrestris.* 1629.

ROHDE, ELEANOUR SINCLAIR. *The Garden of Herbs.* 1920.

—— *The Old English Herbals.* 1922.

—— *The Old English Gardening Books.* 1924.

—— *The Scented Garden.* 1931.

—— *The Story of the Garden.* 1932.

SHUFFREY, L. A. *The English Fireplace and Its Accessories.* 1912.

Index

INDEX

INDEX

Lightning Source UK Ltd.
Milton Keynes UK
UKOW052040030712

195437UK00001B/78/A